SPIKE LEE'S AMERICA

America Through the Lens

SPIKE LEE'S AMERICA

DAVID STERRITT

polity

First published in 2013 by Polity Press

Polity Press
65 Bridge Street
Cambridge CB2 1UR, UK

Polity Press
350 Main Street
Malden, MA 02148, USA

ISBN-13: 978-0-7456-5181-1
ISBN-13: 978-0-7456-5182-8(pb)

A catalogue record for this book is available from the British Library.

Typeset in 10.75 on 14 pt Adobe Janson
by Servis Filmsetting Ltd, Stockport, Cheshire
Printed and bound in Great Britain by MPG Books Group Limited,
Bodmin, Cornwall

For further information on Polity, visit our website:
www.politybooks.com

For Mikita
and Craig
and Jeremy and Tanya

CONTENTS

ACKNOWLEDGEMENTS

I have benefited from the insights of so many gifted friends and colleagues that naming them all would be impossible. Among the most valued in recent years have been my academic colleagues at Columbia University, the Maryland Institute College of Art, and the University Seminar on Cinema and Interdisciplinary Interpretation; my movie-reviewing and essay-writing colleagues in the National Society of Film Critics; and more terrific friends than anyone could deserve. Andrea Drugan, my editor at Polity, encouraged this project at the outset and has been perceptive, supportive, and patient ever since. My son Craig, who lived in the heart of Bed-Stuy when I started this book, was a Brooklyn loyalist when the rest of us lived in Manhattan and embodies the best spirit of both boroughs. Like him, my son Jeremy and my daughter-in-law Tanya Van Sant have brought immeasurable amounts of humor, inspiration, and street smarts into my life. Finally, my gratitude to Mikita Brottman knows no bounds. Without her and The Great Grisby my bamboozlement would be even greater than it is.

INTRODUCTION: CHALLENGING QUESTIONS, NO EASY ANSWERS

Barack Obama doesn't mention it often, but his relationship with Spike Lee's cinema has a personal side. "Our first movie was *Do the Right Thing*, which had just come out," Michelle Obama told a CNN reporter shortly before her husband's inauguration. "That was his cultural side ... he was pulling out all the stops." Beyond this folksy first-date scenario, an old Obama friend called the film a lasting favorite of the president. Why does Obama rarely talk about it, then? In a contribution to The Root, an African-American website of politics and culture, commentator Dayo Olopade hypothesized that the tough-minded, sometimes abrasive politics embraced by Lee in the late 1980s are "awkwardly matched to the president's smooth, carefully cultivated centrism and nonthreatening demeanor," adding that "the first couple's professed distaste for dwelling too much on race" might also be at work.

There appears to be a paradox here: the movie that a politician feels the need to shy away from is the most widely respected movie its director has ever made, and easily the most popular as well. But there is really no paradox at all. First released in 1989 to a chorus of cheers, boos, celebrations, and anxieties, *Do the Right Thing* speaks to wide and diverse audiences today for the same reason it disturbs professional centrists and compromisers – because it raises and examines intractable American problems but *refuses to offer facile solutions* or to wish them away in the feel-good manner that comes so easily to Hollywood cinema. In short, it's an anomaly in American film – a genuinely thoughtful, profoundly dialectical, aesthetically groundbreaking art picture that poses difficult, squirm-inducing sociopolitical questions in terms that are instantly understandable by people along the entire spectrum of American racial and ethnic identity.

Not all of Spike Lee's joints are as penetrating and original as *Do the Right Thing*. (He calls his pictures "joints," which he defines as a "New York word" meaning whatever you want it to mean.) Nor did he singlehandedly launch African-American cinema into a new and unprecedented era; as media scholar Jacqueline Bobo shows (427),[1] films made by black directors or geared toward black audiences fared well at the box office both before and after *She's Gotta Have It* made its big splash in 1986:

1984 *Purple Rain* (dir. Albert Magnoli, dist. Warner Brothers) – Cost: $7 million; Gross: $69 million

1985 *Brother from Another Planet* (dir. John Sayles, dist. Cinecom) – Cost: $.3 million; Gross: $5 million

1987 *Hollywood Shuffle* (dir. Robert Townsend, dist. Samuel Goldwyn Company) – Cost: $.4 million; Gross: $7 million

1988 *School Daze* (dir. Spike Lee, dist. Columbia) – Cost: $6 million; Gross: $14 million

1989 *I'm Gonna Git You Sucka* (dir. Keenen Ivory Wayans, dist. United Artists) – Cost: $3 million; Gross: $15 million

Do the Right Thing (dir. Spike Lee, dist. MCA/Universal) – Cost: $6.5 million; Gross: $33 million

Lean on Me (dir. John Avildsen, dist. Warner Brothers) – Cost: n/a; Gross: $28 million

1990 *Harlem Nights* (dir. Eddie Murphy, dist. Paramount) – Cost: $50 million; Gross: $59.8 million (as of March 1990)

House Party (dir. Reginald Hudlin, dist. New Line Cinema) – Cost: $2.5 million; Gross: $22 million (as of June 1990)

Lee's intervention in contemporary cinema has been tremendously important, but it has not always been excellent in quality or even effective in reaching its target audience. In this book I look at his failures – some just disappointing, a few positively dismal – as well as his successes.

The key point is that most of Lee's movies set forth pointed challenges to conventional ideas of what roles filmmaking, popular culture, and racial discourse are supposed to play in American society. Lee's very career amounts to such a challenge, for that matter – he is the only black filmmaker in history to sustain a major presence in American film over a period of decades, and his output during that time has been both varied and profuse, comprising almost fifty theatrical features, short films, and TV movies and episodes as director, almost as many as producer, and more than a dozen each as screenwriter and actor. His music videos have been commissioned by everyone from Public Enemy and Michael Jackson to Tracy Chapman and Chaka Khan, and he has directed commercials for Nike Air Jordans and American Express, among other clients. He has received two Academy Award nominations – for the original screenplay of *Do the Right Thing* and for the 1997 feature documentary *4 Little Girls*, shared with Sam Pollard, who coproduced it with him. He won an Emmy Award nomination for coproducing *4 Little Girls* and received two Emmys for directing and coproducing the 2006 documentary *When the Levees Broke: A Requiem in Four Acts*. He has won prizes, honors, and nominations at the Cannes, Berlin, Venice, Locarno, and Valladolid film festivals, among others; awards from critics' organizations in Chicago, Los Angeles, and Las Vegas; an honorary César Award in France and a special BAFTA award from the British Academy of Film and Television Arts in the United Kingdom; similar honors from the Independent Spirit, Gotham, and Image Awards; two Golden Globe nominations for *Do the Right Thing*; and this is only a very partial list. In short, he is among the most important and influential filmmakers of our time.

He is also a deeply personal and quintessentially American filmmaker who crafts his movies from the stuff of his own life and the lives of others whom he's met, observed, and interacted with over the years. His original roots are in Atlanta, where he was born in 1957. The family moved to Brooklyn when Spike was still an infant, settling in the downscale Fort Greene neighborhood. He returned to Atlanta for college, but it was during a summer vacation back home that he decided what his profession would be. Roaming around New York City with a Super 8 camera in hand, he envisioned himself trying to "capture the richness of African-American culture that I can see, just standing on the corner, or looking out my window every day" (Lindo 165). That idea has guided his career, which is dedicated to exploring the life, times, ideas, and actions of contemporary America – the comic and the tragic, the enlightened and the backward, the best, the worst, and the ugliest – in all their dizzying variety.

Lee's allegiance to African-American culture has not precluded an acute engagement with other aspects of the American scene at large. While moviegoers rightly regard him as first and foremost a black filmmaker, his artistic practice ranges far and wide through the American experience:

Do the Right Thing is about Italian-American storekeepers in an African-American neighborhood; *Summer of Sam* (1999) centers on Italian-American characters throughout; *Jungle Fever* (1991) deals with romance between the races; *25th Hour* (2002) and *Inside Man* (2006) have predominantly white casts. In these and other films with major white characters, moreover, Lee's insights into their folkways, mores, and mindsets are no less trenchant than the understandings of black culture he displays in movies centering on African-American communities. One of the secrets of his success is his intuitive awareness that African-Americans and Italian-Americans and *Anything*-Americans are socially and psychologically grounded in both parts of their hyphenated racial/ethnic designations: they are African or Italian or Anything by ancestry and they are Americans by birth, residence, or both. Lee's steady alertness to the cultural complexities arising from this doubleness of identity plays a crucial role in his films' ability to touch, move, entertain, and occasionally infuriate such a broad array of viewers. Collectively his films present an expansive, nuanced, proudly opinionated, richly multifaceted portrait of American society, with a particular focus on issues of class, race, and urban life.

This book explores Lee's career to date, from his beginnings as a no-budget independent to his plans for *Oldboy*, slated for release in 2013. My primary focus is the sophisticated representation of American culture, politics, and daily life that begins to form in his early works and continues to deepen and mature (with backward steps and stumbles along the way) through the present day. After this introductory chapter I discuss the production histories, stories, messages, and reception of his films, exploring the topics and ideas that interest Lee and the ways in which his characteristic style allows for an effective balance of narrative variety and aesthetic consistency. I look at the limitations as well as the strengths of his creative personality, focusing mostly on his theatrical features, since I find his documentaries and filmed-theater works a generally unimaginative lot, however fascinating their subjects may be in themselves.

Among the major subjects of the chapters to come are Lee's background in Brooklyn and his reasons for becoming a filmmaker; the early features – *She's Gotta Have It* (1986) and *School Daze* (1988) – that aim satirical darts at African-American idiosyncrasies; the breakthrough to a mass audience with *Do the Right Thing*; the continuing concern with social and political issues in such films as the antidrug drama *Jungle Fever*, the large-scale biopic *Malcolm X* (1992), the topical comedy-drama *Get on the Bus* (1996), and the take-no-prisoners media satire *Bamboozled* (2000); the treatment of different lifestyles in *Mo' Better Blues* (1990), which enters the jazz world, *He Got Game* (1998), a drama about athletics and commercialism, and *Summer of Sam*, about an Italian-American community in a troubled time; the compassion for urban youth manifested in *Crooklyn* (1994) and *Clockers* (1995), contrasted with Lee's failure to create three-dimensional female characters in *Girl 6* (1996) and *She Hate Me* (2004); the mixed success of Lee's most recent features, from the stunningly strong *25th Hour* to the muddled overkill of *Miracle at St Anna* (2008); and his part-time occupation as a big-studio director, beginning with *Inside Man* but stalled since the collapse of his effort to obtain studio backing for a sequel to that film, which has been his most financially successful.

It is a given that not everyone agrees on the merits of Lee's movies. Armond White, perhaps America's most widely known African-American film and culture critic, has often dished out less-than-favorable assessments, as when he told *LA Weekly* reporter Erin J. Aubry in 1999 that Spike is primarily a "first-rate marketer" who "knows what a young audience wants, and . . . supplies it." Lee chooses "hot topics" such as basketball and interracial dating, White continued, "but that doesn't mean you break ground. Barbara Walters picks hot topics every day. The pretense of seriousness doesn't mean you're serious" (2). Amiri Baraka, the African-American poet and essayist, said that for him Lee represented "a recognizable type and trend in American society," to wit, "the quintessential buppie, almost the spirit of the young, upwardly mobile, Black, petit bourgeois professional," more concerned with opportunism than with thinking through a coherent political stance (Strausbaugh 269). In a *Village Voice* supplement devoted to *Do the Right Thing*, the influential black commentator Stanley Crouch wrote under the headline "Do the Race Thing: Spike Lee's Afro-Fascist Chic," calling the film "the sort of rancid fairy tale one expects of a racist" (Crouch 73). Crouch's claim that Lee embraces a "fascist" aesthetic is strangely similar to Pauline Kael's famous charges against director Don Siegel and star Clint Eastwood, whose box-office hit *Dirty Harry* (1971) struck her as a "remarkably single-minded attack on liberal values" that brings out the "fascist potential" in the action genre (148), and against director Sam Peckinpah, whose melodrama *Straw Dogs* (1971) seemed to her "the first American film that is a fascist work of art" (M. Fine 210). Like those great directors of an older generation, Lee brings out fierce emotions in those who cannot or will not get onto his distinctive wavelength.

THEMES

Lee's body of work has three recurring themes. One is his determination to carve out and maintain a resolutely independent presence in a film industry almost entirely controlled by white men with big money. The second is the robust

sociopolitical awareness that inflects and informs all but a
handful of his productions, lending them additional depth
and relevance, and occasionally a touch of social-worker
moralizing that reveals a surprisingly conservative streak
in his creative personality. The third is what I consider the
defining characteristic of Spike Lee's cinema – its continual
willingness to raise hard questions and problems confronting
contemporary America without claiming to have the illusory
solutions and make-believe answers that mainstream movies
constantly peddle. Lee's pictures are designed to challenge
and provoke us, not ease our minds or pacify our emotions.
It's no accident that the last words of *School Daze* and the
first words of *Do the Right Thing* are the same, presenting
the core message of Spike's career in two emphatic syllables:
"*Wake up!*"

As a white critic analyzing the career of America's preemi-
nent black filmmaker, I approach Lee's films as contributions
not only to African-American culture but to *American* culture
in the broadest, most inclusive sense. Some of his movies –
School Daze and *Bamboozled*, for instance – obviously convey
different and more nuanced messages to black audiences
than to white ones, and I can't claim to experience these
films in the same ways African-American moviegoers do. But
culture is no respecter of borders and boundaries; a film or
TV show or magazine aimed at one community will quickly
cross into other communities (if it's any good) and spark
additional kinds of dialogue, discussion, and debate, taking
on new and different meanings that their creators might
never have intended or expected. "Black popular culture is
not just black," the African-American film scholar Manthia
Diawara observes,

> it is also produced through an artistic medium: musical
> genres and film genres. It is ... the critic's task to learn

these genres and to engage them in discussions about the artists. While anybody can criticize a Spike Lee film, it seems to me that the significant criticisms should involve a degree of identification with the argument of the artist and the genre in which the film is produced. (Ross et al. 3)

I concur. Taking my first viewing of *She's Gotta Have It* in 1986 as an example, I found it an accessible and likable picture that spoke to me as a moviegoer with eclectic tastes, a reviewer quite familiar with international film culture, a youngish man with a soft spot for stories of youthful romance and lively, attractive heroines, a male with strong allegiance to the modern feminist movement, and a white male with memories of the 1960s civil-rights movement and a conviction that color-based bigotry had been – and still was, in slightly less virulent forms – the original sin and ongoing blight that must somehow, someday be expiated and redressed if the so-called "American dream" is ever to become something other than a sour, hypocritical delusion. I have no doubt that aspects of *She's Gotta Have It* escaped me in 1986 and continue to escape me now that I am more than a quarter-century older but as white and male as I ever was. Feature films are enormously complicated entities, though, and the ever-shifting perspectives and mindsets of us imperfect mortals preclude *everyone* from grasping *all* the meanings of *any* film. That includes the people who make the movies in the first place; many a towering auteur has told me or one of my academic or journalistic colleagues how completely he or she failed to recognize what a particular film was *really* about at the very time it was being written, directed, and released.[2]

Taking this reasoning one more step, it is also true that Lee's films have been sympathetically and intelligently received by viewers who probably have less in common with him than I do, such as white women – an unexpected

group, perhaps, since creating strong female characters has
not been one of Lee's strong points. One such supporter is
the author and commentator Sarah Vowell, who opines that
Lee's movies may be "hard" and "exasperating," but gets his
American ethos exactly right:

> Lee's ambitious approach is intensely democratic. His
> mosaic storytelling impulse, aided by his talent and ability
> at choosing singular actors, feels like what America is sup-
> posed to feel like. The citizens of his cities are not faceless,
> nameless representatives of the masses. They are unique
> individuals. . . . Ultimately, Lee's films are never going to
> be about any one thing, race included. They're art, not
> politics, and the responsibility of art is to the story, to the
> image, to whatever the artist himself cares about.

Writing about *Inside Man*, film critic Stephanie Zacharek
zeroes in on Spike's indefatigable New York sensibility:

> He has a feel for the city that relatively few other filmmak-
> ers do, a knack for capturing not just the things people say
> to each other and the way they say them, but the way the
> city seems to be carried – maybe even powered – by the
> rhythm of their overlapping sentences: That symphony of
> speech is the city's greatest source of vitality.

Commenting on Lee for the British magazine *Sight and
Sound*, the American critic Amy Taubin calls him "the most
dedicated resistance fighter to infiltrate the Hollywood
system – the film-maker who put the fraught and disavowed
issues of race and racism at the centre of his films and refused
to be ghettoised for doing so" (26).[3] While others – female
and male alike – find much to criticize, dislike, and even
deplore in Spike Lee's cinema, his eagerness and ability to

reach audiences across sociocultural boundaries is a sign that his portrayal of America is insightful, authentic, and true.

In discussing Lee's movies from my own necessarily white perspective I'm also thinking of a passage near the beginning of *Spike Lee: That's My Story and I'm Sticking to It*, an auto-biographical "as told to" book by Kaleem Aftab, a London-based writer and producer.[4] "To pigeonhole Spike Lee on the grounds of his race would be to inflict a great injustice," Aftab writes, arguing that Lee is better seen as "a quintes-sential New Yorker: whether . . . watching basketball games courtside at Madison Square Garden, employing the city as the primary location for most of his films or providing his oft-reported commentaries on . . . politics and life." Shortly after these remarks, however, Aftab contends that Lee's reaction to the terrorist attacks on September 11, 2001, demonstrated that "in both his personal life and his work" Lee cannot be portrayed "as a New Yorker," since he is an integral part of something larger still, "the cultural fabric of America" (3). I agree with Aftab that it's unjust and inaccurate to stereo-type any community – New Yorkers, or Americans, or those shocked and outraged by mass murder – on the basis of race, religion, sexuality, or the other markers used by bigots to separate Us from Them in hazy, lazy, arbitrary ways. And this is a persistent message of Lee's movies, crystallized with special precision by the scenes in *Do the Right Thing* and *25th Hour* where slurs and venom are hurled at the camera with a velocity and force that render them hyperbolically absurd in the former film, bitter and repellent in the latter.

I've known Spike since the 1980s and we've talked many times, informally and in interviews for print and media out-lets; he has never hesitated to speak about race in plain-spoken, no-nonsense terms, and he has never hinted at the notion that a white person might be less qualified than a black one to discuss the subject, remembering of course that the social, cultural, and political experiences of white people unavoidably lack the stink of racist affliction that America has forced on black people throughout its history. All of which underscores the point that Spike Lee is an American artist as well as an African-American one, and that his success in using mass media to reach a sweeping array of black and non-black Americans – plus followers in other countries around the world – opens his work for discussion by observers and critics of every kind. This is the spirit in which I look at, think about, and comment on his usually exciting, sometimes exasperating, invariably stimulating and energizing American movies.

1

THE EARLY JOINTS

Shelton Jackson Lee, nicknamed Spike by his mother as an infant, entered the world in Atlanta on March 20, 1957. His mother was Jacquelyn Shelton Lee, a schoolteacher, and his father was Bill Lee, a musician. Deciding he could have a more successful career if he lived in Chicago, the "jazz Mecca" of the period, Bill Lee moved the family there, and then joined the throng of jazz musicians who relocated to New York in the late fifties. Putting down stakes in Brooklyn, the family settled first in Crown Heights, then in Cobble Hill – where they were the first African-Americans to live – and then in Fort Greene, a neighborhood seen by many outsiders at that time as less than desirable, if not actually dangerous or disreputable. Spike's mother was an important influence on his childhood, exposing him and his siblings to mainstream and African-American culture by way of books, plays, museums, and art exhibitions.

Music was an important part of the picture as well, and Spike sometimes heard his father play the bass at the Blue

Note and other New York clubs. His three younger siblings – sister Joie, born in 1962, and brothers David and Cinqué, born in 1961 and 1966 – went to Saint Ann's School in Brooklyn, a predominantly white private institution where their mother had become the first African-American teacher. Ever independent, though, Spike had already chosen to attend the John Dewey High School, a public school in the Coney Island neighborhood of Brooklyn with a largely black student body. Ever consistent, moreover, after graduating in 1975 he enrolled at the historically black, all-male Morehouse College in Atlanta, where his grandfather and father (a classmate of Martin Luther King Jr. there) had gone. His tuition was paid by his grandmother, Zimmie Shelton, an alumna of the all-female Spelman College across the street from Morehouse, which Spike's mother had also attended.

SPIKE STARTS OUT

Seeing a lot of movies for diversion after his mother's sudden death in 1977, Spike became seriously interested in the possibilities of film for the first time. "I had gotten a Super 8 camera," he recalled later, "so I spent the whole summer just going around New York City and filming stuff. That was really when I decided that I wanted to be a filmmaker" (Lindo 165). Back at Morehouse with two years still to go for his degree in mass communication, he continued his experiments and made *Last Hustle in Brooklyn*, his debut short, before graduating in 1977. Returning to New York, he put an official stamp on his commitment to film, becoming one of very few black students in the graduate film program of the Tisch School of the Arts at New York University, where he spent three years earning an MFA in production. He was not overly fond of NYU, to put it delicately: professors there questioned his grasp of "film grammar," and he sensed an unspoken racial bias in their criticisms. "Any time a black person is in a white environment," he remarked later, "and they are not always happy – smiling, eating cheese [–] then [others] say he's a militant or has an attitude." His first-year film, *The Answer* (1980), did not change that impression. Discussing it with Nelson George, an African-American critic, Lee described it as the story of "a black screenwriter hired to direct a fifty-million-dollar remake of *Birth of a Nation*. We included clips from *Birth of a Nation*. They didn't like that thing at all. How dare I denigrate the father of cinema, D.W. Griffith?" George responded by observing that *The Answer* indicts Griffith's epic Civil War movie as a "racist" work, which of course it is, and Lee replied, "Yeah. No shit, Sherlock." George further observed that the film must have "offended" people to elicit such negative responses, and Lee answered, "Yeah. I didn't care" (Lee 1987, 33–4).

In sum, Lee was ready from the start to work against the grain of mainstream white cinema. Aware that Los Angeles is allegedly the motion-picture capital of the world, he dutifully gave it a shot, traveling west and taking an internship at Columbia Pictures, which he soon left for several reasons: he didn't know how to drive, he "didn't have the resources [there] to make films," and he simply "wanted to come home" (Lee 1987, 33–4). The idea of laboring on money-driven projects dreamed up by other people must also have grated on his sensibility.

SPIKE CUTS HEADS

His dissatisfaction with NYU notwithstanding, Lee made three movies while studying there, including his 1983 thesis film, *Joe's Bed-Stuy Barbershop: We Cut Heads*, a seminal work that sets forth three important clues to his future career. For one, the movie cuts heads – not in the barbering sense but in the sense of revealing and excising the inherited ideas, reactionary fantasies, and unexamined prejudices that Americans too often carry around in their minds. For another, it taps into areas of interest that Spike has been investigating and building on ever since: humor, gangster films, and "the incorporation of negritude" into a familiar movie genre (Lee 1987, 34). For the third, *Joe's Bed-Stuy Barbershop* is very much a New York movie, signaling that Lee's ongoing analysis of America's complicated, mercurial character would always be informed by his experiences in that city, the country's most protean and multifarious urban zone.

Joe's Bed-Stuy Barbershop centers on Zachariah Homer (Monty Ross), who takes over a barbering business after proprietor Joe (Horace Long) dies in a mob-related hit. Zach fares poorly at "head cutting" and his economic future looks grim until he meets the criminal who had set Joe up in the numbers game, a long-established racket whereby people bet on their predictions of the last three digits of the day's total racetrack-gambling figure. Learning that his barbershop will now be a base of operations, Zach has to choose between stooping to their level or standing by his principles.

Spike's decision to make this "semi-gangster" picture was guided partly by the real-world nature of the subject. Numbers-running is a billion-dollar business, he explains in his autobiographical book *Spike Lee: That's My Story and I'm Sticking to It*, and it has "always been a key part of the African-American community" (18). Lee also takes the opportunity to revise the blaxploitation and black-mobster genres, taking them in a more humanistic direction, and to profile some of the character types he encountered in Brooklyn on a regular basis. The movie's attentive portraits of Zach and his social-worker wife, Ruth (Donna Bailey), provided "some of the first sympathetic and detailed glimpses of the borough's

African American faces, personalities, and communities," in the words of film scholar Paula J. Massood (125), who also notes Lee's effective use of rap music and break dancing to pinpoint the story's time and place. Although the story is set squarely in Brooklyn – at the intersection of Flatbush Avenue and Myrtle Avenue, to be precise – *Joe's Bed-Stuy Barbershop* proved anything but parochial in its appeal. It won a student Merit Award from the Academy of Motion Picture Arts and Sciences, shared a prize at a Swiss film festival, and made Spike the first student filmmaker to earn a slot in the highly selective New Directors/ New Films event, presented each year by the Film Society of Lincoln Center and the Museum of Modern Art, two of New York's most important cultural institutions. Spike acquired an agent at the powerful William Morris Agency on the strength of the film. And he had demonstrated his talent for collaboration, a key ingredient in the filmmaking process: *Joe's Bed-Stuy Barbershop* was photographed by Ernest Dickerson, who went on to shoot every Lee picture from *She's Gotta Have It* in 1986 to *Malcolm X* in 1992; the cast included *She's Gotta Have It* costar Tommy Redmond Hicks; and the sound was recorded by assistant director Ang Lee, later to become a major American filmmaker in his own right. Spike's accomplishments with *Joe's Bed-Stuy Barbershop* gave his morale a major boost at a time when prospects for African-American cinema – and for his own career in the industry – seemed, as usual, highly uncertain.

BROOKLYN

Woody Allen is provincial about Manhattan, as reflected in his work; and I am provincial about Brooklyn in mine. Maybe one's [sports] fandom was part of it. Sensibilities must start somewhere.
– Spike Lee (Eliot 107)

A winning element in Lee's filmography is his loyalty to Brooklyn, the city within a city where he grew up, began his career, and maintains his professional nerve center, 40 Acres & A Mule Filmworks, to this day. We should therefore visit Brooklyn before traveling farther into Spike's America as a whole.

Welcome Back, Kotter (ABC, 1975–9), a popular classroom sitcom starring Gabe Kaplan and John Travolta, started each episode with a montage that included a highway sign reading "Welcome to Brooklyn: 4th Largest City in America." The boast is still justified. According to the United States Census, more than two and a half million people lived in Brooklyn in 2010, and although projections suggest that Houston, Texas, may acquire the fourth-largest-city title by 2030, for now it is safely in Brooklyn's hands. All of this comes with the obvious caveat that Brooklyn is not an independent city at all: it is the most populous of the five boroughs that constitute New York City, and the second largest (after Queens, its near neighbor) in geographical size. It is isomorphic with Kings County, one of five counties within New York City, and its population is strikingly diverse. Around 35 percent of its residents are non-Hispanic whites and a slightly smaller percentage – about 877,000 persons – are African-Americans, followed by Hispanics and Latinos at 20 percent, Asians at 10 percent, and others at 2 percent. About 25 percent of Brooklyn's residents have yearly incomes that place them below the official poverty line.

Fort Greene, the uptown neighborhood where Lee's family settled, is in northwestern Brooklyn, not far from the Brooklyn Bridge, which connects the borough with Manhattan to the west. Free blacks lived there long before the Civil War – the slaves in New York State were emancipated in 1841 – and during the Civil War period its largely working-class population was joined by upper-class people moving north from downtown, drawn partly by Fort Greene's reputation for high-grade educational institutions. For about thirty years beginning in the early 1960s, Fort Greene suffered badly from the epidemic of crime, drugs, and poverty that weighed heavily on New York and many other American cities. But reclamation, gentrification, and urban preservation helped the neighborhood regain its footing in the second half of the 1980s, and 40 Acres & A Mule, founded in 1986, was a pioneer in this effort, sparking comparisons between Fort Greene's rising artistic star and the legendary Harlem renaissance of the 1920s and 1930s.

A few years later a sociologist described Fort Greene as "a tolerant, relaxed neighborhood, not a homogeneous one that resists strangers" (Jackson 1). Today it is known for its architecture in the Eastlake and Italianate styles, dating from the middle of the nineteenth century; for such major cultural facilities as the Brooklyn Academy of Music and its annex, the BAM Harvey Theater; and for schools including the Brooklyn Technical High School and the nearby Pratt Institute, which trains creative professionals and artists. Spike moved himself and his family to Manhattan in 1998, buying an Upper East Side townhouse when he and his wife, Tonya, became parents and felt the need for a more secure and secluded residence than they were able to find in their Brooklyn neighborhood. "Here we are much more anonymous," Tonya Lee said in 2004 (Allon). Spike's heart and production company are still in Fort Greene, however, and will probably remain there for good.

SHE'S GOTTA HAVE IT

The Color Purple . . . *is weak . . . but that was no surprise.* WE, I, GOTTA MAKE OUR OWN GODDAMN FILMS. FUCK HAVING

THESE WHITE BOYS FUCK UP TELLING OUR STORIES. WE GOTTA
TELL OUR OWN AS ONLY WE CAN. – Spike Lee (1987, 253)

Dangerous Combination

Brooklyn has not always been as friendly to Lee as he has
been to the borough. He has spoken candidly about the difficulties he ran into while shooting *She's Gotta Have It* there
in 1986, and he has been equally frank about his unhappiness
with some aspects of the film itself. As he later recalled,

> We were cashin' in bottles for change, because we had so
> little money. I remember, we were shootin' in [a] loft in
> the middle of the summer – it musta been a hundred and
> four degrees up there. ... We only shot for twelve days,
> but every night ... I had to think about tryin' to go out and
> raise money for the very next day.

As for the end result, "the acting was bad. ... I didn't really
know how to direct" (E. Mitchell 46–7).

Artists are not always the best judges of their own work,
and while box-office profits are a poor indicator of artistic quality, the success of *She's Gotta Have It* marked Lee's
emergence as a notable independent filmmaker and consoli-
dated 40 Acres & A Mule Filmworks, Inc., as a viable enterprise. (According to Box Office Mojo, the film parlayed its
$175,000 budget into returns of well over $7,000,000.)[1] It
also linked Lee with what Massood calls a "Brooklyn chro-
notope," using theorist Mikhail Bakhtin's term for a unified construction of narrative time and space. Before we see
characters we see the Brooklyn Bridge, then the Brooklyn
building where the heroine lives. Manhattan, the star of so
many Hollywood movies, plays a bit part – it is an Elsewhere
that only one of the film's dramatis personae finds appeal-

ing. The movie strikingly integrates its story with the sights, sounds, folkways, and mores that would surround a young Brooklynite in the mid-eighties. Depicting a "black urbanscape . . . different from any other African-American space screened thus far," as Massood writes (126), the film replaces such iconic locations as Manhattan's fabled Apollo Theater and 125th Street bustle with Brooklyn shots of "identifiable subway stops, the Fulton Mall, the Promenade along the East River, and Fort Greene Park" (129), all filmed on location.

The result is a Brooklyn movie par excellence, making up in authenticity what it lacks in budget and polish. Looking back on *She's Gotta Have It* two years after its premiere, the African-American author and Fort Greene resident Thulani Davis observed that the film "took place in a black neighborhood [and] was about black people and . . . was from a black perspective, but nobody said anything about that within the context of the narrative. It was taken for granted," and a *New York Times* article called the picture "a turning point for both the neighborhood and for Fort Greene's younger generation of creative artists." Lee himself saw the neighborhood as the launching pad for his career as "a black nationalist with a movie camera – and that's a dangerous combination" (Shipp 1988, 3, 5).

The woman who's "gotta have it" in the film is Nola Darling (Tracy Camilla Johns), a freewheeling Brooklynite with an active sex life that signals her refusal of double-standard morality. She begins the story by speaking directly to the audience in one of the self-reflexive shots that Lee calls "confessions," already becoming a trademark in his work. "That's it, that's the word," he wrote in a 1984 journal entry. "CONFESSION. The characters in this film are confessing. Of course, not all of them are telling the truth, only what they perceive as the truth" (1987, 112). Nola says she wants to "clear [her] name," not of being promiscuous but of imputations that her habit of occasionally breaking lovers' hearts is somehow less excusable than similar behavior by a man would be. Over the course of the film she experiments with various approaches to sex and sexuality in relationships with three very different lovers, making mistakes along the way but remaining her own woman in the end.

There are three men in Nola's life, and sometimes in her bed. One is Jamie Overstreet (Tommy Redmond Hicks), who introduces himself in another direct-address shot, saying, "I believe that there is only one person, only one in this world that is meant to be your soul mate, your life-long companion . . . Nola was the one." Jamie thinks this makes him a sentimental sweetheart, but commentator Terry McMillan more accurately describes him as the kind of man who "would try to put the clamps on you after you fucked him real good and . . . would orchestrate and plan out your entire life" (24), which is a good précis of how Lee evidently wants him to be perceived. The second man Nola currently dates, Greer Childs (John Canada Terrell), is a sleek-looking model with a surplus of self-regard. In the screenplay Lee calls him a pretty boy who "takes his good looks for granted, it's a given," adding that if a woman doesn't take notice of this "he automatically thinks there is something wrong with her" (1987, 301). Greer's confession confirms his egotism: "I'm the best thing that ever happened to Nola . . . It was I who made her a better person." As self-regarding as this sounds, it's his later sentences that make him a bona-fide Lee villain. "If she would have only listened to me and moved out of Brooklyn," says the Manhattan dweller, "we would be together this very day. It's not civilized over there." Lee himself plays Mars Blackmon, the third boyfriend.

At first Mars thought Nola was "freaky-deaky," he con-

Mars Blackmon (Spike Lee) visits Nola Darling (Tracy Camilla Johns) in her apartment in She's Gotta Have It, *the movie that launched Lee as an important American filmmaker. (All plates are screen shots made for the author.)*

fesses; but after having "def" sex with her, he decided that "all men wants freaks, we just don't want 'em for a wife." This crisply illustrates yet another kind of male hubris. Mars is the film's most comical figure, uttering his signature plea for Nola's ministrations – "Please, baby, please, baby, please, baby, baby, baby, please!" – like a half-demented rapper whose mind and mouth aren't quite in touch with each other. It isn't clear just why Nola is interested in this scruffy guy, but his presence gives the story added humor, spice, and, above all, energy. Mars is the first of several less-than-admirable secondary characters whom Spike has portrayed; others include the hapless Half-Pint in *School Daze*, the inept Giant in *Mo' Better Blues*, the unreliable Cyrus in *Jungle Fever*, and the dope-dealing Snuffy in *Crooklyn*. His most memorable role is Mookie, the pizza-delivery guy in *Do the Right Thing* who manages the triple threat of being likable, lackadaisical, and fearlessly decisive in the film's most intense moment. Lee's range as an actor is narrow, but he plays

Mars as he plays these others, with a blend of self-effacing wit and attention-grabbing savvy that bespeaks remarkable talent within the circumscribed sphere of character types he has marked out for himself.

Dark Continent

Nola's experiments in sexuality lead to a couple of final ventures that she quickly finds to be dead ends: first celibacy, then going back to Jamie, whom she thinks of as "her best friend in the world." Her last confession sums up both the character's strength of mind and the filmmaker's wish to celebrate her independent spirit. "I got a little crazy," she says of her short-lived return to Jamie, "should have never gone back in the first place. It was a momentary weakness. He wanted a wife, that mythic old-fashioned girl next door. But it's more than that. It's really about control, my body, my mind. Who was going to own it? Them? Or me? I'm not a one-man woman. Bottom line." Whereupon she smiles and jumps into what she calls the "loving bed" in her Brooklyn loft, surrounded by softly glowing candles. Cut to black, roll end credits.

Not everyone is persuaded by Nola's final words. "Autonomy is not depicted as a life-enhancing, empowering choice" in the film, writes the African-American feminist critic bell hooks, claiming that the protagonist's "decision to be self-defining leaves her as vacuous and as empty as she has previously appeared," without even the "savvy" she earlier displayed in her occasional "vamp" persona. Although she has had plenty of sex, hooks continues, "what she has not had is a sense of self that would enable her to be fully autonomous and sexually assertive, independent, and liberated" (2008, 8). Michele Wallace, also an African-American cultural critic, shares hooks's misgivings about the film's negativity toward lesbian sexuality; the lesbian Opal Gilstrap

(Raye Dowell), who unsuccessfully sets her sights on Nola, "comes on like the original serpent in the Garden of Eden," she writes. Wallace likewise declares that Nola often seems "less like a character than a dark continent to be explored and conquered." Nola's language in her direct-address confessions, Wallace adds, "seems inane and self-canceling, as if she were selling something in a TV commercial" (26).

Perhaps most important, hooks and Wallace are both troubled by Lee's handling of the scene in which Jamie forces himself on Nola when she rejects his marriage proposal. Wallace points out that in the journal Lee kept while making *She's Gotta Have It* and published after the film's release, he clearly indicates that Jamie is the "best man" among Nola's lovers and never calls what Jamie does a rape; yet she allows that "these matters work out considerably better in the film than in the notebooks," since Lee ultimately "resists the obvious conclusion, in which the best man marries Nola, the prize" (25). Taking a harder line, hooks observes that Nola refers to the event as a "near rape," as if it weren't really such a bad thing, and contrasts two kinds of responses to the scene. One sort comes from viewers (presumably female) who feel "seduced and betrayed" as well as "passively disgusted, disturbed." The other comes from "sexist male viewers" who, having felt vilified by earlier scenes critiquing male supremacy, vocally cheer Jamie on, "expressing their satisfaction that the uppity black woman [has] been put in her place." So far apart are interpretations of the incident, hooks acknowledges, that many people she spoke with "did not notice that there was a rape scene." She herself felt no such ambivalence, however: for her, the film "impresses on the consciousness of black males, and all males, the sexist assumption that rape is an effective means of patriarchal social control," while simultaneously telling "black females, and all females, that being sexually assertive will lead to rejection and punishment" (2008, 6–7).

Wallace and hooks make valid points, but so do other critics (many of them outside the academic world) who recognize *She's Gotta Have It* as a work of popular art and an intervention in popular culture, not a polemic that fails to make an airtight case for right-minded conclusions. Writing for the *New York Times*, reviewer D.J.R. Bruckner wrote that the characters "are not victims of blind forces; they make choices, defend them and grow in understanding, not always happily, as a result." The entertainment trade newspaper *Variety* (1985) found that the film has everything needed for "an interesting yarn" except a "compelling central figure," but accurately observed that the Nola character "is, clearly, trying to find herself," albeit in ways not interesting enough for the reviewer. Praising the film's "psychological authenticity" in the *Chicago Reader*, critic Peter Keough described Nola as "an earthily charismatic young woman" whose "independence" combines with the "clashing styles" of her three lovers "in comic situations that build into giddy fugues." These are brief but balanced assessments of Nola's sincere yet imperfect and ultimately incomplete quest for knowledge of herself, her sexuality, and what her most gratifying role in black American society might be.

The objections to *She's Gotta Have It* expressed by hooks and Wallace have less persuasive force when placed against the fact that Lee's first feature film is also his first major foray into the dialectical mode of pop-cultural analysis that has remained a constant in his work. As ever, he is not particularly caught up in specific views of right and wrong, good and bad, correct and incorrect; his method is more concerned with setting up situations where different perspectives on moral, ethical, romantic, and other such issues can emerge with roughly equal weight, intersect with one another in comic or dramatic ways, and produce questions and conundrums instead of resolutions and conclusions.

What are the right things for Nola to do ? Should she like lesbian sex better? Crank up her vampishness more often? Try to sound more confident in her confessions? Say "actual rape" instead of "near rape" when she reflects on that traumatic experience? Spike doesn't say, because he doesn't lay claim to neat answers for messy questions. Rape is no less grave a matter than hooks suggests, but Wallace has a more nuanced take on this aspect of the film, realizing that since moral evaluation must always be relative and subjective to a degree, Lee at least merits approval for steering away from the conventionally "obvious solution" and presenting Nola as an aspiring free spirit, if not an actual one, at the end of her story.

In fairness to Lee's less forgiving critics, it must also be said that where I see sophisticated dialectical thinking in Lee's films, others see indecisiveness and dithering. "Lee seems incapable of making a straightforward statement about the social and political issues he depicts," Benjamin Saltman wrote in the early 1990s. "His juxtaposition of anecdotes defines no particular stance, no unified vision. Those who want a definite statement such as 'Fight the power' will not find it, because Lee is himself divided about the nature of the struggle. He will not and perhaps cannot embrace an ideology. He inhabits an aimless political space" (40). This point of view deserves to be taken seriously, although for the most part I don't share it. Lee's practice of putting "definite" and "straightforward" statements into dialogic play with the messiness and irresolution of actual American life makes him a realistic and pragmatic political thinker, not an aimless one.

As a final note about Nola, I will add that she is a dark continent not only to the men in her bed but also in many ways to herself, as are we all in the daily negotiations between our fractured, impulsive selves and the fractured, overbearing world in which we live. Lee takes this as a given with Nola, as he does with virtually all the characters in his films. She is not the liberated woman that hooks and Wallace would like to see, but she is a bravely self-inventing woman whose sense of self is very much a work in progress, as one would expect in a person so young, able, and attractive. While she doesn't always choose her next moves shrewdly or interpret her past mistakes wisely, she deserves the compliment Lee and Johns pay her by giving her personality such a delicate balance of complexity, vulnerability, and charm. "Nola Darling is my heroine," Lee wrote in his production journal. "I love and respect her, and I must show that love and respect in my treatment of her in the script. That's the way it gotta be" (1987, 70).

School Daze

Uplifting the Race

For his second feature, the dark musical comedy *School Daze*, Lee left his beloved New York borough for the South, locating the film at fictional Mission College, a black institution where "Uplift the Race" is the motto, sexual machismo is everywhere, and rampant colorism fuels separation and conflict between African-American students with lighter and darker skins. Although the surroundings are very different from the Brooklyn of *She's Gotta Have It*, Lee again strikes autobiographical chords, since while the Morehouse College he attended was not the crazy house of *School Daze*, it was nonetheless an African-American school in a Southern college town. Lee makes Mission the setting for an obstreperous portrayal of racial politics within a cross-section of the African-American community, sketched out with hyperbole and tendentiousness rather than realism or objectivity in mind. Some find the film biting and truthful; others deem it bitter, self-defeating, and mean. In short, it raised the noisi-est ruckus so far in Spike's career when it premiered in 1988. The story takes place during homecoming weekend, when tensions between the school's opposing camps, the light-skinned Haves and the darker Have-Nots, are running higher than usual. Film scholar Michele Wallace doesn't much like *School Daze*, with its incursions of misogyny and homopho-bia, but she crisply summarizes the dramatis personae who set the tale in motion:

> Dap [Laurence Fishburne], the story's protonationalist hero, and Da Fellas, or male Jigaboos, are participating in a rally to protest South African apartheid and the fail-ure of Mission College to divest. ... Trouble promptly arrives in the form of the stylishly dressed [male] Gamma Phi Gammas, the principal contingent of the Wannabees [sic], led by a proto-Nazi [student, called Dean Big Brother Al-*might*-ty, played by Giancarlo Esposito] and flanked by the glamorous [female] Gamma Rays. They don't give a damn about divestment or the plight of South African blacks. As Julian/Big Brother Almighty so succinctly puts it, "I'm from Detroit! Motown!"
>
> The particular cause of conflict is the display the Gammas are making of breaking in eight, baldheaded, sycophantic, slavelike pledges, who are being led along, chain-gang style, on leashes. "It takes a real man to be a Gamma man!" the Gammites chant at the top of their lungs, "Because only a Gamma man is a real man!"

One of the pledges, Wallace adds, occupies a uniquely limi-nal status in the film, being the only character who appears to communicate effectively with both groups: "none other than the bigeyed auteur Spike Lee, as Half-Pint, Dap's cousin" (27). Wallace's tone implies that the "bigeyed auteur" has somehow outgrown his britches or aspired beyond his station; but to the extent that Half-Pint does serve as a living link between the opposing camps in the story, he is an appropriate analogue for Lee, the filmmaker who creates racially complex fictions on the screen in order to communicate with racially complex audiences in movie theaters. The somewhat similar figure Lee went on to play in his next film, *Do the Right Thing*, does much the same: as the delivery man for Sal's pizza emporium, he divides his time between traversing the story's African-American milieu and working inside the pizzeria itself, seeing the business's Italian-American proprietors more closely and clearly than any of his black neighbors are able to do.

Dirty Laundry

Addressing the film's African-American detractors, sociologist Michael Eric Dyson blames hostility to *School Daze* on the "dirty-laundry theory of racial politics," according to which African-Americans must observe "a tedious etiquette of racial manners" based on the notion that "negative, controversial, or critical news about black folk, especially if its source is other blacks, must be handled in secrecy away from the omniscient gaze of white society" (xxiii). *School Daze* violates this etiquette, Dyson writes, by revealing "the lethal confrontations black folk have over hair texture, skin complexion, class status, and educational attainment" (xxiv). Noting that production of Lee's "morality play" was forced to leave the Morehouse College campus "allegedly due to crossed signals regarding the availability of dorm space for filming," Dyson asserts that "a more likely explanation may be retaliation by Morehouse's administration against Lee's critical look at the rituals of black self-hate dramatized in full color and sketched on a film canvas that the entire public was invited to view." This bespeaks a "racial insecurity" and a "narrowness of racial vision" that must, in Dyson's eyes, "be addressed and opposed" (xxiii–xiv).

Lee's assault on race-based narrowness and insecurity centers on differences – both personal and ideological – between Da Fellas and the Gamma gangs. The students from working-class backgrounds celebrate their racial roots and call their politically complacent peers Wannabe whites, while the more privileged students disdain racial activism. "Back to Mother Africa, that's bullshit," says Big Brother Almighty of the frat-boy set. "We're all black *Americans*. You don't know a goddamn thing 'bout Africa. I'm from Chi-town!" The film's intersecting battles are conducted partly on physical levels, partly on psychological levels, and very much on linguistic levels; the students' cries of "jigaboo" and "wannabe" have provoked a fair share of the animus directed at the film. This aspect of the film suggests a tie between Lee and Frantz Fanon, the philosopher, psychiatrist, and theorist who held that racial alienation and self-hatred are essential products of colonialism, and contended that in racist cultures language is the "primary instrument" through which dominance is exercised *upon* oppressed people and estrangement is expressed *by* them (Sharpley-Whiting 9–10).

Code-Switching

Lee's sophisticated grasp of language codes and linguistic shadings is illustrated particularly well in the scene of *School Daze* wherein Dap and five friends drive to a Kentucky Fried Chicken joint, smoothing over a severe disagreement they've just had by exchanging repartee along the way. The mood turns downward when they arrive at the eatery, encountering black working-class townies who see them as rich kids and outsiders. Dap's brief stab at racial camaraderie goes nowhere, but his group makes an honorable retreat, puzzling about the experience on their way back to the campus. In a detailed study of language variations in this episode, sociolinguist Margaret Thomas observes that speech appears in the different social contexts of language among intimates, conventional service language, and language among strangers. It carries different affects as well, ranging from playful joking on the way to the chicken place, veiled resentment from the waitress, overt hostility during the clash with the locals, and sober conversation as Dap and company drive back to campus. The dialogue also produces many different speech acts, as language is used for purposes of teasing, informing, requesting, rejecting, challenging, conciliating, insulting, denying, attacking, supporting, threatening, reflecting, agreeing, and disagreeing (Thomas 914).

One of the scene's most intriguing features is its display of verbal code-switching, whereby characters mix standard English with what linguists identify as black English or African-American Vernacular, modulating their speech in ways that indicate affiliations of class and ethnicity. Throughout the film, people make spontaneous adjustments in their speech to convey implicit claims about their social identities at that moment; in the chicken-joint scene, they shift between standard English and AAV both to define themselves and to put across unstated propositions about the identities of others. Thomas's analysis of this scene finds many instances of meaningful code-switching, such as those incorporated by the dialogue quoted below. (AAV usages are indicated by nonstandard spellings, italics, and brackets around words the English alphabet can't approximate; the brackets and some slight modifications are mine.) Dap's group includes Grady (Bill Nunn), Booker T. (Eric Payne), Jordan (Branford Marsalis), Edge (Kadeem Hardison), and the relatively inarticulate Monroe (James Bond III), all dressed and groomed with a "natural" look; the locals include an unnamed waitress (Tracey Lewis) as well as Leeds (Samuel L. Jackson) and his crew of Moses (Edward G. Bridges), Spoon (Albert Cooper), and Eric (Dennis Abrams), some of whom wear Jerri curls and garish plastic caps to protect their hairdos. A good example of code-switching occurs when the students ask the waitress for three two-piece meals, all of them "*waht w' frahs*," initiating this exchange:

> **Waitress:** [*using standard English in a deliberately flat tone*] White meat or dark?
> **Dap:** [*after checking with the others*] Yeah he wants white meat.
> **Waitress:** [*flat tone and standard English again*] We don't have any white meat today.
> **Grady:** *Den wah ju as'?*

Since standard English and AAV are on a single linguistic and semantic continuum, with a good deal of overlap, the waitress's adherence to standard English in this informal, conventionalized exchange with black people is a significant choice, asserting her refusal to identify with the students; in response, Grady uses AAV, thereby "communicating to her both that he recognizes the implicit message in her marked choice of code, and that he repudiates it" (Thomas 918, 922).

Another good example takes place after Dap and company have left the restaurant under pressure from the locals, who follow them into the parking lot:

> **Dap:** [*using AAV to diffuse tension by suggesting racial solidarity*] *Yeah brothah, wad d'you wan'?*
> **Spoon:** [*using AAV to fire back*] *You ain no kin t'me.*
> **Leeds:** [*also firing back*] *Thass* [right] *an we ain' yo*

> *brothahs. How come you college muthahfuckahs think y'all run everything?*
> **Booker:** Is there a problem here?
> **Spoon:** [Big] problems.
> **Moses:** *I heard dat.*
> **Leeds:** *You come t'ah town* [year *afta* year] *an' take ovah. We wuz born* [here] *gon be* [here], *gon die* [here], *an'* [can't find] *jobs 'cuza you.*
> **Monroe:** Yeah, right. C-can can we go? OK, can we just go?
> **Leeds:** *We may not haf yo ed-ju-ca-tion but we ain' dirt neither.*
> **Dap:** *It ain' nobody said alla dat, all right?*
> **Leeds:** You Mission folks always *talkin' down t'us.*
> **Dap:** *You look brothah ah'm real sorry dat you feel dat way. OK, ah'm really sorry about dat.*
> **Leeds:** [*explicitly challenging Dap's ethnicity*] *Ah you black?*
> **Eric:** *Take a look inna mirrah, man.*
> **Dap:** Look man, you got a legitimate beef all right but *it ain' wid us, ok?*
> **Leeds:** [*repeating his challenge*] *ah – you – black?*
> **Dap:** [*angrily reversing the challenge by using AAV to signal black authenticity*] *Hey look we don' have a question of fact whether ah'm black. In fact ah wuz gonna ask yo country bama ass wah you got dem drip drip chemicals in yo* [hair].
> [. . .]
> **Leeds:** *N'ah bet you niggahs do think y'all waht. College don' mean shit. Y'all niggahs, an you gon' be niggahs fo-evah. Jus like us. Niggahs.*
> **Dap:** [*slowly and deliberately*] You're NOT *niggahs.*

Having prevailed in the confrontation, for the moment at least, the students walk backward to their car and drive away. Analyzing this moment, Thomas observes that Leeds's highly charged line (*"Y'all niggahs . . ."*) places the college students "under Leeds's own ethnic self-description," changing the argument from "Who is truly black?" to "What does it mean to be black?" Dap frames his response ("You're NOT *niggahs*") in the first phonetically and syntactically standard English he has used in speaking with the locals, reserving AAV only for the final word, which he takes directly from Leed's taunt. Dap thus asserts his difference from the locals, rejects the claim of racial destiny, declares his refusal of the derogatory term, and voices that refusal in a second-person statement that extends it to Leeds and his friends, ascribing more dignity to them than they are ascribing to themselves (Thomas 919, 920, 923).

Lee wrote the *School Daze* screenplay in standard English for the most part, so contributions from the ensemble cast deserve credit along with Lee's scripting and directing skills for the nuances of vernacular speech that enrich the chicken-joint scene and other sequences. Linguistically speaking, Thomas finds the film's uses of AAV and code-switching between dialects to have a wholly authentic ring (925), and she notes that the Kentucky Fried Chicken episode has drawn praise even from otherwise severe critics of the movie, such as essayist and editor Fred Beauford, whose largely negative review grudgingly admitted that the restaurant scene reveals "the Spike Lee everyone was raving about last year" (Beauford, cited in Thomas 914).

Stepping High

The highly significant speech patterns in the Kentucky Fried Chicken scene are underscored and supplemented by knowingly orchestrated details of costume, gesture, and body language. The episode can therefore be taken as a small-scale exercise in a kind of African-American discourse that was riding particularly high in the late 1980s: stepping, a performance ritual – located almost entirely in black colleges and universities, especially among fraternity and sorority members – that is actually a set of interlinked actions known as cracking, freaking, and saluting. Three years after *School Daze* gave stepping the widest, most diversified exposure it had yet received, performance scholar Elizabeth C. Fine estimated that some five thousand Greek-letter chapters with half a million members participated in the practice, a complicated affair (evidently dating back to the 1940s) that involves dancing, singing, chanting, and speaking, with words and music derived from African-American folk traditions as well as advertising jingles, TV theme songs, and current radio and jukebox hits. Sometimes called "blocking," after the block (yard) where students tend to gather and hang out, stepping varies greatly from one region, locale, and venue to another, serving in all its forms as a rite of group identity that manifests the "spirit, style, icons, and unity" of its participants. The main components of stepping are cracking or cutting, whereby groups aim verbal or nonverbal taunts at one another; freaking, which happens when a freaker or "show dog" breaks out of the group activity in a bid for special attention and approval; and saluting, a display of good feeling communicated by one group to another through imitations of its characteristic moves or symbols (E.C. Fine 39, 40, 47–8).

Using a high-spirited step show to encapsulate and dramatize the cultural gap that divides Jigaboos from Wannabes on the Mission campus, Lee constructs a bravura production number: Da Fellas are on the stage; the Gamma Rays start cracking, as do the Gamma Rays in the audience; Da Fellas raise the stakes with a step routine insulting the Gamma Rays, piling them with homophobic and class-based insults; and finally Da Fellas make an outright threat – "Get back, or we'll kick your Gamma ass" – and leave the stage, precipitating a full-out brawl. Pointing to connections between *School*

*Lighter-skinned Wannabes square off against darker-skinned Jigaboos
in one of the uproarious musical numbers in* School Daze.

Daze on the screen and school days in real colleges, Fine says
the film's clashes between dark-skinned and light-skinned
women are "similar to the perceived conflict between Alpha
Kappa Alpha and Delta Sigma Theta at Virginia Polytechnic
Institute and State University, which some students believe
involves skin color." Although women of all shades are found
in both sororities, Fine reports that some students coun-
terfactually think "that one has to have skin the color of a
brown paper bag to be a member of AKA, while the women
of DST are darker" (57).

Pigment Nation

This gets to the heart of the movie. The action of *School Daze*
is sometimes frenetic and often sophomoric, but as Dyson
recognizes when he calls the film a morality play, its main
concern is entirely serious: the philosophical divide between
black Americans who want to embody, refine, and celebrate
their black African identities and roots, and those who want

to integrate, assimilate, and ultimately dissolve into mainstream American society, which is largely dominated and
defined by whites. And the film's chief metaphor for this
divide – colorism – is itself a real and troubling phenomenon. *School Daze* spotlights it as a chronic symptom of the
psychological and spiritual oppression that is largely responsible, in Lee's view, for the African-American insecurity of
which Dyson speaks.

After surveying numerous studies of skin-color stratifica-
tion, sociologist Margaret L. Hunter reported in 2002 that
hierarchies of color, determined by lightness or darkness
of skin tone, are an "enduring part of the US racial land-
scape," supported by "popular understandings within the
Black community about beauty and status." Observing that
the effects of skin color on income and educational level are
determined in part by the prejudices of white employers and
educators, Hunter finds a more disturbing phenomenon to
be the "clear advantage in the marriage market" enjoyed by
light-skinned black women, who are "more likely to marry
high-status men than [are] darker skinned women." Since
this marriage-market inequality has little to do with prejudices among white people, Hunter takes it as evidence for
"the pervasiveness of racist ideologies that value whiteness
and emulations of it" within African-American culture itself
(176, 189). It follows that Lee's attack on pigmentocracy in
School Daze is far from unjustified or gratuitous, however
grating its color-fixated characters and jigaboo–wannabe
vocabulary may sometimes seem.

Sense of Outrage

Critics found much to criticize in *School Daze*. The reviewer
for *Variety* (1987) opined that the film's mixture of forms and
styles "never comes together in a coherent whole,' that Lee's

directing "fails to strike the right note between realism and fantasy," and that "the heavy subject matter just falls with a thud." *Washington Post* critic Rita Kempley (1988) wrote that the "pompous patchwork plot . . . is an arrogant, humorless, sexist mess," and her co-critic Desson Howe (1988) said the film's episodes "are overdrawn when they're not underexplained," building to either "predictable inanity or nothing at all." Janet Maslin's more tempered *New York Times* review (1988) called *School Daze* the work of a "brave, original and prodigious talent," but complained that Lee doesn't let his daring off the leash, creating a hodgepodge of ingredients "bound together only loosely by [his] prevailing sense of outrage."

The most influential critic to speak in favor of *School Daze* was Roger Ebert (1988), who deemed it "the first movie in a long time where the black characters seem to be relating to one another, instead of to a hypothetical white audience." Although he acknowledged "big structural problems" and many "loose ends" in the film, Ebert noted the surprise of finding a "daffy story" treated in a manner that is "revolutionary" in its avoidance of the problems that damage most movies about black people, which seem "acutely aware of white audiences, white value systems and the white Hollywood establishment." Ebert goes on to discuss with refreshing insight the scene that most offended other commentators:

> In its own way, *School Daze* confronts a lot of issues that aren't talked about in the movies these days: not only issues of skin color and hair, but also the emergence of a black class, the purpose of all-black universities in an integrated society, and the sometimes sexist treatment of black women by black men. In one of the movie's most uncompromising sequences, a black fraternity pledge master expresses

concern that Half-Pint is still a virgin (none of the brothers in this house should be virgins), and he supplies his own girlfriend (Tisha Campbell) to initiate the freshman. She actually goes through with it, tearfully, and although the scene was so painful it was difficult to watch, I later reflected that Lee played it for the pain, not for the kind of smutty comedy we might expect in a movie about undergraduates.

In its own way, I will add, *School Daze* accomplishes the task that Mission College finds so difficult. Mischievously and mercilessly, it uplifts the race – not just the very-black race and the not-so-black race and the white race and the other color-based "races" vying for power, freedom, and dignity in today's America, but rather the human race, which is the one that matters.

2

THE RIGHT THING AND THE

LOVE SUPREME

Do the Right Thing

Moviegoers were still debating *School Daze* when Spike Lee completed his third feature. Still widely regarded as his most accomplished work, *Do the Right Thing* had its world premiere in May 1989 at the Cannes International Film Festival, where it was a prime contender for the Palme d'Or, the festival's highest prize. It opened commercially in France and the United Kingdom the following month and reached American screens shortly thereafter, earning an impressive array of honors. These included Academy Award nominations for Spike's original screenplay and supporting actor Danny Aiello; two Image Awards (from the National Association for the Advancement of Colored People) for actress Ruby Dee and supporting actor Ossie Davis; a New York Film Critics Circle Award for cinematographer Ernest R. Dickerson; prizes from the Los Angeles Film Critics Association for director Spike Lee, composer

Bill Lee (Spike's father), supporting actor Aiello, and best picture; a Boston Society of Film Critics Award for Aiello; Chicago Film Critics Association prizes for Aiello, director Lee, and best picture; and Golden Globe nominations for Aiello, director Lee, screenwriter Lee, and best drama. A decade later, in 1999, the National Film Preservation Board and the Library of Congress added *Do the Right Thing* to the National Film Registry of movies with special cultural significance. All of which amounted to quite a haul for a black nationalist with a camera.

Wake Up!

Do the Right Thing represents a considerable change from *School Daze* in terms of filmmaking craft – no other Spike Lee joint surpasses it for visual, verbal, and musical excellence – and accessibility for racially diverse audiences; the latter goal is greatly facilitated by the inclusion of several important white characters, a first for the filmmaker. There are clear continuities of psychology and theme between the two pictures, however, beginning with their shared commitment to prompting social thought rather than promoting particular agendas. *School Daze* does not resolve the racial and sexual issues it raises, concluding instead on a conspicuously open-ended note as Dap forcefully says "*Wake up!*" to the other characters and the audience. *Do the Right Thing* likewise rejects the pretense of "solving" knotty problems and "answering" thorny questions that have stumped real-life America for decades and in some cases centuries. It is therefore appropriate that the last words of *School Daze* reappear as the first words of *Do the Right Thing*, spoken by the disc jockey Mister Señor Love Daddy (Samuel L. Jackson) to the neighborhood he addresses and the moviegoers who overhear him: "*Wake up!*"

Do the Right Thing frames a knockabout New York story in an elegant Aristotelian form, complete with a chorus of corner men who spend their days watching and commenting on current activities from the sidelines. Place: Brooklyn's mostly black Bedford-Stuyvesant neighborhood. Time: the hottest day of the year. Action: the rise of race-based animosities centering on an Italian-American business and the African-American community it serves. The business is Sal's Famous Pizzaria (*sic*), owned and operated in the area for years by the eponymous entrepreneur and his sons Vito (Richard Edson), a relatively hapless and harmless young man, and Pino (John Turturro), an overt and unapologetic racist. Trouble starts when a young black man called Buggin Out (Giancarlo Esposito) tries to organize a boycott of the pizza place because Sal (Danny Aiello) refuses to include pictures of African-American celebrities on the "Wall of Fame" that decorates his establishment. "American Italians only," Sal explains, asserting his rights of ownership. The locals feel a right of ownership as well – they are the raison d'être of the place, after all, and without them Sal's Famous would not exist. Tensions wax and wane as the temperature climbs through the long summer day, culminating when the neighborhood's most resolute rap-music devotee, Radio Raheem (Bill Nunn), plays his ever-present boom box too loudly for comfort in Sal's place of business. Sal unleashes a racist tirade against Raheem; chaos breaks out around them; police barge in, escalating the turmoil; one of them holds Raheem in a chokehold that strangles him to death; Sal's most easygoing employee, the black delivery guy Mookie (Lee), abruptly hollers "*Hate!*" and throws a trashcan through Sal's window; and a full-scale riot erupts, ending only when the building has gone up in flames.

The film concludes with a series of dialectical moments that can be distilled and charted:

1A   In a brief dialogue scene with complex emotional dynamics, Mookie and Sal express mutual distrust and antagonism.

1B   They finish their conversation by partly reconciling with each other, hinting that they might even work together again after Sal rebuilds his business with insurance money.

2   The screen goes dark, allowing the hopeful overtones of (1B) to linger.

3A   Printed text gives a quotation from the Rev. Dr. Martin Luther King Jr., explaining why violence is always self-defeating.

3B   Printed text gives a quotation from Malcolm X, saying violence in self-defense may be necessary and commonsensical.

4A   The screen fills with a photograph of these leaders embracing each other, suggesting that their philosophical differences were skin deep compared with their shared commitment to African-American equality.

4B   Printed text dedicates the film to five people who suffered grave consequences from actual mob and police violence in years prior to the film's release.

Neither separately nor together do these images and words inform us what the right thing is supposed to be. This rich, productive uncertainty is the meaning and "message" of the film, extending from its superbly ambiguous title to a wealth of major and minor details embedded in its fabric.

Race and Rage

Do the Right Thing stirred controversy and debate long before it reached American screens. Its world premiere at the 1989 edition of the renowned and influential Cannes International

Film Festival – where it lost the Palme d'Or to *Sex, Lies, and Videotape*, the debut film by Steven Soderbergh, another American independent director with a formidable future – elicited cheers from observers such as actress Sally Field, a member of the awards jury, who told Lee she fought hard on its behalf, and harsh criticism from others. Attributing such disputes to "the rage of race," the *Time* film critic Richard Corliss summarized the "furor" that surrounded its arrival in American theaters:

> Not since the Black Panthers cowed Manhattan's glitterati 20 years ago has there been such a virulent outbreak of radical chic – or so many political-disease detectives ready to stanch the epidemic. A single issue of the *Village Voice* ran eight articles on the movie, with opinions running from raves to cries of "fascist" and "racist." A political columnist for *New York* magazine charged that Lee's film could undermine the New York City mayoral campaign of a black candidate. Everywhere, the film has polarized white liberals for whom Bed-Stuy is as exotic and unknowable as Burkina Faso. Some see Lee as the movies' great black hope; others tut till they're tuckered. A few fear that *Do the Right Thing* could trigger the kind of riot it dramatizes and perhaps condones. (62)

Lee has answered the latter charge many times over the years, as when he told a *New York* interviewer (Hill) in 2008 how "insane" he finds it that journalists

> like Joe Klein and David Denby felt that this film was going to cause riots. Young black males were going to emulate Mookie and throw garbage cans through windows. Like, "How dare you release this film in summertime: *You know how they get in the summertime, this is like playing with fire.*"

I hold no grudges against them. But that was twenty years ago and it speaks for itself.

Lee feels the film's incendiary elements reflect not only outrage over specific injustices but also a "complete frustration with the judicial system" in the African-American community. One day after the film's premiere at the Cannes festival, Lee told me, "a black man was ... strangled to death ... in New York City, in a police precinct ... This film is not science fiction. All this stuff is happening."

Sesame Street

> *Journalists ask me, "Spike, why aren't there any drugs in your films?" – as if African-Americans are the only people on earth who use drugs and African-American filmmakers are somehow the only filmmakers beholden to tackle that issue in their work. –*
> Spike Lee (1990)

Lee was also accused of portraying a sanitized Bedford-Stuyvesant that amounted to a *Sesame Street* version of ghetto life, as clean and orderly as the well-scrubbed television series for children. Writing in the above-cited piece that he found it "maddeningly difficult" to understand the film's point of view, Corliss went on to say,

> All we know for certain is that *Do the Right Thing* is not naturalistic. Golden sunset hues swathe the street at 10 in the morning. The color scheme is chicly coordinated, as if Jerome Robbins' Sharks and Jets were about to dance onscreen; the picture could be called Bed-Stuy Story, full of Officer Krupkes and kindly store owners. At first, the dilemmas are predictably pastel too: populist cliches brought to life by an attractive cast. Even the racial epithets

have a jaunty tinge, as in a series of antibrotherhood jokes made by blacks, Italians, Hispanics, white cops and Korean grocers – the film's best sequence. On this street there are no crack dealers, hookers or muggers, just a 24-hour deejay .... (62)[1]

I think this criticism has its own prejudicial tinge. On any given day in even the "worst" neighborhoods, most people are just living their lives, not slogging about in dirt, drugs, and crime. It's true that ingrained poverty has taken a mental toll on many of Lee's characters: the corner men and Da Mayor are the most obvious examples. The situation speaks for itself, though, and there's no reason for Lee to exaggerate things by importing worn-down Hollywood views of inner-city misery. "If this film were done by a white filmmaker," he told me, "it would have been all dark. There would've been no loud colors. It would have been raining every day, and in complete despair – with no humor but [with] rapists, crack addicts, drug dealers, pregnant teen-age mothers throwing their babies out of windows." That, he said, is "white people's idea of black ghettos" (Sterritt 1989). Black filmmakers have presented aspects of inner-city life in dire terms as well – including Lee in some of his later work – but his wish to set forth a corrective view is understandable and commendable.

Do the Right Thing has also been accused of downplaying Bed-Stuy's growing diversity, focusing on conflict between blacks and whites at the expense of, for instance, the neighborhood's Asian-American population. This criticism is justified as far as it goes, but it doesn't go very far, since black–white conflict is a substantial enough subject to sustain any number of films, and other tensions are certainly noted in *Do the Right Thing*, especially with regard to the proprietors of the Korean deli across the street from Sal's eatery, who have little patience for complaining customers like Da Mayor and Radio Raheem, but are quick to grab for allegiance – questionable and hypocritical allegiance – with their black neighbors when chaos breaks out at the climax of the story. The deli prompts what might be the bravest gesture of soul searching Lee has ever placed in a film. It occurs in one of the brief episodes showing the corner men – ML (Paul Benjamin), Coconut Sid (Frankie Faison), and Sweet Dick Willie (Robin Harris) – in their usual routine of idle chatter, tired jokes, and expressions of fleeting anger and frustration at their lot in life. They have just been unpleasantly distracted by the sight of two policemen cruising down the street with snarling, suspicious expressions on their faces as they survey the neighborhood. One of them mouths the words, "What a waste," and the following ensues:

ML: Look at that.
Coconut Sid: Look at what?
ML: It's a God damn shame.
Sweet Dick Willie: What's a God damn shame?
ML: Sweet Dick Willie!
Sweet Dick Willie: That's my name.
ML: Damn, man, do I have to spell it out?
Coconut Sid: Come on, make it plain.
ML: Okay, but listen up. I'm gonna break it *down*.
Sweet Dick Willie: Let it be broke, motherfucker.
ML: Can you dig it!?
Sweet Dick Willie: It's dug!
ML: Look at those Korean motherfuckers across the street.
   I bet you they haven't been off the boat a year before
   they open up their own place.
Coconut Sid: That's right, man, it's been about a year.
ML: A motherfucking year off the motherfucking boat and
   they already got a business in *our* neighborhood. A good
   business! Occupying a building that had been boarded

up for longer than I care to remember. And I've been here a long time.

Coconut Sid and Sweet Dick Willie: [*mumbling*] A long time . . . yeah, boy. . . .

ML: And now for the life of me, y'know, I can't figure this out. Either them Korean motherfuckers are geniuses, or you black asses are just – plain – dumb.

Sweet Dick Willie: Fuck you.

Coconut Sid: It's got to be because we are black. There ain't no other explanation.

Sweet Dick Willie and Coconut Sid: [*shouting each other down*] Look, I know, man, ain't it always true . . . they keep the black man without shit . . . Man, I am tired of hearing . . .

Sweet Dick Willie: [*interceding*] You motherfuckers hold this shit down. I'm tired of hearing that old excuse! I'm tired of hearing that shit! Shit!

ML: I tell you, I swear, man, I will be one happy fool when we open our own business, right here in our neighborhood. I swear to God, I will be the first in line to spend what little money I got.

Coconut Sid: I'm right there with you, man.

Sweet Dick Willie: You motherfuckers are always talking that old shit, "I'm gon' do this, I'm gon' do that. You ain't gonna do a God damn thing but sit your ol' monkey ass here on this corner. ML, when you gonna get your business? Huh? Yeah, just like I thought, you ain't gonna do a God damn thing. But I tell you what *I'm* gonna do, you hear me? I'm gonna go over there and give those Koreans some more of my money! Get the fuck outta my way. God damn, it's Miller time, motherfucker! [*walking across the street and muttering*] Old moosehead, fuckin' tell me what to do, and Coconut, you got a lot of damn nerve, you got off the boat too. Leave me alone.

Shoot. [*to Sonny*] Hey, kung fu! Come on and gimme one
o' those damn beers.

Sweet Dick Willie is greeted at the deli by Sonny (Steve
Park) saying, "No more free beer," and continues ambling
down the sidewalk. Back on the corner, ML concludes, "It's
a motherfuckin' shame," to which Coconut Sid responds,
"Man, ain't that a bitch." And the scene is over, having raised
a problem so complicated, emotional, and seemingly intractable that Lee felt he could not sidestep or ignore it in good
conscience, even though his lack of solutions is plainly in
evidence. It is an extraordinarily candid, painful, and moving
moment.

Polyphony

One of the most fertile sites of dialectical expression in *Do
the Right Thing* is the music track, which manifests what
film-music scholar Victoria E. Johnson identifies as Lee's
characteristic position with regard to music and story,
simultaneously in tune with mainstream practices, "promoting familiar black artists for commercial reproduction and
consumption on a mass scale," and forging an oppositional
practice of its own, "voicing black history within a tradition-
ally white industrial context" (19). The film's underscoring
(background music) and source music (present in the world
of the story) act out a complex dialogic pattern as different kinds of music intersect, contrast, and collide with one
another and with the film's dialogue, sound design, and
visual components, echoing three kinds of consciousness that
coexist in the Bed-Stuy personality mix. The two primary
musical modes can be called the historic-nostalgic, composed by Bill Lee in the American style of folk-influenced
romantic music scored for small orchestra and jazz combo,

and the popular-commercial, itself expressed by two dialecti-
cally interacting styles: the rap and hip-hop emanating from
Radio Raheem's boom box; and the soul and rhythm-and-
blues numbers played by Mister Señor Love Daddy on We
Love Radio 108 FM, the neighborhood's own station. The
popular-commercial mode also incorporates the interplay
of music and words, since the boom box songs have lyrics
and the platters spun on 108 FM are linked by the smooth
obbligato of Mister Señor Love Daddy's patter and chatter.

Hip-hop represents the street folks, as the prevalence
of rap on Raheem's boom box suggests. In this variety of
hip-hop, songs are actually "incantations, chants which can
correctly be seen as thematic variations on the question of
power, racism, class," in critic Wheeler Winston Dixon's
words (Dixon 229; Johnson 24). Part of rap's subversive
power comes from its challenge to the traditional bifurca-
tion of word and music in contemporary culture; by blurring
the boundaries between song and speech, and by incorpo-
rating samples from other pop-music pieces, almost any
rap performance or recording is to some extent disjunctive,
disruptive, and dialogical. Lee signals the importance of rap
in *Do the Right Thing* by accompanying the opening titles
with the sound of Public Enemy pumping out "Fight the
Power" and the sight of Rosie Perez dancing to the music
with brightly colored boxing gloves on her expressively
pugnacious hands.[2] The volume is loud and the message is
clear: the movie you're about to see is one that fights the
power with maximum audiovisual muscle. Lee ups the ante
further by celebrating the sonic power of Raheem's boom
box, as when it wins a sidewalk competition with a Latino's
less vigorous blaster and acquires near-deafening volume in
the final approach to the pizza-place melee. Given that traditional ideas of movie music call for it to function "invisibly"
as a mood enhancer of which the audience is hardly aware

– its themes are "unheard melodies," in Claudia Gorbman's accurate phrase – the in-your-face booming of Raheem's box mounts an ultra-scrappy challenge to the audience's ears. Radio Raheem is not the protagonist of *Do the Right Thing*, but in important respects he and his music are its presiding spirits. And while he generally appears to be one of the story's less articulate figures – apart from his "Love and Hate" monologue, which I will discuss shortly – he provides the occasion for some of the film's most subtle word-related humor. My favorite example occurs when he enters the Korean deli to buy fresh batteries for his boom box from Sonny, the clerk who always appears to be on duty:

> **Radio Raheem:** Give me 20 D Energizers.
> **Sonny:** 20 C Energizers?
> **Radio Raheem:** Not C, D.
> **Sonny:** C Energizers?
> **Radio Raheem:** D, motherfucker, D. Learn to speak English first, all right?
> **Kim:** How many you say?
> **Radio Raheem:** 20, motherfucker, 20.
> **Sonny:** Motherfuck you.
> **Radio Raheem:** Motherfuck you? You, you all right, man.

Raheem's face infinitesimally lightens as he says the last line of the exchange, revealing his amusement at the Korean's imperfect mastery of "motherfucker" grammar. Nunn's acting here is superb.

Raheem is inseparable from his boom box, the power and volume of which are sources of extreme pride for him. Discussing his stadium-wattage sound system, film scholar Thomas Doherty calls the boom box "an Ur-symbol of interracial animosity and class style wars" and therefore a "perfect radiator for black anger and white noise (and vice versa)," providing a tool for minority members "to exact vengeance and aggression" (38) on an unwary bourgeoisie. These dissonant urban vibes are definitely not toned down by the choice of Public Enemy's brain-quivering clamor as the soundtrack's most conspicuous component. Founded on Long Island half a dozen years before *Do the Right Thing*, this extremely spirited ensemble managed more successfully than many groups to evade cooptation (at least partially) by the music-industry establishment. Writing not long after the film's first run, Doherty noted that far from being "politically engaged in the approved I-ain't-gonna-play-Sun-City mold,[3] these guys are authentically bad in the Webster Dictionary sense" (38). And so they are, using ferocious lyrics and a jackhammer beat to trash decency, decorum, and propriety at the highest decibel levels enabled by the magic of modern technology.

This is so agreeable to Raheem that he can't imagine the whole world doesn't share his zeal for the group. When the race-minded Buggin Out asks him if this is the only tape he has, Raheem's reply is borderline incredulous:

> **Radio Raheem:** You don't like Public Enemy? It's the dope shit.
> **Buggin Out:** I like 'em, but you don't play anything else.
> **Radio Raheem:** I don't like anything else.

Lee very much likes other kinds of music, though, and some of these also figure in the movie's mix. The most important are romantic string tunes that evoke more conservative tastes in the community, and strains of jazz, soul, and pop that carve out an eclectic ground between middlebrow mildness and street-level aggressiveness.

The triple-pronged musical approach of *Do the Right Thing* – rap and hip-hop, melodious strings, time-tested jazz, soul, and pop – conjures up a virtual history of African-American entertainment, reflecting both Spike Lee's connoisseurship of black music and Bill Lee's experience as the composer of several folk-jazz operas and as a respected bassist who has played in sessions and combos for many jazz, folk, and pop performances. In addition to their artful clashes with Raheem's hop-hop, moreover, the folk-orchestral and jazz-soul-pop modes constitute another dialogic cluster in the movie's sound design. Johnson observes that the folk-opera themes, associated with such older-generation characters as Mother Sister and Da Mayor, use standard tonalities, medium dynamics, and unobtrusive entrances and exits to summon senses of nostalgia for the past and satisfaction with the current status quo, which are attitudes rooted in heritage, community, acceptance, and accommodation with white-dominated society. The black-jazz themes, again associated with Mother Sister and Da Mayor and also with Sal and the mentally disabled Smiley (Roger Guenveur Smith), suggest values of assertiveness, resistance, black pride, black power, and the wish for social transformation. Interspersed with these elements, the records that Mister Señor Love Daddy broadcasts on 108 FM – ballads, dance music, salsa, reggae, a cappella numbers – stand for inclusiveness, multiculturalism, and the ideal of unity among diverse peoples in a changing and complicated community.

Mister Señor Love Daddy's roll call of African-American music stars, heard on the soundtrack against a montage of neighborhood views, is a folkloric oral counterpart to the photographic visual pride expressed by the Wall of Fame in the pizzeria. It is no less plugged into the commercial inter-ests of consumerist America, though, and herein lies another of the film's many dialectical ironies. Buggin Out is right about Sal's wall: Joe DiMaggio, Frank Sinatra, Robert De Niro, Liza Minnelli, Al Pacino, Luciano Pavarotti, Bobby

Darin, and their ilk bedeck the gallery, but there's not a "brother" to be found. Brothers abound on Mister Señor Love Daddy's list, ranging from Little Richard, Chuck D, Janet Jackson, and Stevie Wonder to Thelonious Monk, Otis Redding, Dexter Gordon, Roland Kirk, and beyond.[4] Their differences from Sal's ethnic heroes are grounded in color, style, and audience, not confrontational stances or oppositional politics vis-à-vis the consumers of mass culture. In order to flourish, popular entertainers must maintain an ongoing balance between the contrapuntal values of artistic integrity and commercial bankability, and this goes as much for We Love Radio stars – even for Radio Raheem's beloved rappers – as for Italian-American icons. Sal's idols are gods of the big screen, the concert hall, the opera house; 108 FM's favorites are musicians who thrive on the airwaves, in the jazz clubs, on the stages of jam-packed stadiums. Most of them won't be heard on Raheem's boom box, which is reserved for boom box stars – and they too, however abrasive their sounds and subversive their messages, have struck bargains with the capitalist devil in order to be in the marketplace at all. Aesthetically speaking, nobody in Sal's gallery or on We Love Radio's list is a radical, a revolutionary, a creative outlier, or an ideological extremist. For them as for everyone in Spike Lee's America, artistic freedom and establishment success are like the LOVE and HATE on Raheem's hands, forever at odds yet inextricably conjoined. And all of this applies to Spike's brand of filmmaking, poised as it is between faith in aggressive independence and aspirations to mass-audience popularity.[5]

Many viewings of *Do the Right Thing* over many years have confirmed my early impression that the film's most striking musical moment is one of the most striking cinematic moments as well: the extraordinary single-shot scene in which Sal and his unashamedly racist son Pino have a

heart-to-heart talk across a table in the pizzeria. Their economically written, sensitively acted conversation deserves
quoting at length:

> **Sal:** I'm beat.
>
> **Pino:** Daddy, y'know I've been thinking. Maybe we should
> sell this place, get out while we're still ahead. And alive.
>
> **Sal:** You really think you know what's best for us, Pino?
>
> **Pino:** Maybe we could . . . couldn't we sell this and open up
> a new one in our own neighborhood?
>
> **Sal:** There's too many pizzerias already there.
>
> **Pino:** Then we could try something different.
>
> **Sal:** What am I gonna do? That's all I know. What am I
> doing? I've been here twenty-five years. Where am I
> going?
>
> **Pino:** I'm sick of niggers. It's like I come to work, it's
> Planet of the Apes. Don't like being around them,
> they're animals.
>
> **Sal:** Why you got so much anger in you?
>
> **Pino:** My friends, they laugh at me, they laugh right in
> my face, they tell me go, go to Bed-Stuy, go feed the
> Moulies.
>
> **Sal:** Do your friends put money in your pocket, Pino? Food
> on your table? They pay your rent, the roof over your
> head? Huh? [*Pino says nothing.*] They're not your friends.
> If they were your friends, they wouldn't laugh at you.
>
> **Pino:** Pop, what can I say? I don't wanna be here. They
> don't want us here. We should stay in our own neigh-
> borhood, stay in Bensonhurst, and the niggers should
> stay in theirs.
>
> **Sal:** I never had no trouble with dese people. I sat in this
> window, I watched these little kids get old. And I seen
> the old people get older. Yeah, sure, some of them don't
> like us, but most of them do. I mean for Christ's sake,

Pino, they grew up on my food. On *my* food. And I'm
very proud of that. Oh, you may think it's funny, but I'm
very proud of that. Look, what I'm trying to say, son, is
that Sal's Famous Pizzaria is here to stay. I'm sorry. I'm
your father, and I love you, I'm sorry, but that's the way
it is.

As the dialogue starts, the music starts as well – a slow,
descending piano melody picked up in turn by a violin, a
cello, a soprano saxophone, and more violins. The mode
becomes more jazzy as the saxophone, piano, and drums
kick into freewheeling runs and scalar sheets of sound recalling the improvisational style pioneered by John Coltrane in
the late 1950s, rising in pitch and intensity while remaining
just muted enough to merge and nearly fuse with the actors'
voices rather than contend or compete with them. These
aural elements are calculated to echo the scene's visuals with
unerring accuracy. Sal and Pino are in profile at the table, the
pizzeria's front plate-glass window behind them. At first the
camera symmetrically frames the table and the actors from
a middle distance; then it gradually tracks toward the table,
which grows in proximity and scale as the dialogue becomes
more emotional and the music more passionate. The camera
stops on a fairly close two-shot of Sal and Pino, and stays
in place as the action begins a nuanced shift to the other
side of the window, where Smiley arrives with the photographs of Malcolm and King that he peddles intermittently
throughout the film. Pino angrily slams his hand against the
window to warn Smiley away; when this doesn't work he gets
up and goes outside the building, continuing his harassment
of Smiley and verbally sparring with street people outside
the camera's range while Sal sits exhausted and powerless to
intervene. The music has not changed much in character, but
now its semi-anarchic runs and wails convey the dangerous,

almost feral depths of feeling that surge between the characters and within the neighborhood. This scene stands with the most effective of Lee's career, in its depth of feeling and in its lofty degree of sheer filmmaking craft. It ends with a jolting cut to the first shot of the subsequent scene: Mookie emerging from the shower, pulling back the curtain and hollering a gleeful "Whooo!" I think this is Spike's shout of triumph at pulling off the virtuoso scene we've just watched – a justified burst of self-reflexive cinematic pride.

Raheem

Returning to Raheem, he is central to a pair of additional scenes that deserve attention. One is the aforementioned sidewalk contest between Public Enemy on his boom box, powered by no fewer than twenty D Energizers, and Rubén Blades on that of a young Hispanic man, evidently driven by a less awesome array of batteries. As the two men pump up the volume bit by bit, Lee does not cut between them in the commonplace shot–countershot editing pattern that most filmmakers would use; instead he swings the camera between them in rapid pans, connoting that these two streetwise, music-savvy guys inhabit the same psychological and sociological world even if they establish and affirm their somewhat different positions through acts of competition and contrast. This scene's dialectical complement arrives during the climactic confrontation between Raheem and Sal, where Lee cuts almost violently between the enraged men, one armed with a boom box, the other with a baseball bat. A vast cultural gulf now separates them, and Lee drives the point home with great visual force.

Apart from the climax, Raheem's most memorable moment is surely the "Love and Hate" monologue that he delivers to Mookie during a brief interval in the story. Lee

Radio Raheem (Bill Nunn) reenacts the story of love and hate in Do the
Right Thing, *reprising a memorable scene in Charles Laughton's great
melodrama* The Night of the Hunter.

took the concept of the speech from James Agee's brilliant
screenplay for *The Night of the Hunter*, a classic of American
expressionism that was directed by Charles Laughton
and released in 1955. *The Night of the Hunter* stars Robert
Mitchum as the Rev. Harry Powell, a psychopathic preacher
with the words "LOVE" and "HATE" tattooed on the fingers
of his right and left hands, respectively. Seducing a family
with his preacher masquerade, he sees that the little boy
has noticed his tattoos, and offers an explanation of sorts –
"the story of good and evil" – that Raheem appropriates and
adapts to the Brooklyn streets, displaying the keywords not
with tattoos but on large rings that resemble brass knuckles.
Raheem retains Powell's message but changes the diction a
bit. Samples:

> **Rev. Powell:** H-A-T-E. It was with this left hand that old
> brother Cain struck the blow that laid his brother low.
> L-O-V-E. You see these fingers, dear hearts? These fingers
> has veins that run straight to the soul of man.

Radio Raheem: HATE! It was with this hand that Cain iced his brother. LOVE! These five fingers, they go straight to the soul of man.

Rev. Powell: Now watch and I'll show you the story of life. These fingers, dear hearts, is always a-warrin' and a-tugging, one agin' t' other. Now watch 'em. Old brother left hand, left hand HATE's a-fightin', and it looks like love's a goner. But wait a minute. *Wait* a minute! Hot dog, love's a-winnin'! Yes, siree! It's love that won, and old left hand HATE is down for the count!

Radio Raheem: The story of life is this. *Static!* One hand is always fightin' the other hand. The left hand is kicking much ass. I mean, it looks like the right hand, LOVE, is finished. But hold on, stop the presses, the right hand's comin' back. Yeah, he got the left hand on the ropes, now, that's right! Ooh! Ooh, it's a devastating right and HATE is hurt! He's down! *Ooh! Ooh!* Left-hand HATE KO'ed by LOVE!

Rev. Powell illustrates his spiel by pitting his hands against each other in imitation of the struggle. By contrast, Radio Raheem interlaces his fingers while saying the word *Static*, and then enacts the conflict as a slugfest, jabbing his four-letter brass knuckles toward the camera like a prizefighter in the ring. Broadly speaking, Raheem's monologue accomplishes two things. One is to reaffirm the essentially good nature – the innocence, even – of this burly, lumbering, normally laconic man who appears to have no ambition in life beyond striding the Bed-Stuy streets with the blasting box and "Fight the Power" jive that will soon catalyze ruination for him and anguish for everybody else. He is clearly thrilled by the notion of Love knocking Hate off its pins, and he shares the story with the zeal of an evangelist.

The monologue's other function is to underscore Raheem's role as a conduit for cultural currents originating from sources far outside himself, not from a self-generated voice with worthwhile things to say about Brooklyn, or the neighborhood, or Sal's Famous, or Buggin Out's boycott, or even the Public Enemy song that leaps from his speakers all day long. His lack of meaningful things to *say* does not signal a lack of meaningful things to *feel* and *believe* and intuitively *know*, however. Like the Public Enemy song, the words of his monologue come from a source not encompassed by his first-hand experiences: they are spoken by a fictional character – an evil, unhinged character – in a movie made before Raheem was born, and it is anybody's guess where Raheem first heard them, how he came to memorize them, and why he takes such joy in repeating them. But they are *his* words now, as much a part of his mind, heart, and spirit as the other sights, sounds, impressions, and influences that flow to him and from him in the course of his daily rounds. After reciting them he addresses Mookie in similar terms:

Radio Raheem: [*showing his right-hand rings*] If I love you, I love you. [*showing his left-hand rings*] But if I hate you . . .

Mookie: [*having no idea what to say*] There it is, love and hate.

Radio Raheem: [*reaching out to shake Mookie's hand*] I love you, brother.

Mookie: Radio Raheem, check you later. Peace.

This exchange quietly foreshadows the paired quotations from Martin Luther King and Malcolm X that appear at the movie's end. It is thus one of the many politically charged moments that recur throughout the story.

Politics

Da Mayor, played by Ossie Davis, is a very sweet, very lacka-daisical man, capable of jumping into action when a little boy is about to get mowed down by a car, but mostly concerned with keeping up his supply of Miller High Life or whatever inferior substitute the Korean deli on the block currently stocks. The choice of Davis pays excellent dividends in terms of top-flight acting, and it enriches the film with associations stemming from his off-screen life. He was married to Ruby Dee, who plays Mother Sister, always skeptical of Da Mayor but gradually won over by him; and he was a civil-rights activist who delivered a eulogy at Malcolm X's funeral, which is printed as an addendum in *The Autobiography of Malcolm X* and is repeated in part in Lee's biopic about the leader. In addition to giving *Do the Right Thing* a considerable portion of its charm, Da Mayor is a walking, talking satire of the man actually reigning over New York City's government at the time: Edward I. Koch, first elected to the office in 1978 and nearing the end of his third consecutive term. (He ran for a fourth term in 1989 but lost the Democratic primary to David Dinkins, who then defeated Rudolph Giuliani in the general election, becoming the only African-American mayor the city has had to this day.)

Like many black people, and more than a few white people, Spike Lee had come to dislike Koch intensely, and he hoped *Do the Right Thing*, slated for release not long before the start of the campaign season, would help to bring him down. "In terms of the racial climate in the city at that time, Mayor Koch had really polarized a lot of New Yorkers," he said later. "We knew that when the film came out, it would be right before the Democratic primary for mayor. We felt that we could have a little bit of influence . . . and every time we could nail Koch, we would" (Aftab 76). The presence of Da Mayor is one such gesture, and a mild one, linking "mayor" with a harmless, even likable, but clearly ineffectual and shiftless old codger. Another jibe at Koch is Sonny's exaggerated impersonation of his thumbs-up, "How'm I doin'?" way of greeting the public during the interlude of direct-to-camera racial epithets in the film – this is one slur Spike agrees with and approves. Even the African-American cultural critic Armond White, normally a Spike Lee skeptic, calls *Do the Right Thing* "the movie [he] was born to make" and cites its anti-Koch activism as one of its main virtues. "*Do the Right Thing* didn't just sum up frustration with Ed Koch's legacy of neglect and implicit disdain," White wrote in 2006, "it did groundwork for the upcoming David Dinkins term and strengthened what little resistance there would be to the hostility of the upcoming Rudy Giuliani putsch."

Another, more controversial political gesture is the sight of "TAWANA TOLD THE TRUTH" spelled out in huge spray-painted letters on a wall in the scene where Mookie tells his sister Jade to stay away from Sal and the pizzeria. Tawana Brawley was a fifteen-year-old black girl who lived with her family in Wappingers Falls, New York, a Dutchess County town fifty miles north of New York City with a hundred black residents and five thousand white ones. After disappearing for four days in 1987, she was discovered "curled in a fetal position inside a plastic bag behind an apartment house," in the words of a *New York Times* report.

> Miss Brawley, who is black, had been beaten. "Nigger" and "'KKK" had been written in charcoal or marker on her torso, feces had been smeared across her body and her hair had been chopped off, the police said. She later told her family and law-enforcement authorities that she had been abducted and sexually assaulted by six white men – one of whom wore a police badge. (Iverem)

The case stirred up enormous public outrage and curiosity, only to become an enduring and contentious mystery when Brawley took the advice of her advisers and attorneys to end cooperation with those investigating her claims. A grand jury discredited her claims in 1988, reporting "an avalanche of evidence that [she] had fabricated her tale of abduction and sexual assault in the hands of a gang of racist white men" and had "concocted the degrading condition in which she was found . . . by smearing herself with feces, writing racial slurs on her body and faking a traumatized daze" (McFadden). This conclusion was based on hundreds of exhibits and thousands of pages' worth of testimony to the effect that when she was found her clothing but not her body was burned; she showed no evidence of being malnourished; the racial epithets were written upside down as if she had scrawled them herself; and more along these lines.

Spike's show of support via the prominently displayed graffiti accords with the perspective of commentators such as Patricia Williams, who wrote that the teenager "has been the victim of some unspeakable crime. No matter how she got there. No matter who did it to her – and even if she did it to herself" (169–70). The name Tawana Brawley in the film stands for all of the African-American girls and women who have been physically brutalized, psychologically traumatized, and spiritually dehumanized during centuries of enslavement and second-class citizenship. Some critics raked Lee predictably over the coals for promoting the "truth" of what they considered a manifestly false tale, but he stood by his words. "No one is ever going to find out what the true story is," he said during a college appearance in Dutchess County in 2001, "but I still find it hard to believe that Tawana Brawley, at that age, would have covered herself with feces and thrown herself in a garbage bag" (Rush et al.). I find it hard to agree with Lee's defense of the girl's literal truth, and even he has hedged his bet at times, as when he said on the 2001 commentary track for The Criterion Collection's release of *Do the Right Thing* on DVD that "the slogan was not a show of support" but was simply "the kind of statement he thought would be spray-painted on a wall in Brooklyn in 1989" (Aftab 75). Be this as it may, Williams's vindication of Brawley's story as symbolic, sociohistorical truth is valid and compelling for me. Whether or not Tawana faked her ordeal, Lee's film unfolds a larger truth about the oppression visited on black women and men ever since their forced arrival on the North American continent.

Martin and Malcolm

The most meaningful and dialectical of all the political elements in *Do the Right Thing* are found in the four documents that appear in succession between the last scene in the story and the start of the closing credits. The first and second are texts quoted from speeches by two African-American leaders; the third is a photograph; the fourth is Lee's dedication of the film.

The quotations from the civil-rights leaders have such weight and dignity that they deserve to be quoted in full. The first is a paragraph from the Nobel Lecture delivered by Martin Luther King Jr. on December 11, 1964, during the ceremonies marking his receipt of that year's Nobel Peace Prize for his leadership in the American civil-rights movement:

> Violence as a way of achieving racial justice is both impractical and immoral. I am not unmindful of the fact that violence often brings about momentary results. Nations have frequently won their independence in battle. But in spite of temporary victories, violence never brings

permanent peace. It solves no social problem: it merely creates new and more complicated ones. Violence is impractical because it is a descending spiral ending in destruction for all. It is immoral because it seeks to humiliate the opponent rather than win his understanding: it seeks to annihilate rather than convert. Violence is immoral because it thrives on hatred rather than love. It destroys community and makes brotherhood impossible. It leaves society in monologue rather than dialogue. Violence ends up defeating itself. It creates bitterness in the survivors and brutality in the destroyers. (King)

The second comes from a speech by Malcolm X titled "Communication and Reality," which he delivered to an assembly of domestic Peace Corps volunteers on December 12, 1964, a little more than three months before his assassination on February 21, 1965 at the age of thirty-nine:

I think there are plenty of good people in America, but there are also plenty of bad people in America and the bad ones are the ones who seem to have all the power and be in these positions to block things that you and I need. Because this is the situation, you and I have to preserve the right to do what is necessary to bring an end to that situation, and it doesn't mean that I advocate violence, but at the same time I am not against using violence in self-defense. I don't even call it violence when it's self-defense, I call it intelligence. (X 313)

These are characteristic statements by their respective speakers, setting forth complementary positions on the question of violence in the cause of human rights. If analysis went no further, their appearance here would represent the kind of "balanced" discourse habitually brokered by mainstream movies, public-broadcasting outlets, and the establishment press.

The statements are not neutrally presented, however. Their order on the screen frames Malcolm's avowal as a response and a risposte to King's declaration, signaling Lee's greater allegiance to Malcolm's call for "self-defense" and "intelligence" than to King's warning about the "bitterness" and "brutality" produced by violent action. Malcolm's words gain still more emphasis from their obvious relevance to the lengthy narrative and harrowing climax preceding them: moviegoers (especially white ones) have been asking since the film's premiere why Mookie throws the garbage can that sparks the riot that destroys Sal's place of business, and part of the answer lies in the film's vivid depiction of smoldering tensions and overpowering emotions that inevitably tilt the black community's default position toward the urgent need for self-defense rather than the time-consuming processes of dialogue and understanding across racial lines. And of course we now know that Lee would complete a massive biopic about his hero Malcolm just three years later.

The third of the film's concluding documents is a photograph showing the two leaders sharing a warm handshake with broad smiles on their faces – the "Malcolm and Martin" photo that Smiley, representing the inarticulate masses in the film, has been peddling in their neighborhood throughout the story. From all appearances, this is public-broadcasting discourse in its purest form, setting up a contest between conflicting points of view and then offering a "balanced" and "even-handed" perspective that "resolves" the conflict in emotionally appealing pseudo-utopian terms. But once again Lee's dialectical imagination is at work. The photo's content is clear: two giants and rivals of the civil-rights crusade setting aside their differences in a moment of mutual respect, understanding, and goodwill. What complicates

Smiley (Roger Guenveur Smith) displays his lovingly adorned photo of "Martin and Malcolm" in Do the Right Thing.

the moment, however, is the fact that Malcolm and King met and were photographed together only *this single time* during their careers, and the encounter itself lasted only a minute. Describing it on the occasion of Malcolm's eighty-fifth birthday in 2010, journalist John Blake wrote that King was leaving a news conference one afternoon when Malcolm stepped out of the crowd and approached him. "Malcolm X, the African-American Muslim leader who once called King 'Rev. Dr. Chicken-wing,' extended his hand and smiled. 'Well, Malcolm, good to see you,' King said after taking Malcolm X's hand. 'Good to see you,' Malcolm X replied as both men broke into huge grins while . . . photographers snapped pictures."

This information about the photo's provenance short-circuits any interpretation putting too much stress on ideo-logical agreement or personal closeness between the men. Yet to dismiss the image as a product of mere historical happenstance – and to dismiss its appearance in the film as a sort of dark inside joke on Lee's part – is also a mistake, since the two leaders actually *were* moving toward greater agreement on strategies and tactics in the movement they both served. "Malcolm X was becoming more like King – and King was becoming more like him," Blake wrote, citing historian David Howard-Pitney's conclusion that Malcolm was "moderating from his earlier position" while King was becoming "more militant" in his views. Blake's account continues,

> Malcolm X was reaching out to King even before he broke away from the Nation of Islam and embraced Sunni Islam after a pilgrimage to Mecca, says Andrew Young, a member of King's inner circle at the Southern Christian Leadership Conference, the civil rights group King headed.
>
> "Even before his trip to Mecca, Malcolm used to come by the SCLC's office," Young says. "Unfortunately, Dr. King was never there when he came."

All of these considerations were surely on Lee's mind when he planned the last moments of the film, and also when he prefaced the published screenplay (although not the movie itself) with words from *The Autobiography of Malcolm X* that again deserve quoting in full:

> The greatest miracle Christianity has achieved in America is that the black man in white Christian hands has not grown violent. It *is* a miracle that 22 million black people have not *risen up* against their oppressors – in which they would have been justified by all moral criteria, and even by the democratic tradition! It is a miracle that a nation of black people has so fervently to believe in a turn-the-other-cheek and heaven-for-you-after-you-die philosophy! It *is a miracle* that the American Black people have remained a peaceful people, while catching all the centuries of hell that they have caught, here in white man's heaven! The *miracle* is that

the white man's puppet Negro "leaders," his preachers and
the educated Negroes laden with degrees, and others who
have been allowed to wax fat off their black poor brothers,
have been able to hold the black masses quiet until now. (X
and Haley 251; Lee with Jones 1989, 120)

In a 1993 interview, the politically concerned critics Gary
Crowdus and Dan Georgakas told Lee that they saw not
a contradiction but rather a "dialectical tension" between
Malcolm and King, and that near the end of his life Malcolm
seemed to be saying to white leaders and citizens, "You'd
better deal with King, because, if you don't, you'll have to
deal with me." Lee readily agreed with this analysis, saying
that Malcolm's work complemented and supported King's
work, and that Malcolm wanted King to know that. Lee also
looked back at the quotations that concluded *Do the Right
Thing* four years earlier. "I wasn't saying it was one or the
other," he remarked. "I think one can form a synthesis of
both. When Malcolm was assassinated, I think they were
trying to find a common ground, a plan they could both
work on" (75). But time ran out, regrettably for them and
for us all.

Dedication

The last text to appear in *Do the Right Thing* is the dedication
of the film: "Dedicated to the families of Eleanor Bumpurs,
Michael Griffith, Arthur Miller, Edmund Perry, Yvonne
Smallwood, Michael Stewart." All were African-American
residents of New York City, and all died wrongful deaths –
like Radio Raheem in the film – at the hands of white people.
Eleanor Bumpurs died at age sixty-six on October 29, 1984,
shot twice with a 12-gauge shotgun while authorities were
evicting her from her Bronx apartment. The mentally ill

woman owed about $400 in back rent. You hear her name
from the crowd during the confrontation between the residents and the pizzeria guys after Raheem's death. (Her name
is misspelled "Bumpers" in the dedication.)

Michael Griffith lived in Bedford-Stuyvesant and died in
the Queens neighborhood of Howard Beach on December
20, 1986, hit by a car after leaving a pizzeria and being chased
onto a highway by white men chasing him and his companions with baseball bats. He was twenty-three years old, and
his death sparked enormous protests in the black community. Attorneys for Griffith and the other victims included
the Rev. Al Sharpton, mocked by Vito as "the Reverend
Mister Do, Al Sharp-tone," in the film, as well as Alton H.
Maddox and C. Vernon Mason, famously combative law-
yers centrally involved in the Tawana Brawley case. Twelve
people (not including the driver of the car, who wasn't at
fault) were indicted on charges related to the death; three
primary defendants were convicted of second-degree man-
slaughter and six others were found guilty of lesser offenses.
In the film, the mob trashing the pizzeria starts a chant of
"Power to the people," a phrase often heard in youth protests of the 1960s, but it soon changes to "Howard Beach!
Howard Beach!"

Arthur Miller, a construction contractor and community-
development leader, was choked to death by police in 1978
after a traffic stop in the Crown Heights neighborhood. The
incident led a local minister, the Rev. Herbert Daughtry, to
establish the Black United Front, a Brooklyn political organization that has expanded in subsequent years to become the
National Black United Front with headquarters in Chicago.

Edmund Perry, a seventeen-year-old graduate of Phillips
Exeter Academy, was preparing to attend Stanford University
on a scholarship when he was shot and killed by a plain-
clothes police officer in the Morningside Park neighborhood

of Manhattan on June 12, 1985. The policeman was cleared of wrongdoing when witnesses supported his assertion that Perry and another man were trying to mug him.

Yvonne Smallwood, twenty-eight years old, entered a dispute between a livery-cab driver and police and traffic agents that resulted in her arrest on December 3, 1987 on charges of assault, resisting arrest, obstructing government administration, and disorderly conduct. She died in custody at a Queens hospital six days later. Friends said she had been severely beaten by police. Nobody was indicted by the Bronx grand jury who considered the case, but the African-American official David Dinkins, then president of the Borough of Manhattan and soon to be the New York City mayor, called it "one in a long list of shameful incidents involving abuses against minority people by the New York City Police Department and the Transit Authority Police" (Uhlig).

Michael Stewart was twenty-five when he was arrested by Transit Police on September 15, 1983 for spray-painting graffiti on a Manhattan subway-station wall. He lay in a coma for thirteen days before dying. The city's chief medical examiner averred that death did not result from injuries suffered while in custody; a month later he amended his report in the face of massive public uproar over the report. The new version stated that the decedent had collapsed while in police custody and died from a physical injury to the spine in the upper neck, but the medical examiner would not say what might have caused the injury. All officers involved were cleared of all charges by a grand jury in 1985. Two years later, an audit report from the city comptroller stated that Transit Police officers had acted with excessive force (Chronopoulos 113). Stewart's name is also heard from the crowd when the neighbors confront Sal and his sons right after Raheem's death.

This roll call stands in melancholy contrast to the list of African-American greats spoken by Mister Señor Love Daddy and the collage of Italian-American greats celebrated on Sal's wall. None of these slain New Yorkers could be called great in a conventional sense, but in Spike Lee's America their memory lives on.

Natural Violence

The violent climax of *Do the Right Thing* was directly inspired by the mournful histories of the six dedicatees along with other, less imposing factors. Spike attributed the idea that "people get crazy when it's hot" partly to a TV episode of *The Twilight Zone* wherein a scientist proves that "the murder rate goes up after the temperature hits ninety-five degrees," and Raheem's confrontation with Sal recalls "a big incident in Brooklyn College, where black students and white students were fighting over what music was being played on the jukebox" (Aftab 76). But background details like these have not subdued the ongoing debate about the tone, appropriateness, and meaning of the melee.

Perhaps the most frequently raised question is why Mookie throws the garbage can through his employer's window, thereby touching off a riot that might otherwise not have happened. One theory is that Mookie does it for altruistic reasons. "At the moment of Mookie's decision," suggests art theorist W.J.T. Mitchell, who entertains other hypotheses as well, "the mob is wavering between attacking the pizzeria and assaulting its Italian-American owners. Mookie's act directs the violence away from persons and toward property, the only choice available in that moment. Mookie 'does the right thing,' saving human lives by sacrificing property" (897). That's a nice try, but when I put the idea to Spike on a Monitor Channel broadcast in 1989, he scoffed at it. Until that moment, he said, Mookie is designed to be the nice black guy whom white people would take home for dinner, so when he shouts "*Hate!*" and smashes the window, white people feel more comfortable thinking he's doing it for *them*.

Mitchell is on much stronger ground when he writes that on the scene's most fundamental level, Lee does the right thing by "breaking the illusion of cinematic realism and intervening as the director of his own work of public art, taking personal responsibility for the decision to portray and perform a public act of violence against private property." The decisive action by Lee/Mookie liberates the film's climax from cause-and-effect logic and political-justice morality, allowing it to become "a piece of Brechtian theater," which is to say, "a pure effect of *this* work of art in this moment and place." The conclusion Mitchell draws from this strikes me as exactly right:

> We may call *Do the Right Thing* a piece of "violent public art," then, in all the relevant senses – as a representation, an act, and a weapon of violence. But it is a work of *intelligent* violence, to echo the words of Malcolm X that conclude the film. It does not repudiate the alternative of nonviolence articulated by Martin Luther King in the film's other epigraph (this is, after all, a film, a symbolic and not a "real" act of violence); it resituates both violence and nonviolence as strategies within a struggle that is simply an ineradicable fact of American public life. . . . The film exerts a violence on its viewers, badgering us to "fight the power" and "do the right thing," but it never underestimates the difficulty of rightly locating the power to be fought, or the right strategy for fighting it. . . . Like the Goddess of Liberty in Tiananmen Square, the film confronts the disfigured public image of legitimate power, holding out the torch of liberty with two hands, one inscribed with HATE, the other with LOVE. (897–8)

For me the scene's violence is not only intelligent but also natural, in the sense put forth by social philosopher Paul Goodman in his essay "Natural Violence," first published in 1945. There he distinguishes between two kinds of violence. "Natural" violence is rooted in human nature and erupts spontaneously out of deep-seated drives, as when parents use violence to defend their children against physical attack. "Unnatural" violence is artificially provoked, as when a government whips up desire for war against a country that poses no immediate threat. Natural violence sets in motion "the destruction of habits or second natures" so that contact can be regained with "primary experiences" such as "grief and mourning for death," which are affects felt profoundly by the Bed-Stuy crowd after Raheem's murder. "Deeper than their fears," Goodman continues, "civilized people yearn for and welcome" catastrophes that "strip them of their possessions and touch routine to the quick." If the rioters in *Do the Right Thing* are anarchic, they are so in the sense meant by Goodman when he likens an anarchistic situation to a "fertile vacuum . . . where heavy masses fall of their own weight and . . . seeds germinate." The true anarchist, Goodman concludes, "speaks a word that *heals* as it violates" (26–8). I think the "word that heals as it violates" must sound very much like "intelligence."

Mo' Better Blues

Once you become aware of this force for [order in the universe and] unity in life . . . you can't ever forget it. It becomes part of everything you do. . . . My goal on meditating on this through music, however, remains the same. And that is to uplift people, as much as I can. To inspire them to realize more and more of their capacities for living meaningful lives. Because there certainly is meaning to life. – John Coltrane, 1965 (Hentoff)

The working title for Lee's next film was "Love Supreme," borrowed from one of John Coltrane's most progressive, popular, and unprecedented jazz recordings. This was changed to *Mo' Better Blues* early in the film's production process, but both titles signal the movie's main subject: music and musicians. Spike asked Universal for a budget of $11.5 million but received only $10 million, thanks to the poor box-office performances of Bertrand Tavernier's *'Round Midnight* (1986), starring tenor saxophonist Dexter Gordon as a jazz musician, and Clint Eastwood's *Bird* (1988), starring Forest Whitaker as Charlie Parker, the greatest sax player of them all. This was still the healthiest budget of any Spike Lee joint to date (Aftab 109), but it's ironic that Lee, who considers jazz "the music [he feels] closest to," intensely disliked the films that indirectly cramped his jazz movie's funding. "Every musician I know hated *Bird*," he says in his book on *Mo' Better Blues*, adding, "Not only was the tone grim, but the film was so dark you couldn't see a damn thing. . . . On all fronts, *Bird* just rang false." He finds Tavernier's film "slightly better," but still a narrow view of a black musician through white filmmakers' eyes (Lee with Jones 1990, 39).

The protagonist of *Mo' Better Blues* is Bleek Gilliam (Denzel Washington), a Brooklyn jazz trumpeter who "enjoys a life of laid-back hedonism," as Owen Gleiberman (1990) puts it in his review, which goes on to summarize the plot:

> Bleek, who whiles away the afternoons practicing, leads his quintet through nightly sets at a plush local club and Ping-Pongs between two women who adore him – the modest, devoted Indigo (played by the director's sister, Joie Lee, who bears a disarming resemblance to Prince), and Clarke (Cynda Williams), a flirtatious beauty who sees right through him . . . .

*With a poster of legendary jazzman John Coltrane looking on,
trumpeter Bleek Gilliam (Denzel Washington) gives his little boy Miles
(Zakee L. Howze) a music lesson in* Mo' Better Blues.

Onstage, the Bleek Quintet are inheritors of many decades of hipster showmanship. . . . Offstage, they're black
urban professionals (buppies) who live in sleek, expensive
pads. What they've grown past (what, some might say, Lee
wipes clean) is the fabled decadence of the jazz life: the
drugs and the excess . . . .

Bleek, a control freak, needs to dominate every relationship he's in. Now his girlfriends are getting fed up with him,
and he has been drawn into an explosive rivalry with his
saxophone player, Shadow Henderson (the terrific Wesley
Snipes), a more flamboyant – and maybe more talented
– musician than he is. Their conflict springs in part from
Bleek's loyalty to the band's flaky manager, Giant (Spike
Lee), a compulsive gambler who loses thousands betting on
baseball games when he should be out negotiating a better
contract for his clients . . . .

Bleek eventually suffers a beating that permanently dam-
ages his lip, ending his career but inducing him to reinvent

himself as a dependable husband and parent. The first part of Coltrane's composition, "Acknowledgment," swells on the soundtrack during the last part of the film, a montage sequence that shows and celebrates Bleek's new dedication to home and family. We are encouraged to see this as the love supreme that has hitherto been missing from his life.

A Love Supreme

The significance of this musical choice extends far beyond its connection with the main character's profession. Coltrane recorded *A Love Supreme* with his classic quartet in December 1964 and Impulse! Records released it in February 1965. It is a four-part suite with a strong spiritual agenda, of which Spike was very much aware. "The album is . . . a very spiritual work," he writes in the movie's companion volume, "and I used it as inspiration for the film. The love in *A Love Supreme* goes beyond romantic love. It's love for God and the human community" (Lee with Jones 1990, 42).

To his disappointment, however, Coltrane's widow, Alice Coltrane, denied permission to use "Love Supreme" as the movie's title. Lee explained in 1991 that

> Mrs Coltrane, who's a very spiritual person, felt that because of the profanity and nudity in [the film], it would not be in her late husband's best interest to allow us to use the title of *Love Supreme*. She felt that *Love Supreme* was her husband's most spiritual song. And she said, "Spike, any other title you could have had. But not *Love Supreme*." And we obeyed her wishes. If I had the choice between the song and the title, I was just happy that she still let us use the song. (Lee and Gates 1991, 191)

Searching for a different title, Lee considered borrowing the title that jazz bassist Charles Mingus gave to his autobiography, *Beneath the Underdog*, and then chose *Variations on the Mo' Better Blues* because it "sounds like the title of a jazz composition." This was shortened to *Mo' Better Blues* at the behest of Universal Pictures and Spike's personal advisers.

Perhaps bearing out the Coltrane estate's misgivings, "the mo' better" is a slang term for sex. "One day I want to write a book containing every single expression for making love," Spike says in his book on the film. "There must be a million of them. Number one on my list is 'the mo' better'" (Lee with Jones 1990, 42). This said, however, Lee's use of "making love" in this passage softens the sensual import of "the mo' better" and implies the "spiritual" dimension that sexuality can have when love, gentleness, and humanity are also present. Music from Coltrane's composition is heard only when those qualities are enabling Bleek to get his life back together via marriage, the birth of a son, and a sincere commitment to respectable middle-class domesticity.

Uplift

> *I know that I want to produce beautiful music, music that does things to people that they need. Music that will uplift, and make them happy.* – John Coltrane, 1962 (Wilmer)

It is nonetheless reasonable to ask whether the finale of *Mo' Better Blues*, affirming Bleek's new allegiance to home and family, represents the kind of inspiration and "uplift" that Coltrane identified as his aspiration when creating *A Love Supreme* and *Meditations*, a 1965 recording (released in 1966) that he called an "extension" of the former piece. Since his music of this period evokes his ever-evolving conception of a "force" that brings unity and order to the cosmos (Hentoff), transplanting it into a movie should not be done casually or carelessly. My answer is that Lee's use of *A Love Supreme* is wholly appropriate. Although the soaring splendor of "Acknowledgment" has (like other late Coltrane recordings) an all-embracing sublimity that only a few masterpieces of world cinema (none of them by Lee) can claim to equal, the conclusion of *Mo' Better Blues* is earnest and enthralling enough to justify the superb music accompanying it.

That said, however, the word "uplift" has a history that casts ironic light on the film's finale, if not on the music that Coltrane created in accordance with *his* concept of the term. The idea of uplift is "consistent with the imagery of transcendence in Coltrane's work," culture historian James C. Hall observes – another Coltrane album from this period is called *Ascension* – and it is further consistent with "a whole body of African-American folk material on 'rising' and 'flying.'" Yet the word "uplift" also reflects what Hall describes as "a (black) middle-class ideology of mobility and change," which holds that "moral perfection, entrepreneurial aptitude, and leadership" provide vehicles by means of which "the race can be raised up." For many people, Hall continues, this ideology has been a stimulus to "getting on with the business of bourgeois acquisition," and even its more spiritualized forms can lead toward "the (potentially) comfortable complacency" of middle-class religiosity. Hall therefore concludes that the music's deservedly hailed aesthetic and spiritual qualities do not preclude a sense "that the recording and composition [are] just slightly behind the social relevance curve" (142). For me this recalls sociologist Todd Gitlin's analysis of "individual subjectivity" ideologies of the 1960s, which "not only stabilized shaky selves, they had the side value of channeling devotees back to conventional middle-class existence, giving them rationales for putting aside the travails of politics" (412).

The manner in which Bleek resolves his problems and regenerates his life – which is to say, the manner in which Spike Lee resolves Bleek's problems, ties up the narrative, and offers uplift to the audience – is to elevate and venerate precisely the conventional middle-class existence of which Gitlin speaks. The sociopolitical conservatism of this gambit is reinforced by the cautionary thrust of the story as a whole, which follows the well-established Hollywood pattern of associating jazz with decadence and instability. "Spike Lee was acting within prescribed cultural/cinematic practice," observes Krin Gabbard, a scholar of film and jazz, "when he equated the jazz life with self-destructiveness (the attack upon Bleek's mouth is the most gripping moment in the film) and then indicated his hero's redeemed masculinity through the perennially effective spectacles of a wedding and the birth of a child" (57). So incompatible are jazz creativity and middle-class respectability in the eyes of mainstream cinema that Lee himself declares, "I really don't think Bleek could have been a happily married family man if it weren't for the accident" that ruins his embouchure and ends his musical career (Lee with Jones 1990, 68; Gabbard 57). Lee doesn't even allow the jazz life to offer Bleek a meaningful network of professional peers; there is "no real jazz community in *Mo' Better Blues* outside of Bleek and his sidemen," Gabbard points out, and Bleek never interacts with a musical mentor or "strong poet," in literary critic Harold Bloom's terminology (Gabbard 56).

Lee has defended the bourgeois leanings of *Mo' Better Blues* with a variation of his counterargument against the charge that *Do the Right Thing* presents a *Sesame Street* version of the African-American ghetto, garnishing it with another potshot at his jazz-movie *bêtes noires*, as in this exchange with the African-American cultural scholar Henry Louis Gates Jr.:

HLG: Some people have said – and I've thought this myself – that you put a fairy-tale ending on *Mo' Better Blues*. And that the film lost touch with reality at that point.

SL: I don't know why it's unrealistic for a couple, a black couple, to be happily married and have a child at the end of a movie. We suppose to end up broke and OD-ing in some little funky hotel in the lower east side?

HLG: So you wanted to break the stereotypical image of black reality, which was a kind of didactic effect.

SL: Yeah, because just look at the two previous films about jazz. *Around* [*sic*] *Midnight* and *Bird*. That's something we definitely wanted to get away from. (Lee and Gates 1991, 196–7)

I think the fairy-tale quality adduced by Gates and others is precisely what rescues *Mo' Better Blues* from the quicksand of middle-class conformity and conservatism that might otherwise swallow it up. Losing touch with reality can be a salutary maneuver when the reality at hand is a matter of "didactic effect" rather than complex, conflicted social truth. The aesthetics and the ideology of *Mo' Better Blues* are of a piece: conventional, comfortable, and as inescapably square as its protagonist is ostensibly hip. This is both the movie's fatal flaw and the source of its enduring charm.

Moe and Josh

An accusation Lee has found harder to fend off centers on the anti-Semitic bigotry that numerous critics see in his treatment of the comic characters named Moe and Josh Flatbush, owners of a jazz club in *Mo' Better Blues*. The case against Moe and Josh, who are played by the real-life brothers John and Nicholas Turturro, was summarized well by critic Caryn James in a *New York Times* article:

The Flatbush brothers [are] loaded with despicable traits typically used to disparage Jews. . . . They become rich by gouging others; they are deceitful; when challenged they threaten to sue. In thick New York-Jewish accents they accuse the underpaid black musicians of "trying to take food from my children's mouth.". . . These caricatures are wildly out of synch with the film's other roles. The blacks . . . are flatly depicted, but unintentionally so. The other white characters . . . are relatively harmless clichés. . . . But the Flatbush brothers are the film's villains, their greed inseparable from their Jewish identity. And because there are no other Jews to offset them, they become tokens of an entire ethnic group.

James also quoted the Anti-Defamation League, which declared that the Jewish characters "dredge up an age-old and highly dangerous form of anti-Semitic stereotyping" and expressed its disappointment "that Spike Lee – whose success is largely due to his efforts to break down racial stereotypes and prejudice – has employed the same kind of tactics that he supposedly deplores" (1990a). Among other dubious achievements, the Flatbush brothers brought forth a lot of colorful language from movie critics: David Ansen called them "shylocks" in *Newsweek* (1990), and James herself described them as "money-grubbing, envious, ugly stereotypes with sharks' smiles" in her *Times* review (1990b).

"Many people who know [Lee] only from the pages of *The New York Times*," another observer wrote, "have decided that he is a vicious and dangerous anti-Semite who panders to Black racism and allies himself with divisive people like the Reverend Al Sharpton" (Stone). Cultural critic Jerome Christensen, whose analysis of Lee's work owes little to opinions in the *Times*, reached a similar conclusion via more imaginative reasoning. He regards the "crude . . . vulgar" prejudice in *Mo' Better Blues* as an expression of

Lee's "dramatized opposition" to Hollywood in general and Universal Pictures in particular, using the club owners as "stand-ins for the parasitic Jewish moneymen (for example, Lew Wasserman of Universal) who run the film studios." Through these caricatures Lee assures us that while he may be bankrolled by Universal and its ilk, this circumstance "does not soil his art or compromise his independence" any more than the vile club owners contaminate Bleek's integrity. Lee's opposition to the studio system is a fantasy and a fraud, however, because in Christensen's view that system is in terminal disorder anyway, captive to corporate conglomerates whose movies are merely vehicles for image management and product plugs. It follows that Lee can both "do business with the studios and maintain his independence" because, Christensen concludes, "they share the same social ontology (in the glitzy *Mo' Better Blues* every shot is either derived from or destined for a television commercial) and belong to the same corporate intertext: Forty Acres and A Mule aspires to the status of Touchstone Pictures; Spike's Joint is a nascent Disney World" (590).

Lee refutes the anti-Semitism charge by invoking yet again his claim that black films, or at least his films, should receive a sort of educational exemption from the requirements of ordinary Hollywood practice. His most prominent statement on Moe and Josh appeared in a *New York Times* article titled "I Am Not an Anti-Semite" (1990), which reads in part:

> There is a double standard at work in the accusations of anti-Semitism. . . .
> Negative images of black people are presented on film and television every day and there is no great uproar. . . .
> Just for the sake of argument, let's say that Moe and Josh Flatbush are stereotypes. Let's compare their 10 minutes of

screen time with 100 years of Hollywood cinema. . . . I've gotten more press for being a "racist" and an "anti-Semitic" filmmaker for the 10 minutes of Moe and Josh than a slew of really racist, anti-Semitic filmmakers . . . .
  [I]f critics are telling me that to avoid charges of anti-Semitism, all Jewish characters . . . have to be model citizens, . . . that's unrealistic and unfair.

As always, Spike sticks to his guns. I have no interest in defending Moe and Josh, but they seem to me such one-dimensional cartoons that I can't get worked up over them. On the larger issue of racial and ethnic stereotyping as an offensive weapon and a dispenser of offensiveness, I'll give the last word to the African-American political commentator Clarence Page, who weighed in more than once on *Mo' Better Blues*. After opining that the picture "stereotypes almost every group in it, including the blacks it is supposed to be about," Page (1990) wrote that Spike's defense reminds him of "white filmmakers who have waxed nervously defensive when accused of stereotyping blacks as clowns, Italians as criminals, Jews as greedy, homosexuals as swishy, Asian women as geishas or Native American Indians as savages, to name just a few Hollywood standards. Surely brother Spike does not think the sins of whites now allow blacks to commit the same sins." A year later, when *Newsweek* ran a cover story about Lee's just-released *Jungle Fever*, Page (1991) returned to the subject, noting that nineteen feature films by black directors – more than the total output of the preceding ten years – were slated for release in 1991. "But the new clout of Hollywood's new 'black pack' brings with it new responsibilities and new choices," he continued.

One hopes, for example, that the new black directors will do as Lee has done in demanding that craft union jobs and other positions be opened up to blacks. . . . And one also hopes Hollywood's new black moguls will be sensitive enough about stereotypes to set new standards of sensitivity, if sensitivity in Hollywood is not too much of a contradiction.

That's fair enough, I think.

Bigger-Budget Blues

Among the criticisms relating to both substance and style in *Mo' Better Blues*, some of the most crisply stated come from Ed Guerrero, a practiced observer of minority cinema who understands the double bind faced by a staunchly independent filmmaker who starts plugging more directly into patterns and practices of mainstream film. "Lee's films have grown progressively larger in budget," Guerrero wrote in 1991, "more consonant with industry production standards and dominant cinema's narrative and visual conventions, more persistent in seeking out the appreciation of a broad popular audience." Like all of Lee's films since *She's Gotta Have It*, he continues, *Mo' Better Blues* demonstrates that "films made about the black world from a black point of view can appeal to a heterogeneous popular audience." Lee pays a heavy price, however, infecting the film with a "trite sense of nostalgia" that flows from its "romanticized view of black music, its slick glossy images and its opulent overripe sense of visual beauty." More sweepingly, Guerrero finds the film guilty of flirting with temptations to convert potentially resistant modes of style, story, language, and music into specimens and servants of the "dominant cinema paradigm" (2).

It seems to me that Guerrero's reasoning builds a double bind of its own, calling for African-American narratives to set forth "an honest, uncoopted perspective" and finding Lee wanting in this area, yet conceptualizing the "plural, multiverse experience" of "the vast social construct we call 'blackness'" in a manner that subsumes such films as John Sayles's *The Brother from Another Planet* (1984) and Steven Spielberg's adaptation of Alice Walker's novel *The Color Purple* (1985), both written, directed, and creatively controlled by white filmmakers. Guerrero even damps down his skepticism about Lee by acknowledging that Spike has succeeded in expressing an auteurist vision while mobilizing "enough money, talent and resources to make a brilliant series of diverse feature films exploring his commitment to the African American experience." Concluding his survey of black film in the early 1990s by comparing the trope of "the young boy struggling to learn the trumpet" in *Mo' Better Blues* and in Charles Burnett's marvelous 1990 drama *To Sleep with Anger*, Guerrero prefers the latter for its "finely tuned independent vision," yet winds up heaping praise upon *Mo' Better Blues* as well, since it too reveals "the truth of the blues idiom so relevant to black life and cinema, that of creativity and grace shaped under pressure of limitation" (3, 2).

I cite the zigs and zags of Guerrero's analysis not to discredit it but rather to illustrate the perils that even smart, dedicated criticism can encounter when it tries to measure values like honesty, authenticity, autonomy, and cooptation in terms of "dichotomies or dualities" determined by "black 'independent' cinema," on the one hand, and "the 'mainstream' employment of black creativity in the dominant studio system," on the other (2). *Mo' Better Blues* and every other Spike Lee film is a work of artful *synthesis*, modifying Hollywood-derived elements of camera and editing style, dialogue and narrative structure, character development, and so on, with an array of inflections, mannerisms, eccentricities, and idiosyncrasies distinctive enough to be widely recognized as Spike's personal (auteurist) signatures. Although he has never made a movie as radically individualistic as, say, Burnett's remarkable debut feature *Killer of Sheep* (1979) or Haile Gerima's *Sankofa* (1993), even a comparatively tame and well-behaved joint such as *Mo' Better Blues* expresses more about contemporary African-American experience than almost any blaxploitation melodrama (e.g., Barry Shear's *Across 110th Street*, 1972), black chop-socky (Jack Starrett's *Cleopatra Jones*, 1973), black horror film (William Crain's *Blacula*, 1972), black western (Jack Arnold's *Boss Nigger*, 1975), black crime film (Larry Cohen's *Black Caesar*, 1973), black pimp movie (Michael Campus's *The Mack*, 1973), black vigilante picture (Jack Hill's *Coffy*, 1973), black biker movie (Matt Cimber's *The Black Six*, 1974), black policier (Gordon Parks's *Shaft*, 1971), et cetera, ever to reach the screen.

I choose those examples from the 1970s to recall that when Spike Lee was growing up, "black movies" were almost always made by white men who unambiguously aimed to redirect African-American energies, talents, subjects, and subjectivities toward the explicitly commercial aims of an industry almost entirely dedicated to the purpose of filling white men's pockets with money. While calculating the relative merits of a particular trope as handled by Spike Lee and Charles Burnett is a worthwhile exercise in narrative aesthetics, the baseline against which both filmmakers should be assessed is the mostly appalling state of "black movies" before they and a handful of peers gained the opportunity and wherewithal to put their skills into practice, sparking a transformative moment in black cinema. The ensuing developments were spearheaded most conspicuously by Lee in the crucial years when *Do the Right Thing* brought his work to the attention of a large mainstream audience and *Mo' Better Blues* confirmed the staying power that has made him a unique presence in American cinema. His accomplishments are rife with impurities, but stressing these too strongly slights his distinctively progressive impact on American popular culture.

My original review of *Mo 'Better Blues* in *The Christian Science Monitor* (1990) anticipated some of the complaints leveled against the film after its release. The performances "often seem more jokey than pungent," I wrote,

> and Lee's camera keeps cutting away, trying to work up rhythms that should grow spontaneously from the acting and dialogue. Some scenes of violence ... are handled with a half-humorous quality that doesn't work as comedy or irony. The whole plot wanders, moreover, to the point where you sometimes wonder where it's going and what it has on its mind. And when you find out, it isn't always worth the wait.

On the plus side I felt that "even its weakest moments show no evidence that Lee is ignoring his own vision or catering to mass audiences." I wouldn't claim today that Spike didn't have mass audiences very much in mind, but I reaffirm my opinion that "even his second-best work has an awful lot going for it."

3

DEEPER INTO POLITICS

Lee created two of his most strikingly political films in 1991 and 1992. The first, *Jungle Fever*, is an interracial romance, a family melodrama, and a dissection of American hypocrisies, but it is also Lee's first all-out assault on the scourge of drugs in the African-American community. The second, *Malcolm X*, is a historical biopic that follows a man, a movement, a religion, and a turning point in American race relations through tumultuous vicissitudes over many years. These ambitious movies are among Lee's most outspoken and deeply felt creations, and they remain key works in his filmography.

JUNGLE FEVER

Spontaneity

Upon its release in June 1991, *Jungle Fever* was publicized as a taboo-breaking look at interracial romance. In fact, the picture broke no taboos and was about much more. The main characters are Flipper Purify (Wesley Snipes), a married and successful African-American architect, and Angela Tucci (Annabella Sciorra), an Italian-American office temp.[1] Roger Ebert described the basics of the story in his 1991 review:

[Angie] comes to work in [Flipper's] Manhattan office one day, their eyes meet, and the fever starts. Their halting, tentative conversations expand into "working late," eating Chinese food from the take-out, and finally having sex right there on top of the blueprints. . . .

[Flipper] comes from a traditional, God-fearing Harlem family. His father . . . is a self-righteous former preacher called the Good Reverend Doctor Purify [Ossie Davis] by one and all. His mother [Lucinda, played by Ruby Dee] . . . is loving and sensible. There is another son, Gator [Samuel L. Jackson] . . ., who is a crackhead [and] has gone as far down as Flipper has gone up. . . .

The office worker comes from . . . Bensonhurst. [She] is engaged to Paulie [John Turturro] . . . who works all day in the luncheonette owned by his father [Lou, played by Anthony Quinn] . . ., a hidebound old man who sits around upstairs praying to the photograph of his wife. When word gets back to the local communities about the new romance, it does not go over well. Flipper's wife [Drew, played by Lonette McKee] is enraged and his father deeply offended (not least by the adultery), and all of Angie's relatives and friends react with shock. . . .

Later we learn that Drew is half-white, and when Flipper leaves her, she fears it's because he married her for her light skin, and has now succumbed to the lure of even lighter skin. By contrast, Paulie doesn't particularly mind losing Angie; but when he then grows fond of an African-American woman who gets her coffee at the luncheonette, his friends beat him up. Angie's father beats her up, too.

   Critics generally agree that the film's most striking set piece – and it is definitely a set piece, with a tone noticeably different from the movie's other scenes – is a conversation among Drew and her female friends after she has kicked her unfaithful husband out of their home. Lee's screenplay describes the scene as "a WAKE. A MOURNING for another SISTER who has been WRONGED. [They] sit in the living room, laughing, crying and discussing the state of THE BLACK MAN." According to their diagnosis, the state of the black man is not good. Samples:

> Most of them are drug addicts, in jail, homos. . . . The good ones know they the shit so they got ten women at a time, leaving babies all over.

> How many men do you know . . . black men . . . who can effectively deal with a mate who has more education . . . and makes more money? Not many. They freak.

> Everything in society . . . we keep doin' the same thing over and over; we keep telling ourselves, negatin' ourselves. Look at the brothers who are successful. Look at them! Most of the brothers who have made it . . . got white women on their arms. That's true.

Much of this was improvised by the performers. "For the actresses," journalist Samuel G. Freedman reported," the performance ventured deeply into their personal lives." Lee rehearsed the scene for three days before filming it with two cameras over the course of a whole day. The sequence stands out by virtue of its spontaneity, which is both a plus and a minus – a plus because the conversation rings remarkably true, a minus because it isn't of a piece with the movie's other scenes, and its immediacy isn't necessarily superior to the moderately stylized tenor of the picture as a whole. But however one judges its quality as cinema, one should credit Lee with knowing his limitations on this occasion. As he remarked later, "I can't write dialogue as good as they're gonna say it" (Freedman).

The dialogue in *Jungle Fever* is less finely tuned than that of *Do the Right Thing*, and a sociolinguistic analysis of the sort conducted by Margaret Thomas vis-à-vis *School Daze* would most likely produce fewer revealing insights. At times it's almost fatuous. More samples:

> **Gator:** [*on meeting Angela*] She's white!
> **Flipper:** No shit. Yeah, she's white.
> **Gator:** She got any money? Real long money?
> **Flipper:** No, she doesn't have any money. She's a temp.
> **Gator:** A secretary? You mean to say my brother got him an ofay who ain't got no mo-nay?
> **Flipper:** Shh!

> **Flipper:** There's something you should know. I'm having an affair.
> **Cyrus:** [*Flipper's friend, played by Lee*] H-bomb! H-bomb!
> **Flipper:** It gets worse – she's white.
> **Cyrus:** Nuclear holocaust!

The dialogue can't get much worse, but it sometimes does when Italian-Americans speak.

> **Lou:** [*to his son Paulie*] You hate your own father!
> **Paulie:** I'd like to kill you, but I don't hate you.

> **Lou:** If your mother was alive she would turn over in her grave.

Character names of the order of Flipper and Gator Purify further reduce the sense of narrative authenticity in a film that never quite settles on experiential realism or Brechtian distanciation as its major discursive mode, oscillating uncertainly between the two.

Crack

The other big set piece in *Jungle Fever* is Flipper's search for Gator through the horrific hellholes of New York's hard-drug underground, culminating in a crack house that resembles a circle of Dante's Inferno – perhaps the third, which is populated by gluttons. Dante pictures their sin as "a cold sensuality, a sodden and filthy spiritual wretchedness," as Dorothy L. Sayers writes in her commentary. "Here is no reciprocity and no communication; each soul grovels alone in the mud, without heeding his neighbors – 'a sightless company', Dante calls them" (Alighieri 107). While this descent into a heart of darkness is clearly Lee's belated response to the charge that *Do the Right Thing* overzealously cleansed its portrait of drugs and other inner-city ills, it is also the most powerful portion of *Jungle Fever* in its own right. Lee claims, in fact, that black–white romance was merely the "hook" for the film. "I think a lot of people got tripped up into the whole interracial thing," he said later, "but for me, that wasn't . . . the most important part of the story. For me, the thing was the devastation that crack is afflicting [*sic*] upon families, and generations and generations just being wiped out" (Lindo 169). Lee is incontestably right about the ravages of crack cocaine, which appeared in poverty-plagued inner cities in the early 1980s, marketed for as little as five dollars in small "rocks" to be smoked in pipes. "Users found themselves bingeing for hours or days," according to an authority, "smoking up hundreds of dollars of the product."

Gator Purify (Samuel L. Jackson) and his girlfriend Vivian (Halle Berry) are desperate crack addicts in Jungle Fever, *Lee's first film to deal seriously with America's drug epidemic.*

Efforts by crime networks to safeguard their profits "produced significant spikes in rates of homicide and assault," while users turned to "theft and sex work" to finance their habits (Anderson 137).

Importantly, however, the film's two spheres of interest – interracial relationships and the crack-cocaine epidemic – are not as distinct from each other as they may first appear. The vast, labyrinthine crack house of *Jungle Fever*, called the Taj Mahal by its denizens, proves to be a multiracial community, populated by black and white users who, judging from appearances, represent more than one class, ethnic, and professional status. The crack house is a "mausoleum and abode for the living dead," but it is a "happily integrated" one where "black hustlers and hookers, white businessmen and laborers, black and white couples . . . have realized a dystopia of interracial intimacy," in the vivid words of philosopher Ronald R. Sundstrom, whose analysis captures some – not all – of the complicated psychosocial dynamics at play in the Taj Mahal scene.

It is possible, Sundstrom speculates, that if such characters as the Good Reverend Doctor and Angie's father Mike
(Frank Vincent) were to visit the Taj Mahal and witness its
mingling of races and classes in circumstances of addiction
and squalor, they might regard the spectacle as an embodiment of "the nightmare brought on by miscegenation."
These and other characters feel the same about the affair
between Flipper and Angie, an exercise in racial mixing
that is undermined and destroyed by the conflicted, guilt-
laden mindsets of the participants, but strikes onlookers as
a self-evident instance of the spiritually fatal malady known
as jungle fever. Considered from this perspective, the multiracial apparitions in the Taj Mahal are at once tangible casu-
alties of a society gone insanely off the rails and projections
of what Sundstrom calls "the generational disappointment of
the fathers . . . as they confront old age and reconsider the
goals for which they fought" (153–4).

The archetypal father in *Jungle Fever* is the Good
Reverend Doctor, whose chosen honorific title bears a certain similarity to that of the protofascist Julian – Dean Big
Brother Al-*might*-ty – in *School Daze*. The Good Reverend
Doctor is no fascist; he is, in fact, a veteran of the civil-
rights struggle as well as a retired minister who has presumably done his best to follow the ways of the actual Almighty
both personally and professionally. Lee does not take the
strength, the dignity, or even the decency of civil-rights-era
veterans for granted, however. Returning home one night,
the Good Reverend Doctor comes upon Gator trashing his
home and terrorizing Lucinda for money; telling his stoned,
desperate son that he is better off dead, he shoots the young
man and leaves him to die a whimpering death in the arms of
his bewildered mother.

This scene and its repercussions underscore the sav-
agely ironic meaning of the family name: the Good Revered

Doctor has physically purified the household by extinguishing its most disruptive element; he has symbolically purified the clan by firing his deadly bullet into Gator's genitals; soon Flipper will reaffirm his racial purity by relinquishing Angie and white romance; and in the film's last moments he will begin to morally purify his neighborhood by embracing a pathetically young crack whore and shrieking "*Noooooooo!*" to her and all she represents. Except for the last, every one of these purifications is rash, fatuous, and heartbreaking, and even Flipper's wail of protest is more a reflexive cry of rage than a sign of social or psychological transformation. It's true that the Good Reverend Doctor would probably see the Taj Mahal as a contradiction and betrayal of the sociopolitical goals his generation fought to actualize; but by committing filicide he contradicts and betrays them all over again, revealing himself as a tired and terrified old man rather than the upstanding American purifier he once thought himself to be.

Actually, of course, the Good Reverend Doctor does not reveal his own failings; it is Spike Lee who reveals the lamentably defective father as what the Bible calls a whited sepulcher. And it happens that Spike made *Jungle Fever* during a very fraught period in his dealings with his own father, Bill Lee, who had composed the music for all of his previous films but was not involved in this one. It also happens that drugs and interracial romance played key roles in the conflict that undermined their relationship. Tensions apparently began as early as 1976, when Spike's mother died and Bill moved in with Susan Kaplan, a white woman whom he later married; they began living together when "my mother wasn't even cold in her grave," Spike said later, in a remark redolent of *Hamlet*. Strains increased when Spike went to work on *Jungle Fever*, a film "directly talking about me and my wife," Bill angrily told Jonathan Mandell of the

Los Angeles Times. It didn't help that Bill Lee was busted for heroin possession in 1991, and that early the next year Spike refused his request for a loan of a few thousand dollars to help with household expenses, saying no with what Bill claimed was a "very insulting . . . attitude."[2] Spike tried to remain above the fray – "Why should I dignify comments my father said or play it out in a public forum?" – but Bill Lee never did music for a Spike Lee joint again, and Lee did state publicly that he and his family were devastated by his father's arrest.

   With chronic resentment over the timing and perhaps the nature of Bill Lee's relationship with the white woman who became his wife, and acute resentment over Bill's surrender to the narcotics that were defiling the African-American community, Spike may well have infused his new movie with bitterness toward his father's generation in general and his own father in particular. The sarcastically named Good Reverend Doctor and the roughly named Gator are thus the symbolically scrambled Jekyll and Hyde of a single corrupt personality: the drug-abusing son betrays the father in the film much as Bill Lee fell short of Spike's expectations in real life, whereupon the momentarily berserk father murders his degenerate offspring with a bullet in the groin, actualizing the worst unconscious fears of every conflicted son by night-marishly reversing the normal outcome of the oedipal struggle. One needn't be a vulgar Freudian to see this scenario as a harrowing variation on a well-established psychoanalytic theme, the resonance of which is felt in many other Spike Lee father–son scenes, starting with the mingled love and antagonism of Pino and Sal in *Do the Right Thing* and the contrasting first and last scenes of *Mo' Better Blues*, which opens with the father of little boy Bleek failing to moderate the mother's strict trumpet-practicing schedule and ends with Bleek allowing *his* little boy to run off and play against the mother's better judgment. Father–child psychodynamics also play out importantly in such later films as *Crooklyn* and *Get on the Bus*, and the major turn they take in *25th Hour* is one of the factors making that 2002 drama such a milestone in Spike's career.

Continuity between *Jungle Fever* and Spike's earlier films comes through in other respects as well. Much as the ending of *Do the Right Thing* paid tribute to fallen victims of white-power brutality, for instance, the first image in *Jungle Fever* is a photograph of Yusuf (spelled Yusef in some sources) Hawkins, a sixteen-year-old black boy who was murdered in 1989 by a mob of thirty or so white men armed with baseball bats and the handgun that fired the fatal bullet. The killing occurred in Bensonhurst, the predominantly Italian-American neighborhood of Brooklyn where Sal and his family reside in *Do the Right Thing*; those involved in its aftermath included the Rev. Al Sharpton and the Rev. Jesse Jackson, who accurately predicted that the tragedy would help David Dinkins get elected as New York City's first African-American mayor. Hawkins was not murdered for wandering into a white neighborhood, but rather because he was mistaken for the companion of a white woman who was despised for dating black and Hispanic men,[3] and this plays into the theme of the movie, wherein the old civil-rights warrior speaks about the 1955 murder of Emmett Till, a fourteen-year-old black boy lynched in Mississippi for whistling at a white woman. Lee links such incidents with "sexual inadequacy," noting that "black men who got lynched . . . usually got castrated, too. There's something about black men being with white women that threatens white men. And that's why Yusuf Hawkins was killed." It is also why Angie and Paulie get beaten up in a film that explores, in Freedman's words, "the nexus of race, sex and place that in one instance cost a 16-year-old innocent [Hawkins] his life and in a broader historical scheme has tormented America for centuries."

Jungle Fever is a conservative film in some respects, as the race and literature scholar Celia R. Daileader has demonstrated. On one hand, she observes, Lee's depiction of African-American sexuality as natural and positive reverses the dominant cultural narrative. Yet, on the other hand, he makes no essential change in "the position of the white female in the inter-racial dyad: Angela is the white devil – or 'that white bitch,' as Drew calls her repeatedly." While this is true as far as it goes, I see a more dialectical set of forces at work, countering the white woman's subordinate position with recognitions of her authenticity and selfhood. Daileader acknowledges this when she notes the film's candid treatment of schisms in attitudes toward racial pedigrees within the African-American community. "No children . . . No half-black, half-white babies for me, no," Flipper says to Angie in a moment when his hopes for their romance are collapsing. Angie turns the tables on his hypocrisy, though, pointing to the mixed blood of his own child and wife, and finishing with, "You know, you're not much different from my family." Flipper rejoins, "Except that *your* family is *racist*." "And what's this stuff coming out of *your* mouth?" rejoins Angie in turn. The film thereby "gives her the last word," as Daileader rightly declares (210). Spike often disappoints when it comes to creating strong female characters, but this moment in *Jungle Fever* redounds to his credit.

The genuineness of both protagonists is central to *Jungle Fever*, which stands or falls for many moviegoers on its quality as a haunted love story, supercharged with sociohistorical complexities but reaching out to the hearts as well as the minds of its viewers. On this Lee himself deserves the last word. "What's important about this film," he remarked in 1991, is that the characters . . . are not drawn to each other by love but by sexual myths. When you're a black person in this country, you're constantly bombarded with the myth of the white woman as the epitome of beauty – again and again and again – in TV, movies, magazines. It's blond hair, fair skin, blue eyes, thin nose. If you're black, you never see yourself portrayed in that way – you don't fit that image, you're not beautiful . . . [Angie] bought into the myth that the black man is a stud, a sexual superman with a penis that's two feet long. So those are the two sexual myths that bring these two people together.

Despite all this, Lee adds, "We're not saying that a black man with a white woman won't work. I think if two people love each other, that's great," and if Flipper and Angie had built their relationship on a deeper, firmer foundation, "love would have enabled them to withstand the onslaught of abuse from their family and friends and the two neighborhoods they live in" (Richolson 28–9). The absence of that foundation is what dooms them to split apart, two more sad victims of America's vast and ineluctable racial mythos.

MALCOLM X

Hopeful and Angry

An outstretched American flag goes up in flames as the opening credits roll, intercut with shots of urban friction and violence, including the beating of Rodney King, which sparked ferocious riots in Los Angeles earlier in 1992. The viewer is set up for all the pyrotechnics one might expect from the combination of filmmaker Lee, black leader Malcolm X, and the never-ending tensions of American race relations. But as the credits end and Malcolm's story starts to unfold, the

Denzel Washington delivers a searing portrayal of the title character in
Malcolm X.

unexpected happens. Turbulence and confrontation fade, and in their place appears a biopic in the old Hollywood tradition, telling the story of a hero's life in straightforward, conventional terms.

Following the outline of *The Autobiography of Malcolm X*, written by the eponymous leader with the assistance of author Alex Haley, the film begins with flashbacks to Malcolm's early life, showing him as a child (Matthew Harris) with a loving mother (Lonette McKee) and a deeply dedicated father (Tommy Hollis) whose defiance of white supremacy leads to his untimely death. The movie then follows Malcolm as an adolescent (Zakee Howze) and an adult (Denzel Washington), evolving from a street hustler to a prison inmate to a Nation of Islam convert – and chief public spokesman for Elijah Muhammad (Al Freeman Jr.), the movement's leader – to a free thinker whose discovery of Elijah Muhammad's hypocrisy drives him to split with the organization and establish an Islamic institution of his own.

Through these events the film traces Malcolm's gradually shifting conception of the white power that dominates his social and cultural background. First he shows a sad capitulation to white hegemony by straightening his hair in a painful and degrading process. Later he grows hostile to the entrenched strength of white people, deciding they are literally "devils," as Elijah Muhammad's paranoid theology calls them. In the end he explores the roots of traditional Islam and learns that men and women of all colors and races can be united in divinely inspired love. A quest for harmony and understanding replaces the separatism that surged through his earlier teaching. And just then Malcolm is gunned down by forces that may include hate-mongers from the Nation of Islam, the FBI, the CIA, or all of them. But his lately found message of love and hope lingers. Lee points up its continuing relevance to American society by recruiting contemporary public figures, black and white, to play cameos in the film: among them are Bobby Seale, a founding member of the Black Panther Party, and the Rev. Al Sharpton, both cast as street preachers; the radical left-wing activist and attorney William Kunstler as a judge; and Ossie Davis, the towering black actor, activist, filmmaker, and cultural icon, who repeats in voiceover words from the eulogy he delivered at Malcolm's actual funeral in 1965, concluding, "Our own black shining prince who didn't hesitate to die, because he loved us so."

Most strikingly of all, the film includes an appearance by the antiapartheid militant Nelson Mandela, the soon-to-be president of South Africa, who had recently been freed from his long captivity as a political prisoner in his native country. In the final scene, an African-American schoolteacher (Mary Alice Smith) in Harlem celebrates Malcolm's birthday by saying to her class, "Malcolm X is you, all of you, and you are Malcolm X!" Pupils then stand and shout, "I am Malcolm

X!" and the film jumps to a classroom in Soweto, the township that was an internationally known embodiment of South Africa's governmentally enforced racism, where children are seen identifying with Malcolm as enthusiastically as their New York counterparts.[4] Explaining this moment, Lee said, "We make the connection between Soweto and Harlem, Nelson and Malcolm, and what Malcolm talked about – pan-Africanism, trying to build these bridges between people of color" (Rule).

Lee's decision to end the film on this upbeat note stemmed from his strategy of deemphasizing the "angry black man" image often pinned on Malcolm and other African-American activists by a white majority that prefers the racial status quo to prospects of meaningful change. "I think one can be hopeful and angry at the same time," Spike told me and a few others when the film premiered, "because that's what I am. I think any black person in this country has a right to be angry, [but] we've got to give people hope. We want people to come out of the theater uplifted."

Indeed, countering impressions of Malcolm's angry, violent nature was a high priority for many people involved in producing and promoting the film. Among them were Malcolm's widow, Dr. Betty Shabazz, the director of communications and public relations at Medgar Evers College of the City University of New York and a consultant to the production, and Malcolm's oldest daughter, Attallah Shabazz, who ran a theater and film production company called Nucleus Incorporated with Martin Luther King's daughter and helped with the film's launch. "My husband was not violent," said Dr. Shabazz in the same discussion.

He was never part of any violence. The only violence was his death, and he did not commit it. ... He said [there should be] freedom and respect for members of the African diaspora ... by any means necessary. That's not a violent statement, it's a comprehensive statement. ... It means you might accomplish your ends by political or social or religious or academic activities. ... Malcolm's point was that if you are a member of the human family, as we are all made in the image of God and the likeness of God, then all of us should be able to aspire to positions of influence and gravity.

Attallah Shabazz sounded a similar theme, saying the biggest misconception about her father was "that he was inspired by anger, motivated by vengeance." Malcolm was "serious, focused, dedicated," she said. "He knew his self-worth and was hoping that people would get a sense of their own self-worth. ... But when he came home, I saw a warm human being – not in spite of his day's work, but inclusive of his day's work. I got to see someone who loved my mother, who nurtured his children" (Sterritt 1992b). This is the Malcolm whose spirit is evoked in the later stages of the film.

From Malcolm Little to El-Hajj Malik El-Shabazz

An epic biopic of Malcolm X was Lee's longstanding dream project, and, true to its subject and main character, the venture stirred up controversy long before its premiere in November 1992. More than a year prior to that, for example, the African-American activist and author Amiri Baraka, speaking for the United Front to Preserve the Legacy of Malcolm X, held a widely disseminated press conference on the project in Harlem, where he called Lee a "buppie" and a "petit bourgeois Negro," and urged moviegoers to resist the blandishments of Lee's forthcoming "exploitation film," which he presumed would "trash" the Malcolm X story "to make middle-class Negroes sleep easier."[5] This was unsurprising in itself, since Baraka had previously chastised such pictures as *She's Gotta Have It* and *Do the Right Thing* for trivializing social issues as important as women's rights and police violence against minorities. "Based on the movies I've seen," Baraka said at the press conference, "I'm horrified [at] seeing Spike Lee make Malcolm X. I think Eddie Murphy's films are better."[6] Spike responded in similarly unsurprising terms, charging that Baraka had "appointed himself the grand pooh-bah of all blacks." Observing that Baraka was hardly a Malcolm X expert, Lee said that when Malcolm was alive, "Amiri Baraka was LeRoi Jones running around the Village being a Beatnik. He didn't move to Harlem until after Malcolm X was assassinated. So a lot of these guys – not all – weren't even down with Malcolm when he was around. . . . I was seven years old so I had an excuse. I had to be home by dark" (Ansen 1991). In pretty much the same breath, however, Lee exercised uncharacteristic caution by promising to engage in dialogue with the African-American community – and no less important, the Muslim community – about the many sensitive spots against which his film would inevitably brush.

Many filmmakers wanted to tell Malcolm X's story in the seventeen years between 1975, when he was assassinated while delivering a speech in a Harlem auditorium, and the advent of Lee's movie in 1992. Rights to *The Autobiography of Malcolm X* were owned during much of that time by Marvin Worth, a Hollywood producer who had known Malcolm, and whose documentary *Malcolm X* was nominated for an Oscar in 1973. Those who wrestled with the idea included black writers James Baldwin and David Bradley, white writers David Mamet and Calder Willingham, and white directors Stuart Rosenberg, Bob Fosse, Mark Rydell, and Sidney Lumet; all had solid records and reputations, but none could get the venture off the ground.[7] There are two main reasons for this. One is that Malcolm X was a hugely complex figure whose forty years were crammed with an enormous range of activities. Even his name and nickname were constantly in flux (Thompson 26). He was called Malcolm Little as a child; Detroit Red as a young hoodlum; Satan as a prison inmate; Malcolm X as a leader of Elijah Muhammad's Nation of Islam movement; and El-Hajj Malik El-Shabazz as a follower of traditional Islam, to which he converted before breaking with Muhammad's group. How would one go about condensing so much physical adventure, intellectual growth, psychological deepening, and spiritual exploration into a screenplay that captured not just the appearances but the *meanings* of Malcolm's transformation from an unthinking thug into a white-hating radical and then a resolutely moral humanist and Pan-Africanist who rejected racism? The second big challenge facing would-be movie biographers was that many in the African-American community felt – and still feel – that their understanding of Malcolm X's life was the correct one, and therefore other points of view were either actively harmful or beside the point. This is a common feeling within any group that combines diversity of membership with strong commitment to a person, philosophy, or cause. But recognizing the social dynamics of such a situation is a far cry from knowing how to correct the resulting tensions and dissensions. Hence the years of delay between Malcolm's death and the movie of his life.

Acting from personal commitment, or as a sort of spiritual insurance policy, or both, Lee kept his promise to dialogue with blacks, Muslims, and Black Muslims as his project unfolded, and he did this internationally. In 1991 he went to Jiddah, Saudi Arabia, for several days, explaining to interested parties back home that his government hosts "realize that millions and millions of people are going to see this film, and this will be their first introduction to Islam, and they hope it will be a positive treatment of the religion and it will be." Whether such efforts were primarily a public-relations exercise or were sincere expressions of respect was an open question. When the production arrived in Cairo for a few days of shooting, a newspaper introduced the team to Egyptians with the headline "Malcolm X crew converts to Islam," a very loose interpretation of the facts. This was the first time a commercial film production had received permission to shoot in Mecca, where non-Muslims are not allowed to go, and some members of the technical crew found it expeditious to convert to Islam a few weeks beforehand.

Lee wasn't with them at the time, and later he spoke with reasonable candor about his own relationship with religion. "Most black [American] people are Southern Baptists," he told an interviewer. "I only went to church when I went down South to visit my grandmothers. I have always been honest about [my views on] organized religion. There's a difference between religion and spirituality. It comes down to a personal choice." Asked by Cairo journalists about the converted crew members, Spike gave a smart-alecky response, saying, "Robert De Niro gained eighty pounds for [Martin Scorsese's 1980 film] *Raging Bull*." Perhaps realizing that irreverence was not the ideal stance under the circumstances, he then changed his tone. "I have the utmost respect for the religion of Islam," he said, and added later, "It's no joke. You can't mess up. It's not just Islam; look what they did to Martin Scorsese – they [Lee presumably means Christians] wanted to hang him for [the 1988 film] *The Last Temptation of Christ*" (Berger). It remains unclear whether Spike's utmost respect was motivated by spiritual stirrings in his soul or pragmatic stirrings in his mind telling him to avoid Scorsese's quagmire by any means necessary.

Beyond his rhetorical gestures, Lee shored up the film's credibility by bringing in Betty Shabazz as a consultant. He also enlisted the Nation of Islam's defense arm, the Fruit of Islam, to provide security for the production. And he spoke to interviewers of the extensive reading and research he had done, as did Denzel Washington and other prominent contributors to the film. Washington also gave extra weight to the religious dimensions of Malcolm's ever-evolving life. In a conversation with me and a few other journalists at the time of the film's premiere, he said he put "a lot of prayer" into this aspect of his portrayal. "I had some very strong, spiritual men around me when working on this film. . . . Every day we started and ended the day with a prayer. I did anyway. There was a lot of spirituality involved" (Sterritt 1992b).

Pooh-Bahs

It is likely that no number of books read, research hours logged, prayers uttered, and knowledgeable people consulted would have stilled the apprehensions of Baraka and other African-American spokespersons who feared that Lee would turn Malcolm's mighty life into an anodyne commercial product. By this time Lee was firmly established as a serious and groundbreaking filmmaker, however, and one can hardly blame him for proffering scrappy responses to his harsher critics. Still, a great irony of his rejoinder to Baraka was that Lee himself could hardly claim to be free of cultural hubris, being something of a *soi-disant* grand pooh-bah in his own right. So unshakeable was his confidence in the eventual excellence of his biopic, and so strong was his addiction to the American film industry's most mercenary habits, that he was marketing Malcolm X commodities tied in with the still-unmade epic as early as the fall of 1991. Equally to the point, Lee too had been known to criticize an unmade movie when he didn't like the cut of its jib or the color of its director.

Exhibit A is his 1990 attack on the veteran Hollywood filmmaker Norman Jewison, who had declared his intention of filming Malcolm X's life from a screenplay by the African-American playwright Charles Fuller, the writer of Jewison's well-respected 1984 movie *A Soldier's Story*. Jewison was white, Fuller was black, and they made a formidable team. Jewison had built an important part of his career on socially conscious films with a left-liberal slant, such as the racially concerned *In the Heat of the Night* (1967), the labor-union drama *F.I.S.T.* (1978), and the criminal-justice satire . . . *And Justice for All* (1979); later he would make *In Country* (1989), about Vietnam War veterans, and *The Hurricane* (1999), based on the true story of Rubin "Hurricane" Carter, a black prizefighter (played by Denzel Washington in the film) wrongly convicted of murder. *A Soldier's Story* was adapted by Fuller from his stage drama *A Soldier's Play*, which had won the Pulitzer Prize, a New York Drama Critics' Circle Award, and numerous other honors in 1982.[8] Academy Award nominations went to Fuller for best adapted screenplay, to Adolph Caesar for best actor, and to the movie for best picture. How could these people possibly do justice to Lee's favorite African-American leader? He was livid at the very idea.

And he said so, promptly and publicly, insisting that such a quintessentially African-American topic should never be entrusted to a white director. "I have a big problem with Norman Jewison directing *The Autobiography of Malcolm X*," he told a *New York Times* interviewer.

> That disturbs me deeply, gravely. . . . Blacks have to control these films. . . . With a film of this magnitude, I wouldn't trust a white to direct – to be honest – they just don't know what it feels like. There's stuff I go through every day – I still cannot get a cab in New York! I don't care how many

books they read, or if they grew up with a black nanny, or what friends they had.

Consciously or not, Lee was recycling the views of August Wilson, the African-American dramatist whose 1987 play *Fences* was a recent Pulitzer Prize and Tony Award winner. In a special edition of the rock magazine *Spin*, which Lee edited, Wilson recalled the response he gave Paramount Pictures when the studio proposed a movie adaptation of *Fences*:

> I declined a white director not on the basis of race but of culture. White directors are not qualified for the job. The job requires someone who shares the specifics of the culture of black Americans. . . . Let's make a rule: Blacks don't direct Italian films. Italians don't direct Jewish films. Jews don't direct black-American films. That might account for 3 percent of the films that are made in this country. The other 97 percent – let it be every man for himself. (Thompson 57)

To mention just one of this argument's ridiculously obvious problems, it fails to tell us what makes a film "Italian" or "Jewish" or "black-American." The characters' skin color? Their accents? Their clothes? The food they eat? And how do all sorts of Spike Lee films, made before and after *Malcolm X*, fit into this scheme? Such movies as *Summer of Sam* and *25th Hour* are surely "white," which means Lee should have passed his scripts along to white directors, also calling one in to direct Sal and his sons in *Do the Right Thing*. And speaking of "every man for himself," can a male direct a "female film," can a homosexual direct a "heterosexual film"? Difficulties galore!

Of course it was Wilson, not Lee, who propounded the

above-quoted "rule," and Lee has never said anything quite so simplistic, on this subject at least. (Wilson asked him to direct *Fences* but his schedule precluded it.) Other movie people chimed in about the issue, many taking Lee's side, some not. James Earl Jones: "Spike said the director ought to be black, which was Spike's way of saying it should be Spike. When an important subject comes along and a Spike Lee suggests he must be involved, I think that's destructive." Sidney Lumet: "I understand the black point of view: what does a white know? But what does Spike know about life in 1942 – the Detroit period shaped everything. Where do you stop? Only an Irishman can direct Eugene O'Neill?" David Bradley, author of *The Chaneysville Incident* and writer of three drafts of a Malcolm X screenplay that didn't pan out: "It's the story of a man who learns to transcend race. The history of Malcolm X has mostly to do with the forces brought to bear on him by whites. It's a stupid notion that there's a black aesthetic, black experience. Malcolm never was a Christian – does that means you have to have a black Muslim director?" (Thompson 57).

All this aside, Lee lobbied fiercely to wrest Malcolm from Jewison's hands. "I'm the guy. I'm the guy," he chanted to Jewison on the phone (Denby 50). Their feud, such as it was, petered out when the screenplay Jewison commissioned from Fuller proved unacceptable to the director. "If I knew how to do it," Jewison said when he gave up the project near the end of 1990, "I would move heaven and high water tomorrow to do it." He also admitted that Malcolm remained "an enigma" to him. "I just haven't licked it," he said. "I know Spike Lee wants to get involved and, at the moment, I would encourage him to do it because the film should be made." Lee immediately signed with Warner's to write and direct the picture (Thompson 29). He wrote it with Arnold Perl, whose diverse credits included the 1959 documentary *Jazz on a Summer's Day* and Ossie Davis's directorial debut, *Cotton Comes to Harlem* (1970), adapted by Perl and Davis from Chester Himes's novel. Perl had also collaborated with James Baldwin on his "Malcolm X" script in the late 1960s. That screenplay was the best of the early efforts, Lee told critic David Denby a few weeks before his film's premiere. "But Elijah Muhammad was still alive when they wrote [it] and they dodged the breakup between the Black Muslims and Malcolm, as well as the assassination. I put all that back in. Malcolm was always in search of truth. He was in that one percent able to repudiate their past [lives] because of what was no longer true" (50).

Among its other effects, putting all that back in ballooned the movie's cost. Warner's budgeted it at $20 million, and Lee raised another $8.5 million by selling overseas distribution rights. Costs then rose another $5 million or so, and Lee let it be known that he would not keep the final cut to the running time of two hours and fifteen minutes stipulated by the studio. At this point the Completion Bond Company, which provides insurance protecting studios from cost overruns, refused to allow additional funding and shut down the postproduction process. Lee made a direct appeal to Bill Cosby, Oprah Winfrey, Janet Jackson, Magic Johnson, Michael Jordan, Prince, and other African-American celebrities, who invested in the production and kept it in business (Denby 50). Final cost: about $34 million. Running time: three hours and twenty-two minutes. Domestic gross through 2011: $48,169,910.

Man, Myth, Movie

America was ripe for a Malcolm X movie, and Lee's preoccupation with the project grew from his sharp awareness of its timeliness. In the three years or so before the film's arrival, sales of *The Autobiography of Malcolm X* rose three hundred percent, and four of Malcolm's books published by Pathfinder Press had a ninefold rise in sales between 1986 and 1991 (Ansen 1991). Lee acknowledged this factor when he claimed that "the studios were scared" of the topic until "the rising popularity of Malcolm," paired with the box-office appeal of Washington and himself, "made it economically feasible for them to invest in the project" (Lee and Gates 1992). The film rode this swelling wave to considerable success, grossing almost $10 million in its opening weekend; this was considerably less than the pictures that opened at the same time – *Home Alone 2: Lost in New York* earned three times that figure, and *Bram Stoker's Dracula* took in $15 million – but it was impressive for a historical drama almost three and a half hours in length. "No artist . . . has commodified Malcolm X's identity more effectively than Spike Lee in his . . . superb cinematic portrayal," a scholar of religion and black culture wrote later, adding that the film "inspired renewed interest and debate about Islam and black nationalism in black America" (Turner 240).

Among the honors accorded *Malcolm X* were Academy Award nominations for best actor (Washington) and best costume design; awards for best actor (Washington) from the New York Film Critics Circle, the Berlin International Film Festival, and critics' organizations in Boston, Chicago, Kansas City, and elsewhere; Image Awards for outstanding motion picture as well as Washington for best actor and Angela Bassett and Al Freeman Jr. in supporting roles; selection in 2010 by the Library of Congress for preservation in the National Film Registry, to which twenty-five "culturally, historically, or aesthetically significant" movies are named each year; and more. Although it was neither a box-office blockbuster nor an unalloyed critical success, *Malcolm X* quickly established itself as one of the most broadly influential interpretations of its protagonist's life, times, and career ever to enter the sphere of American popular culture. Reviews were generally good. Rita Kempley (1992) of *The Washington Post* called it "a spiritually enriching testament to the human capacity for change" and "surely Spike Lee's most universally appealing film," presenting an "engrossing mosaic of history, myth and sheer conjecture." She added that Lee "directs the way other people order Chinese food," bringing "all manner of styles and moods to the film's four chapters," but she praised Washington for pulling all the elements together with "uncanny ease." *Chicago Sun-Times* reviewer Roger Ebert (1992) called it "one of the great screen biographies" and saluted Lee as "not only one of the best filmmakers in America, but one of the most crucially important, because his films address the central subject of race," not via sentimentality or slogans, but by showing "how his characters live, and why." Ebert later deemed it the year's best film, and later still he listed it among the ten best films of the decade. Vincent Canby used his *New York Times* review to embrace it as "an ambitious, tough, seriously considered biographical film that, with honor, eludes easy characterization." Ansen (1992) wrote in *Newsweek* that the film brings Malcolm "very much to life again, both as man and myth," and *Entertainment Weekly* critic Owen Gleiberman (1992) lauded the film as "an intimate and engrossing . . . saga that is also one of the most passionate political films ever made in this country."

In a more ambivalent review, Desson Howe (1992) of *The Washington Post* criticized Lee for shining too bright a spotlight on himself in the secondary role of Malcolm X's sidekick, Shorty, and for confusing the concept of epic filmmaking with merely making an overlong film; yet he also suggested that the film might "do for Malcolm X what the federal holiday did for Martin Luther King: legitimize his beliefs nationally." On the negative side, *Variety* critic Todd McCarthy (1992) wrote that while the film is "ambitious, right-minded and personal," the climactic "montage of footage and stills of the real Malcolm proves infinitely more powerful than any of the drama that has preceded it." Wittingly or not, Jonathan Rosenbaum's review in the *Chicago Reader* harkened back to Baraka's lament, opining that the need to create "a pious 'official' (i.e., middle-class) portrait squeezes out too many aspects of Malcolm's varied experience and mercurial intelligence." My review in *The Christian Science Monitor* (1992a) took a similar view, calling the film "more inspirational than inspired" and "respectful to the point of hagiography, detailing [Malcolm's] weaknesses (mainly in his misspent youth) so that his goodness will seem all the more triumphant in the later scenes." Like almost everyone, though, I praised Washington's acting, saying it was "never less than riveting to watch and hear, capturing the subtleties of Malcolm's personality and the magnetism of his public persona without lapsing into shallow imitation or showy grandstanding for an instant." I have the same opinion today, and I still find it highly ironic that after forcefully explicating why only an African-American filmmaker could properly handle this quintessentially African-American topic, Spike Lee created a movie that is true in every respect to the most time-honored Hollywood traditions of the biopic genre – traditions that were originated, developed, and locked into place by the white men who have controlled the white-dominated studio system since the beginnings of modern American cinema.

4

BROWNSTONES IN THE NABE, PROJECTS IN THE HOOD

Spike Lee said late in 1992 that he considered *Malcolm X* to be "a nice little coda" to the first part of his career (Sterritt 1992b). Nice sprawling coda would be more like it, but perhaps Lee's choice of words was inspired by the nature of his next production, *Crooklyn*, one of his more intimate films – modest in scale, in cost, and in achievement, although I think most critics have underrated its importance as Lee's most concentrated examination of middle-class family life in an African-American environment that strongly resembles the one in which he grew up and for which he has never lost his affection. In a fine example of Spike Lee dialectics, this 1994 production was followed in 1995 by *Clockers*, an emotionally wrenching drama where the decent neighborhood of *Crooklyn* is replaced by an impoverished housing project that couldn't be more different – a place where crime, crack, and craziness reign supreme over junkies, children, and others too weak, ignorant, or foolish to keep control of their lives.

CROOKLYN

Family Life

The screenplay of *Crooklyn* originated with Spike's sister Joie Susannah Lee and his brother Cinqué Lee, neither of whom expected Spike to embrace it as a project he wanted to direct. Spike was looking for a venture at the opposite end of the size spectrum from *Malcolm X*, however, and the intimacy of *Crooklyn* neatly filled the bill. Spike both produced and directed the picture, with his siblings as associate producers. All three shared credit for the final version of the script.

Named after a slangy nickname for Spike's favorite borough, *Crooklyn* revolves around the Carmichaels, a black family living a reasonably contented life in a Brooklyn brownstone during the 1970s. The mother, Carolyn (Alfre Woodard), is a hard-working schoolteacher with five energetic kids to handle at home. The father, Woody (Delroy Lindo), is an out-of-work musician whose artistic ideals get in the way of practical matters such as earning a living and supporting his household. At first the story concerns all seven members of the household, but it soon becomes apparent that ten-year-old Troy (Zelda Harris), the princess of this little kingdom, will be the main character of the loosely knit narrative. As imperfect as she is adorable, she uses her status as the only girl in the house to coax special treatment from her parents, meanwhile indulging her penchants for nagging, fighting, and shoplifting for the thrill of it. Most of the film unfolds in Brooklyn, but a key segment depicts a visit to a Southern branch of the clan, which agrees to take Troy in when financial hardships break her nuclear family apart. There she copes with a straitlaced aunt (Frances Foster) and a high-spirited cousin (Patriece Nelson), learning lessons about life and maturing a little in the process. Near the end of the story she needs all the maturity she can muster, since her return to Brooklyn coincides with the descent of a serious illness on her mother. Before long, Carolyn dies, and the film's conclusion is bittersweet.

Crooklyn is a conservative film, exploring middle-class family life in mostly positive and affectionate terms. In this context it's surprising to encounter one of the most experimental stylistic gestures in Lee's entire body of work. The centerpiece of the film, comprising Troy's adventures in her temporary Southern home, was filmed with an anamorphic lens that squeezes a wide-screen image into a narrower full-frame space; in normal practice, the image would be unsqueezed by a compensating lens as it was projected, but Lee leaves the image in its compacted shape, giving this portion of the movie a deliberately distorted look that matches Troy's feelings during her sojourn as a stranger in a strange land. Reception for this device was decidedly mixed. In my 1994 review I linked it to the adventurousness of Arthur Jafa's cinematography throughout the movie, calling *Crooklyn* an "inventively cinematic film . . . with a camera that tracks, travels, swoops, and glides into every nook of its Brooklyn surroundings and every cranny of its characters' lives." By contrast, *New York Times* critic Janet Maslin (1994) derided "the bizarre trick of compressing images by using the wrong aspect ratio," saying this "affectation" was "less likely to evoke Troy's mental state than to prompt hasty trips to projection booths in movie theaters across the land." I find the device quite effective, but Maslin was surely right about the projection-booth part.

Lee thought of *Crooklyn* as "a distillation of things that are remembered and imagined" about an important moment in his childhood and that of his siblings. "It really wasn't my intent to make a film that reminisced about this grand old time back in the 1970s," he told Roger Ebert in 1994.

I just wanted to tell the story of this young girl who was coming of age during that time. And also to show an African-American family that was not dysfunctional; that was headed by two parents. The mother and the father were there and none of the children were on drugs or rapists or murderers, whatever. And despite the fact [that] there's a lot of conflict amongst the siblings, there's a great amount of love in this family for each other.

Dying and Death

The black cultural commentator bell hooks might not like my précis of the narrative or my account of Lee's accomplishment in this film. This is because I see *Crooklyn* as a moderately nuanced and thoughtful comedy-drama with reasonably well-developed characters and a variety of more or less revealing incidents relating to the joys and sorrows of African-American family life in a middle-class urban milieu. For hooks, however, the film's raison d'être and meaning are completely tied up with one event – the death of Carolyn, an afflicted and underappreciated black woman – and the fatal flaw of the movie is Lee's inability to take the death of a black woman with due seriousness. Making her case in a 1996 essay called "*Crooklyn*: The Denial of Death," hooks herself has trouble making up her mind about the film, finding it a crypto-racist melodrama in some sentences, a paradigm-shattering breakthrough in others. She focuses attention on a key question, though: what degree of *authenticity* can we properly ascribe to the story, the characters, and Lee's manner of presenting them? She also admonishes *Crooklyn* for indulging in such lazy inclinations as naïveté and sentimentality, and while other observers have done the same, I choose hooks to engage in dialogue with because she is among the most pointed in her criticisms, which she throws at the film from unusual and provocative angles. Her essay's uneasy fusion of praise, reproach, lucidity, and orneriness captures the density and complexity of *Crooklyn* in ways she may not have anticipated.[1]

Assessing the picture as a whole, hooks finds a jumble of worthy and unworthy elements. On the plus side, Lee is "positively radical" in his willingness to see the world through a little black girl's perceptions, "to enter the spaces of her emotional universe, the intimate world of family and friends that ground her being and give her life meaning." The film also triumphs when it presents "fictive representations of black subjectivity rarely seen in mainstream cinema, images that both counter racist stereotypes [and] facile notions of positive images of 'the black family'." The parents in the story are "property-owning, artistic, progressive" as well as "not obsessed with upward mobility, with the material trappings of success." They are unique and even countercultural, representing "a mixture of the nationalist movement for racial uplift and a bohemian artistic subculture." They dwell comfortably in a multiethnic, multicultural world (36–7). In all of these particulars, hooks is right on target.

Within this seemingly progressive film about a seemingly progressive family, however, hooks detects the odor of patriarchy, misogyny, and white cultural hegemony. Lee looks at the Carmichaels through "rose-colored glasses," but he can't hide the fact that they are "seriously dysfunctional" in hooks's eyes, afflicted by eating disorders, uncontainable rage, domestic violence, and Woody's inability to hang onto money (40). Troy's cuteness embodies "all the desirable elements of sexist-defined femininity," except when she goes South and meets a light-skinned cousin, whereupon she assumes a "bitchified" persona rooted in stereotypes of evil dark-skinned females (41–2). Worst of all is Lee's treatment of Carolyn's death and Troy's subsequent entry into a new stage of life. He portrays Carolyn as "a modern-day Sapphire with direct lineage to the Amos 'n' Andy character," and her death is "upstaged by the passing of the torch to Troy," itself a manifestation of "patriarchal thinking that females are interchangeable [and] undifferentiated" (40, 43). Neither of these tragedies – Carolyn's death, Troy's loss of girlhood – is properly mourned by the other characters. Death and dying are merely a "diversionary ploy" in *Crooklyn*, providing "a passive emotional backdrop" for Lee's vision of the black family – an "insidious anti-woman, anti-feminist vision" aligned with "the beliefs and values of white mainstream culture" (45).

It's ridiculous to link Alfre Woodard's multilayered Carolyn with the one-dimensional Sapphire on the bygone *Amos 'n' Andy* comedy shows, but apart from this and hooks's generally overheated tone, her critique raises issues worth considering.[2] *Crooklyn* is certainly darker, moodier, and more psychologically intricate than many commentators have recognized; hooks goes after critic J. Hoberman at some length, saying he is mostly interested in the "comedic aspects" of the picture (37). And it is plausible, perhaps even defensible, to charge Lee with putting more emotional weight on such well-worn *Bildungsroman* tropes as "passing the torch" and "coming of age" than on the existential anguish of an adult woman, mother, wife, worker, friend, and community member who is annihilated by disease in the prime years of her life. As in the critique of *She's Gotta Have It* that I discussed earlier, though, hooks is basically complaining that Lee made the movie he wanted to make, not the movie she wanted to see. She says the film's most interesting aspects are those "rooted in Lee's own life story," and that the story loses its appeal "when he exploits those memories to create a counter worldview . . . that will advance patriarchal thinking" (45). I can't speak as confidently as hooks about Lee's

uses of African-American cultural and social values, but I
know enough about memory and about patriarchy to suggest that he doesn't depict Woody's "irresponsibility and
misuse of resources" (43) just so he can extol that character's
"artistic sensibility" by excusing these failings as endearing
idiosyncrasies; as we've seen, Spike was not so forgiving with
his actual jazz-musician father. Nor does taking on heavier
household responsibilities as a girl appear to have damaged
Joie, who was fourteen years old when cancer killed their
mother. My point is that Lee intends *Crooklyn* as a memory
movie, not a manifesto or declaration of principles. Much
other evidence within the film could be adduced to this
effect.

In sum, *Crooklyn* is not a documentary or even an autobiography or auto-biopic. It is a memoir – composed in
partnership with loved ones – in which facts, events, people,
places, things, ideas, and feelings are not captured as records
and representations but are glimpsed as mercurial impressions, filtered and altered by the haze of time and mutability
that surrounds us throughout our days. I agree with hooks
that *Crooklyn* works best when it seems most deeply, passion-
ately rooted in the authentic recollections of Spike and his
siblings, and in these moments, which comprise most of the
film, the experiences and personalities we see and hear are
not only African-American phenomena, they are *American*
phenomena as well. In one of her more effective and evoc-
ative passages, hooks writes that Troy, taking the place of
her dead mother, "is no longer adventurous. She no longer
roams the streets, exploring, discovering. ... Gone is the
vulnerable, emotionally open girl who expressed a range of
feelings. ... [She] becomes a spectator, standing behind the
gate looking out at life, a stern expression on her face" (43). I
think hooks overstates her case again, but to the degree that
this description rings true, *Crooklyn* transcends racial and

ethnic boundaries to become an American family portrait in the fullest sense.

CLOCKERS

Honestly, I don't think I've ever done an adaptation of a novel.
. . . What I did was a combination of three things: there is stuff
that I liked in the book that wasn't in the script; there is stuff that
I changed in the script; and there is stuff that I added. – Spike
Lee on *Clockers.* (Aftab, 188–9)

Change of Focus

Based on the eponymous 1992 novel by Richard Price, a specialist in narratives about urban life, *Clockers* was originally slated to be directed by Martin Scorsese, also an urban specialist, from Price's own screenplay, with Robert De Niro playing a homicide cop investigating a drug-related murder. Since all of these artists are white, the screenplay would presumably have followed the novel in giving approximately equal attention to Rocco Klein, the white cop, and Strike Dunham, a black drug dealer who may have committed the slaying to which his straight-arrow brother has confessed. Scorsese and De Niro then decided to make their brilliant *Casino* (1995) instead, and *Clockers* flew onto Spike Lee's radar screen. "I was leery of directing in this black gangsta, hip-hop, shoot-'em-up genre," he later told a *New York Times* writer, who found Lee similarly wary of the white-male midlife-crisis angst that pervaded the story. The departure of white, middle-aged De Niro opened up new possibilities, however, which Lee quickly turned to his advantage. "No disrespect to De Niro," he said, "but when he left, I was able to change the focus" (Bradley). While the screenplay written by Price and revised by Lee retained Rocco as an important character, Strike now became the movie's main character.[3] Scorsese produced the picture with Lee and Jon Kilik, who was then shoring up his status as Spike's regular producer; but the finished film departs in many ways from the version Scorsese would likely have made.

In a major alteration straight from the Spike Lee playbook, Lee moves the story from the New Jersey town of the novel (loosely based on Jersey City) to a slummy district in Brooklyn, depicting his beloved borough with a grittiness and gloominess without precedent in his work. Ronald "Strike" Dunham (Mekhi Phifer) is a nineteen-year-old clocker, a street-level dealer in crack cocaine who peddles his product in front of the housing project where he lives. The local drug lord is Rodney Little (Delroy Lindo), a psychopathic criminal whose front, a neighborhood junk shop, well suits his personality, which hovers just a few pimped-up mannerisms above the gutter. Strike has a vulnerable streak – in fact, he has an ulcer, which explains the chocolate Moo he swigs – and Rodney protects him from the worst hazards of his trade, racking up implied IOUs from Strike in the process. The story kicks into gear when Rodney orders Strike to kill another young dealer, Darryl Adams (Steve White), who's been stealing from the till. The latter's corpse turns up soon after in the parking lot of a fast-food joint, ripped into by four bullets that have splashed his blood and brains upon the pavement where he lies. For most of the cops on the scene, the killing of a black crack peddler is a routine and even risible event.

It appears to be an uncomplicated case as well, since a young black man from the area – Victor Dunham (Isaiah Washington), who happens to be Strike's big brother – promptly confesses, saying that he killed Darryl in self-defense. Victor is a very improbable suspect, however. He's conspicuously clean and sober; he's a solid family man; he's never had trouble with the police; and he's been reliably holding down two jobs, working like mad to earn enough money for a new home outside the projects. To the lead investigator on the case, Detective Rocco Klein (Harvey Keitel), the confession is too fishy to take at face value. If it's true that Victor fired the deadly bullets, he must have done it to protect his younger brother from Rodney's psychotic wrath; and if he *didn't* do the killing, he may be confessing to protect Strike from the law. Buying into the latter theory, Rocco puts relentless pressure on both brothers, hoping that the truth will eventually emerge. He turns out to be wrong, and the screenplay implicitly explains Victor's violence with a kind of "black rage" theory, contending that the pressures of being a dutiful black man in a brutalizing urban environment caused Victor to accrue rising antisocial impulses that could not be kept under control forever.

Other characters in the story include Larry Malilli (John Turturro), the second detective on the case; Iris Jeeter (Regina Taylor), a rage-filled mother in the projects; her son Tyrone "Shorty" Jeeter (Pee Wee Love), who is Strike's protégé and hanger-on; André the Giant (Keith David), a housing cop with a high regard for African-American history; and Thomas Jefferson Byrd (Tom Byrd, aka Errol Barnes), an addict with AIDS who wants everyone to know he caught the disease via needles, not gay sex. The editor was Sam Pollard, who had worked on *Mo' Better Blues* and *Jungle Fever*, and has done five more Lee pictures to date. The cinematographer, by contrast, was a first-timer: Malik Hassan Sayeed, an electrician and gaffer (lighting assistant) getting his break into big-time camerawork from Lee, who took the gamble because the young man's "uncontaminated" style appealed to him (Pizzello 102). The bet paid off, and Sayeed went on to photograph several more of Spike's films. Their collaboration on *Clockers* produced colors that swing between eye-dazzling luxuriance and metallic harshness; lens choices that bring symbolic symmetry to scenes that might otherwise have seemed chaotic or confused; and eruptions of pure delirium from time to time, when deliberately contorted images conjure up an implicitly subjective tense intimating unrealized possibilities for the characters.

The Flip Side

No element in *Clockers* is more essential than its setting: a housing project erected with public funds to provide theoretically secure and decent homes for families with incomes at or near the poverty line. Lee shot the picture at the Gowanus Houses, a complex in the Boerum Hill area of Brooklyn, renamed the Nelson Mandela Houses in the film – an artful moniker, since Mandela's place in the history of modern South Africa represents both long-lasting captivity and ultimate empowerment. The drug-dealing heart of the place is a raised platform in the courtyard that film critic Amy Taubin likens to both a theatrical stage and a place of imprisonment, "an inversion of [philosopher Michel] Foucault's panopticon" that holds Strike in an iron grip, keeping him "under constant surveillance, vulnerable to aggressors who enter from all sides" (G. Brown and Taubin 71).[4] Building on this insight, Paula Massood asserts that the plaza and housing units amount to "a carceral city, where the surrounding buildings act as sentries . . . guarding the boundaries" (194). The sentries presumably keep people in, not out, since aggressors are evidently free to enter the place.

Although these are productive ideas, the setting of *Clockers* does not strike me as quite so carceral. We are introduced to the Mandela Houses in a shot marked by strong visual symmetry, suggesting not only the entrapping qualities of the complex but also a sense of solidity and safety that may be comforting for the solid citizens who live alongside the drug peddlers and their ilk. A number of Lee's films open by ushering viewers into a New York neighborhood, and while *Clockers* does so more ambivalently than, say, *Do the Right Thing* or *Crooklyn*, it nonetheless implies that we are entering civilized terrain, however precarious the civilization may sometimes seem. The buildings do have a touch of the observation tower about them, and the clockers are aware of being visible to residents and police. Yet the buildings are people's homes, after all, and if spying were indeed their main function, the criminals would have no hope of ever getting away with anything. We are in a "bad" section of Brooklyn, to be sure. Still, we are in Brooklyn, and for Lee that is never a fundamentally bad thing.

Sometimes it comes close, though, and this movie offers one of those occasions. *Clockers* is the appalling flip side of *Crooklyn*, and to underscore this dreadful inversion, Lee precedes the first encounter between Strike and Darryl with a tabloid headline saying "Crooklyn" in close-up. *Clockers* continues the earlier film's interest in neighborhood personalities and local color, but here Lee replaces bittersweet memories with foul realities.

Power Relations

Anticipating the deservedly acclaimed HBO miniseries *The Wire* (2002–8), for which Price later wrote several scripts, *Clockers* vividly outlines the hierarchies and bureaucracies that organize power relations on both sides of the law. Rodney is an insanely evil man, but his drug operation is rigidly structured and controlled, with high-powered suppliers at the top and no-power dealers at the bottom. Strike is a hard worker with an active mind and personal habits that border on puritanical; in a more civilized milieu he could easily achieve the kind of success and respectability that Victor has been striving for in the period leading up to the story. But some incalculable combination of forces – social, cultural, psychological, even cosmic, for all we know – has snagged him in Rodney's mercilessly effective web, where he isn't a full-fledged criminal, just a miserable clocker, endlessly racing an imaginary two-minute clock as he services inner-city addicts and thrill-seeking suburbanites while dodging cops, turf-conscious rivals, and assorted predators and losers who dwell around him. The crack scene in *Jungle Fever* was harrowing enough to mark a turning point in Lee's treatment of urban life, and seen on its own it's a vision out of Dante, as I remarked earlier. But it's more of a way station in purgatory when set alongside the all-consuming inferno seen here.

The journey into hell begins with the opening credits, which are accompanied by a montage of photographs showing young African-American men lying dead in pools of gore, foreshadowing Darryl's death early in the story. After a second prologue, with five black teenagers commenting in hip-hop rhythms on life in the project where they live, Strike enters the picture and the plot gets under way. The decision to focalize the narrative entirely through Strike, rather than switching between Strike and Rocco, is one of three changes from the novel that are particularly important to the film's meaning, as Paula Massood's analysis persuasively shows. Seeing things from Strike's perspective makes it easier for viewers to identify and sympathize with him, sensing his pangs of conscience (or at least twinges of doubt) over his line of work and gaining a bit of insight into the moment-to-moment thoughts and feelings that underlie and motivate his actions. Comparing him with characters in such contemporaneous African-American films as John Singleton's *Boyz N the Hood* (1991), Ernest R. Dickerson's *Juice* (1992), and

Albert Hughes and Allen Hughes's *Menace II Society* (1993),
Strike is "more three-dimensional ... in the sense that he
possesses a well-defined psychology," manifested in behaviors colored by his youth and inexperience, such as his love
for model trains and his defenselessness when threatened by
authority (Massood 190–1).

In addition, the change of venue from New Jersey to New
York resonates beyond the look and feel of the story's locations. When he transplanted the tale to a Brooklyn setting,
Lee said that cost, convenience, and efficiency were the only
reasons for the move, since "projects are projects" (Bradley)
wherever you go. In fact, however, the semiotics of the move
are very rich. For one thing, the location inserted *Clockers*
into the historiography of black Brooklyn that Lee had been
developing, discontinuously but lucidly, since his earliest
films. For another, low-income projects in the Gowanus
Houses mold were a factor (along with real-estate specula-
tors, apathetic authorities, and the like) in the growing ghet-
toization of the black community in New York and other
big cities. Conducting research for his novel, Price had been
amazed at how projects had gone in a relatively short time
from "launching pads for working-class families to just ter-
minals where generations are stacked up in the same apartment because there's no place to go" (Werner 10). Related
to this, Brooklyn has become a metaphorical end of the
line for many black people – the last stop for the hopes and
dreams of African-Americans who had left the segregated
South, transitional cities such as Chicago and Memphis,
and the declining purlieus of Harlem in a search for better
things that breathed its last in the human warehouses Price
describes. These are among the subtextual and extratextual
matters that enter *Clockers* by way of its Brooklyn setting
(Massood 193–4).

In a third salutary alteration to Price's original story,

Strike gets to have a hobby. Whereas the novel portrays him as a money-minded guy with no interest in sports, music, or even girls, the movie gives him a collection of model trains that means more to him than anything except selling his dope and keeping Rodney at bay. Trains are another signifier of the migration that has marked so much African-American history, and they are also an emblem of the oppression black Americans have endured. The rise of railroading across the continent played a powerful role in constructions of masculinity during the late nineteenth and early twentieth centuries; yet for blacks the railroads brought whole new kinds of second-class citizenship, symbolized by constricted employment opportunities – being a Pullman porter was the only realistic option – and the humiliations of Jim Crow segregation, now extended to the fresh arena of railway cars. Within the film, Strike's trains subtly accentuate his status as a violator of boundaries forced into dangerous passage between lawmen on one side and lawbreakers on the other. Finally, the presence of the trains deepens the emotional tone of two other memorable moments in the film. One is André the Giant's remark to Strike about the pathetic limitations of his world (Massood 199, 195). "There's more than just these projects out there, you know?" the housing cop says to the hopelessly provincial young adult, pointing out that for all his love of trains, the only kind he's actually ridden is the subway. "Don't you want to go someplace you've never been before?"

The other moment is the end of the film. Forced to get out of town in a hurry, Strike doesn't hop on a bus at Port Authority as in the novel; instead he heads for Penn Station and boards a train, taking a smooth ride to somewhere that can't help being a step up, or at least an energizing step sideways, from the hellhole he's escaping at long last. Some critics find this finale sentimental and false, but it rings true for those who understand the fundamentally optimistic vision that is nested within even the bleakest and unhappiest Spike Lee joints. The open-ended ending of *Clockers* anticipates that of *25th Hour*, which again uses New York as the point of departure for a mythically tinged journey toward an unfamiliar corner of the American scene. Neither conclusion offers any certainty that problems will be solved or sorrows overcome, but both rank with Lee's most invigorating scenes. And it's fair to conjecture that the *Clockers* finale has special meaning for him, offering the possibility of new fulfillment for a character who almost shares his name. The equation is simple: Strike ≈ Spike.

Capping a Decade

I didn't fully appreciate *Clockers* at first. My 1995 review applauded Sayeed for his stunning cinematography and Pollard for his energetic editing, and I praised Lee as one of the few current filmmakers who seek "not merely to represent but to reinterpret our contemporary world" through the lens of personal insight and experience. I criticized the film as well, however, finding deficiencies of narrative and style. In condensing the 600-odd pages of Price's book into about two hours of screen time, I wrote, Lee omits subplots that flesh out and enrich the novel's main concerns, disrupting the story's flow and turning slow-building revelations into abrupt surprises or arbitrary twists. Noting that *Clockers* was the first Lee film devoted entirely to realistic depictions of underclass poverty, violence, and despair, I added that Lee's artistic sensibilities had become so deeply ingrained that he couched even the most wrenching subjects in aesthetic as well as dramatic terms, allowing his cinematic style to call as much attention to itself as to the real-world problems at the center of the film. *Clockers* is a major work by a major artist, I concluded, but its achievements are diminished by shortcomings of story and psychology.

My opinion of *Clockers* has soared in subsequent years, thanks to deeper acquaintance with the film and further thought about the ways in which its style helps develop shades of narrative and thematic meaning that I undervalued on first viewing; in a 2007 essay I called it one of Lee's most important New York City films. I see it now as the culmination of the first and finest period in Lee's career, capping ten years of filmmaking that was frequently brilliant, invariably exciting, and inventive, provocative, and memorable even when it fell below his usual high level of accomplishment.

Among their other merits, Lee's movies of this decade comprise a remarkably coherent vision of American life, centered on the city and filtered through an African-American's eyes, ears, heart, and mind, but clearly meant to engage with Americans of every kind, hyphenated or not. Lee has been outspoken about the decisive role played by black identity in his personal life and professional practice, and his forthrightness about this has provided ammunition (sometimes artificially souped up by distortion, exaggeration, misrepresentation, and selective quotation) for those who find his films insular, parochial, aggressive, argumentative, self-indulgent, self-regarding, or simply not their cup of tea or chocolate Moo, as the case may be. Look at the actual films, though, and as likely as not you'll find a *consciousness* of race that fair-minded people will find hard to confuse with the quarrelsome, obsessive racism or racialism that tendentious viewers, critics, and (occasionally) scholars read into them.

The next chapter examines the films that Lee has directed since the end of his first decade as a feature filmmaker. His output has grown more diverse in subject, theme, and location – focusing more intently on women and white people, for instance – and it has grown less consistent in quality, popularity, and ambition. Its low points, found in unfortunate projects like *Girl 6* in 1996 and *She Hate Me* in 2004, are major let-downs; its high points, found in stunningly original films like *Bamboozled* in 2000 and *25th Hour* in 2002, stand with the finest achievements in twenty-first-century cinema. In sum, Spike's second decade and a half has been as unpredictable as the years that preceded it, and its volatility makes it all the more fascinating to explore.

5

WOMEN AND MEN, BLACKS AND WHITES

The respect he has earned from female critics such as Amy Taubin and Georgia Brown notwithstanding, Spike Lee has never excelled at creating female characters. In the ten years after *She's Gotta Have It* launched his feature-filmmaking career, he created only one – the ten-year-old Troy in *Crooklyn* – who could rival Nola Darling as a fully developed three-dimensional figure. Perhaps to rectify this insufficiency, he embarked on *Girl 6*, the first movie he directed from a screenplay he had not written or cowritten himself. The script was by Suzan-Lori Parks, a young African-American dramatist whose first full-length play, *Imperceptible Mutabilities in the Third Kingdom*, staged by the Brooklyn Arts and Culture Association in 1989, had won an Obie Award for best new work. *Girl 6* is her only screenplay to date, and the failings of the completed film are attributable to the script as well as to Lee's handling of it. It is neither a popular movie nor an artistically successful one.

GIRL 6

Judy (Theresa Randle) is an African-American actress with a shoplifter (Isaiah Washington) for an exhusband and a sponger (Lee) for a neighbor and friend. The acting career she dreams of grows more improbable than ever when her chronic lack of money and a bungled audition for a movie part – the director (Quentin Tarantino) says he needs to see her breasts, and she grows visibly upset while acceding to the request – induces her white agent (John Turturro) and her black acting coach (Susan Batson) to part company with her. After faring just as badly in some ordinary low-wage jobs (passing out handbills, checking coats), she starts looking for work on the phone-sex circuit. This means more auditions, but the standards are less than exacting, and she even turns down a couple of opportunities that seem too sleazy for comfort. Then she agrees to be Girl 6 for a phone-sex operation headed by Boss 1, also known as Lil (Jenifer Lewis). Judy doesn't have the right instincts for this line of work, though. It's hard for her to tell when a client is lying, and racism manages to rear its head even in a profession where anonymity is supposedly the rule. She finally calls it quits when a caller turns into a stalker. Making up with her exhusband, she moves to Los Angeles for another try at acting. There she learns that West Coast auditions are as bad as East Coast auditions, but at least she's a little older, wiser, and more savvy about the countless ways modern society has devised to exploit the bodies and images of women.

Lee wasn't particularly savvy about that very subject, much to the film's disadvantage. It doesn't take a sociologist or a semiotician to see how the movie's entire conceptual scheme is sabotaged by the disastrously ill-wrought audition scene at the beginning: Judy is objectified, demeaned, and humiliated by the director's demand to see her breasts, and

Lee shows his sympathy for the mortified actress by – showing her breasts! On top of this, the dialogue Judy reads in the audition comes from *She's Gotta Have It*, which showed Tracy Camilla Johns's breasts! It is just barely possible that Lee thinks he is exposing the patriarchy of American popular culture by owning up to the same sexist impulses and male-chauvinist practices that motivate Quentin Tarantino and his ilk, but this already far-fetched explanation falls apart when one imagines a version of the scene where Judy feels the same distress but doesn't actually bare her breasts, or where Lee's camera stays on her expressive face without filming her below the shoulders.

This is Movie Directing 101, and it's amazing that Lee either didn't think this episode through or thought it through with a carelessness that is not characteristic of his work; either way, it fouls the atmosphere for everything that follows. He certainly thought about other aspects of the film, but the results aren't much more satisfactory. In a stab at feminist aesthetics, for instance, he photographed the sex-line callers in hi-def video and shot the women on proper 35mm film, theorizing that the video image diminishes the "power" of the men while "the 35-mm. look and texture heightens [the] strength" of the female characters (cited in Ebert 1996). Nice try.

Roger Ebert, one of Lee's most articulate supporters, faulted the film on several grounds, including its unsuccessful effort to suggest that a female phone-sex worker might easily get attached or even addicted to her job – a development that has no doubt come to pass, but surely does not happen often enough to sustain a pro-woman, anti-exploitation fable. *Girl 6* is indeed a fable, or perhaps an allegory, attaching labels rather than names to most of the characters – Madonna plays Boss #3, Michael Imperioli plays Caller #30, Naomi Campbell plays Girl #75, etc. – in the manner of a medieval morality play. This further contributes to the film's shallow, chilly feel. Critics panned it, and its grosses have never reached the $5 million mark. Ebert sees the picture just the way I do, and he deserves the last word. "Spike Lee is a great director," he wrote in 1996, "but his strong point is not leading expeditions into the secret corners of the female psyche." We're back on Nola Darling's dark continent, and it's dismaying to find that our intrepid guide has less of a grasp on its geography in 1996 than he did as a neophyte directing his first feature film.

GET ON THE BUS

We can't bring our families to the movies because the American people have an appetite like a swine. And you are feeding the swine with the filth of degenerate culture. We got to stop it. – Louis Farrakhan (1995)

The Million Man March

By design or by happenstance, Lee turned next to a story populated almost exclusively by men. *Get on the Bus* was his tenth feature in ten years, and his third release in thirteen months: the admirable *Clockers* arrived in September 1995, followed by the unfortunate *Girl 6* in March 1996, and the surprisingly engaging *Get on the Bus* debuted in October 1996. Moviegoers with no special interest in the Nation of Islam, the controversial leader Louis Farrakhan, or the Million Man March on Washington, DC, expected little from a film about what seemed a parochial topic; but *Get on the Bus* proved to be a lively and intelligent visit with a group of men who represent an array of masculine personality types without resembling (like the *Girl 6* women) tokens in a sociopolitical board game. Once again Lee worked with a script by another writer, Reggie Rock Bythewood, and once again the budget (a little less than $2.5 million) was very low. But this time the situations, characters, and dialogue ring true.

Almost all of the action takes place on a chartered bus carrying its passengers to the Million Man March, a massive rally of citizens, activists, and social, cultural, and political leaders that took place on October 16, 1995.[1] Although it was organized by Benjamin Chavis, a former executive director of the National Association for the Advancement of Colored People, and a committee representing a number of African-American religious and civil-rights groups, the event was closely associated with Nation of Islam chief Louis Farrakhan, its keynote speaker, de facto leader, and most fervent proponent. Farrakhan's prominence in connection with the event "raised fears that the huge numbers at the march would propel [him] to the status of a central figure in American politics," Lee's biographer writes; but as things turned out, the march may better be seen as "the apex of Farrakhan's career, before a speedy fall back from the mainstream toward the margins" (Aftab 221).

Although celebrities as different as Bill Cosby and Jesse Jackson endorsed the march, Lee did not personally attend it. "I had just had a knee operation, arthroscopic surgery, so I couldn't go," he explained. The idea for *Get on the Bus* came from movie producer Reuben Cannon and his colleagues. Lee liked the idea and suggested that they fund the picture with "black seed-investment for a black business," using "strictly African-American finance" in keeping with the race-based principles of the march itself. Choosing not to approach the same people who had donated to *Malcolm X*, and insisting that backers would be making "an investment – not a gift, like *X* was," Lee raised $2.5 million from a fresh list of participants including actors Danny Glover and Wesley Snipes, screenwriter Bythewood, and Johnnie Cochran, then famous as the lawyer who got O.J. Simpson acquitted on his murder charges. The budget was tiny and the schedule was correspondingly tight, but Lee and company managed to complete it just in time for release on the first anniversary of the march. "It was [shot] in eighteen days," recalled Roger Guenveur Smith, who plays Gary in the film, "and I think that was perfect – because these were characters who really didn't know each other." Photography took place in four different states at a rate of ten to eleven pages of script per day (Aftab 217, 218). The production process was fast, cheap, and firmly controlled by a director, cast, and crew well suited to guerrilla filmmaking.

Get on the Bus is a fully character-driven film, providing only the ghost of a storyline – the passengers go from Los Angeles to Washington, the first bus breaks down and another one continues the voyage, a white driver is replaced by a black driver, an elderly passenger dies while en route – on which to hang the personalities, ideas, and feelings that are its real interests. Each passenger is going to the march for his own reasons.

Jeremiah (Ossie Davis), the old man of the group, is a former alcoholic who hopes the event will give his weary spirit a jolt of hope and inspiration. Jamal (Gabriel Casseus), a reformed gangbanger, is now a devout Muslim who works with at-risk children. Xavier (Hill Harper) is a UCLA film-school student documenting the trip on video. George (Charles S. Dutton) is the organizer of the journey. Wendell (Wendell Pierce), who joins the group along the way, is a car salesman eager to peddle his wares among the marchers. Gary (Roger Guenveur Smith) is a mixed-race LA police officer whose black father, also a cop, was killed by a black gang member. Evan Thomas Sr. (Thomas Jefferson Boyd) is a well-meaning father and Evan Jr. (De'aundre Bonds) is his troublesome son. Flip (Andre Braugher) is an actor with an exceedingly high opinion of his talents, although they haven't gotten him far in his profession. Kyle (Isaiah Washington) is a veteran of the Persian Gulf War who was hounded and harassed in the service for being gay, and Randall (Harry J. Lennix) is his about-to-be-ex-lover. Also present is a Nation of Islam member (judging by his clothes) who never speaks or identifies himself, keeping his own counsel throughout the film.

Like the march, which Farrakhan described as a call for "a million sober, disciplined, committed, dedicated, inspired black men to meet in Washington on a day of atonement," the film is a single-sex affair. Women appear briefly in a handful of scenes, but they are two-dimensional tokens, not three-dimensional persons. This limits the movie's scope and lends still more ammunition to those who correctly fault Lee for an inability to develop female characters. I will add, however, that since men (of all races and ethnicities) are primarily responsible for the wars, violence, crimes, and other ills in the world, it makes sense to single them out for special scrutiny from time to time.

Except for the women and the mute Muslim, we learn a good deal about the characters by listening to their conversations, by hearing their answers to questions posed by Xavier behind his video camera – someone calls him "Spike Lee Junior" in an amusing dig – and by following the alliances and quarrels that develop among them during the journey. Flip derides Kyle for being "a gay black Republican" and mocks Randall for his demeanor. The reformed gangbanger Jamal has an intimate conversion with Gary the cop, candidly expressing his remorse for the killings he committed when he was a member of the Crips, one of LA's most notorious gangs; one might expect Gary to honor the trust Jamal places in him when he confides this secret and reveals the profound shame he feels about his past, but instead Gary tells Jamal that he will arrest him for murder as soon as they reach LA and step out of the bus. In a more short-lived subplot, the Lexus dealer Wendell proves to be not only a Republican but a loud-mouthed conservative and blustering capitalist who takes obnoxious pleasure in chanting the word "nigger." The others get fed up and literally fling him out the door, producing the film's punchiest comic moment.

Boiling Water

Get on the Bus gains much of its sociological heft from Lee's usual practice of setting forth moral dilemmas as food for thought and reflection rather than conventional dramatic situations to be resolved in artificially satisfying ways. We never learn, for example, whether Gary follows through on his pledge to arrest Jamal when they return to their home city. Lee also treats the story's racial politics with the dialectical complexity that is one of his trademarks. The driver of the replacement bus is a Jewish man named Rick (Richard Belzer) who grows increasingly uncomfortable with the passengers, less for reasons of generalized racism than from unhappiness about indirectly helping a project headed by Farrakhan, who was perceived by a good many observers as an anti-Semitic ideologue.[2] Deciding to walk away from the job during a stop in Nashville, Tennessee, he asks George to take over the driving and cover for his absence, prompting a lengthy exchange between the two that goes in part like this:

> **Rick:** If the base calls in, you tell them I got sick.
> **George:** Why?
> **Rick:** Because I'm not coming back.
> **George:** Shit, what the hell do you mean you're not coming back?

Rick: I can't do it.

George: Oh, come on, you're bullshitting. You're just trying to go to Graceland.

Rick: I'd be safer there.

George: Meaning what? What do you think we're gonna do, put you in a pot of boiling water and have you for supper?

Rick: [*referring to Jeremiah's drum beating on the bus*] You already got the damn African drums in there.

George: You know, Rick, that's the epitome of cultural disrespect. I could come back at you with something anti-Semitic or I could whip your ass. Which would you prefer, Rick?

Rick: I'm sorry. All right, George, here it is. Maybe I am a little bit prejudiced against blacks but no more than you're prejudiced against white people. You want me to stay on and prove how liberal and shit I am? I don't have to prove anything to anybody. I mean, I think affirmative action has been fucked up. I think O.J. was guilty. He's a cold-blooded murderer who slaughtered two innocent human beings. Okay. There it is.

George: I bet you wish there were more white players in the NBA, too, huh? Well, okay, let's just get it out in the open. I bet you'd like to call me a nigger or, what do you call it, a schwartzer or whatever the fuck it is. Well, I'm going to allow you to say it. Go ahead.

Rick: I never called anybody that in my life. All I'm saying is that if this bus is going to the Farrakhan march, I can't be a part of that.

George: This is not just Farrakhan's march.

Rick: I don't want to debate this thing. He called Judaism a gutter religion; he said Hitler was a great man. I wouldn't expect you to drive a bus to a Ku Klux Klan rally, so don't expect me to do this.

George: So now you're comparing this to a Klan rally.

Rick: Look, George, either you're gonna kick my ass, you're gonna cover for me or I'm gonna get fired. But no way am I getting my white ass back in that bus, so what's it going to be?

George: Well, if you feel that way, then you shouldn't get your white ass back on that bus. I'll cover for you, Rick. See you in LA.

Each guy gives as good as he gets, and if George seems more fair, reasoned, and articulate than his interlocutor, it's partly because Rick is repeating commonplaces – affirmative action isn't fair, O.J. Simpson was guilty, the march is comparable to a Klan rally, and so on – rather than looking more deeply into his "little bit prejudiced" mind and heart. The end of the scene leaves George and Rick neither friends nor enemies, recalling the final encounter between Mookie and Sal in *Do the Right Thing*.

In a later scene that complements this one, the passengers enter a restaurant and bar in a Southern locale, where they are surrounded by whites who seem ominously interested in the dark-skinned strangers. Lee allows just enough of a foreboding mood to develop before letting the locals reveal themselves as a perfectly nice bunch of folks, curious about the travelers because they're travelers, not because they're black. This is Lee at his even-handed best; yet in another scene that complements *this* one, a pair of clearly antagonistic state troopers board the bus with police dogs near Knoxville, Tennessee, in search of drugs, weapons, or other contraband, brushing away Gary's effort to intercede as a fellow cop. The bus comes up clean and the troopers depart, but the atmosphere they leave behind positively stinks of unspoken racist animosity. The interplay of these and related moments throughout the film weaves the kind of intricate

Two of the passengers in Get on the Bus *are Evan Thomas Sr.*
(Thomas Jefferson Byrd) and his son Junior, aka Smooth (De'aundre
Bonds), who has been in trouble with the law and is chained to his
father by a judge's order – a potent symbol of race-based justice and
intergenerational tension.

social-psychological dialectic that Lee creates and manages
so expertly. Other questions also generate provocative dialectics in the film. Is a males-only event like the Million
Man March a healthy spur to black self-improvement, or
yet another way of keeping women out of the public arena?
Is discrimination against homosexuals rooted in legitimate
moral principles, or does it echo other forms of bigotry that
blacks should be the first to recognize and deplore?

Get on the Bus also presents one of Lee's most forthright
treatments of the father–son dynamics that play important roles in a number of his films, as we have seen. Evan
Jr., who prefers to be called by his nickname, Smooth – or
rather Smoove, as he pronounces it – was arrested for a petty
crime shortly before Evan Sr. was due to get on the bus for
Washington, and the judge in Junior's case ordered that he
be shackled to Senior for seventy-two hours in lieu of jail
time. So the son is literally chained to the father, and vice

versa, enacting a pitch-dark parody of the ties that bind. The ordeal does not appear to wreak further havoc on what was already a very strained relationship, but it does not bring much in the way of better mutual understanding, either, apart from Senior's realization that Junior's misbehavior has been an inchoate plea for more parental attention, which should have been obvious all along. A greater question is whether a court-ordered spectacle like this calls useful attention to the need for fathers to be better role models, or simply spews an offensive reminder of black slavery and oppression into the public sphere.

Ossie and Jeremiah

A more complicated and resonant variant on the father–son motif centers on Jeremiah, a veteran of the civil-rights glory days whose own glory days have long been over. Failures and frustrations drove him to drink, and alcohol fueled further distress, causing his family to flee and leave him permanently on the skids. He sees this trip as a last chance to make up for missing Martin Luther King Jr.'s historic march on Washington three decades earlier, and he hopes it will somehow revive his enthusiasm for life. He represents the race-relations equivalent of the so-called "Greatest Generation" that fought World War II, and while younger African-Americans respect what their elders accomplished in the 1950s and 1960s, their imaginations may give those long-ago deeds an abstract, not-quite-real quality that smacks more of myth and legend than of actual flesh-and-blood experience. (This is a trans-racial phenomenon, of course; yesterday's heroic exploits tend to become today's boring stories that grandpa won't stop telling.) One senses that Jeremiah is perturbed by the shortage of appreciation expressed by the bus's younger passengers (i.e., all of them)

Get on the Bus *features Ossie Davis as Jeremiah, an over-the-hill activist with fond memories of the civil-rights era – a fitting role, since Davis delivered a eulogy at Malcolm X's funeral in 1965.*

toward the kind of person he fancies himself to be, a living reminder of a brave and militant past. It is fascinating to observe that Ossie Davis, who plays Jeremiah, felt as luke-warm about Louis Farrakhan in real life as the youngsters on the bus feel about Jeremiah in the film. Davis was a no-nonsense thinker whose eulogy at Malcolm X's funeral was eloquent enough to be memorialized in Alex Haley's epilogue to *The Autobiography of Malcolm X*; in another contribution to that volume, an afterword simply titled "On Malcolm X," he wrote that the great leader was

refreshing excitement; he scared hell out of the rest of us, bred as we are to caution, to hypocrisy in the presence of white folks, to the smile that never fades. Malcolm knew that every white man in America profits directly or indi-rectly from his position vis-à-vis Negroes, profits from racism even though he does not practice it or believe in it. He also knew that every Negro who did not challenge on the spot every instance of racism, overt or covert, committed against him and his people, who chose instead to swallow his spit and go on smiling, was an Uncle Tom and a traitor. (X and Haley 494, 498)

For his part, Malcolm had called Davis "one of the finest black men" (X and Haley 438).

Davis did not feel so warmly toward Farrakhan and the Nation of Islam, however. "I think that the march was an acknowledgment that the world had changed," he explained, in remarks that might echo Jeremiah's feelings in *Get on the Bus*. "A world that was created to some degree by Malcolm was now being overtaken by another figure." Davis went on to say that his own attachment to Malcolm's memory and achievements prevented him from being "fair and logical with those who, in some sense, are detractors." Since he understood "the pain and anguish that Malcolm felt when he looked upon the behavior of Elijah Muhammad," he continued, he could not "say with Louis Farrakhan that Elijah Muhammad is the great moralist, the great spiritual leader, the great son of Allah and all that." Davis recognized that Farrakhan had exerted "a positive effect on the life of the black community," and he had sent money (with Ruby Dee, his wife) to fund a bus carrying people to the march. But he could not whole-heartedly support the event. If they had gone about building "a first-class university or a first-class hospital," he said, "where all the qualities of which they thought so highly were put into practice, then I would have been prepared to drop all my differences and climb aboard. But I don't believe that will happen as a result of the Million Man March," because it was not a venture that "spoke eloquently to the community" in a lasting way.

Why, then, did Davis agree to act in *Get on the Bus*? For three reasons: because Lee asked him, because he loved the character of Jeremiah, and because Lee let him write some of his own material. As Davis remarked, "It was what Jeremiah was trying to say when he was beating on the drums about the power and the necessity of African people of the world to be proud of who they are and to accept some responsibility." The character, he felt, "could help explain the movement and the purpose [of the film] to the general African-American audiences and to the white audience too. Jeremiah could give it depth and perspective" (Aftab 216, 218). In the end, however, Lee belongs to a generation considerably younger than Davis's, and as often happens in a Spike Lee joint, the father figure must flare out or fade out so youth can shine more brightly. Not only does Jeremiah succumb to a heart attack on the bus, he does so at a very inconvenient moment, causing several fellow passengers to miss the march they've come so far to experience because they choose to mount a vigil at the hospital where he lies dying. This provides a grimly ironic climax for what is, beneath its entertaining repartee, an earnest and serious-minded film.

HE GOT GAME

Lee turned to another masculine milieu in *He Got Game*, his most ambitious film since *Malcolm X* six years earlier. The title comes from an eponymous Public Enemy song that advises one to "fuck the game if it ain't sayin nuttin." The main focus is sports, but no film better illustrates why even critics who admire Lee have likened his movies to overloaded trucks careening down narrow streets with hairpin turns, steered by drivers who don't mind leaving a mess in their wake as long as they reach the destination, or someplace near it, in the end. Its overstuffed story is matched by experimental stylistic touches, such as out-of-sequence montage and unmotivated flashes of light.

The protagonist is Jake Shuttlesworth (Denzel Washington), a basically decent man serving a prison stretch in Attica after inadvertently causing the death of his wife, Martha (Lonette McKee), during a bout of domestic violence. The warden, Wyatt (Ned Beatty), approaches him with an unexpected offer: Jake can drastically reduce his sentence if he can persuade his own son Jesus (NBA star Ray Allen), a nationally renowned basketball player now finishing high school in Coney Island, to join the team of the college that the governor attended, Big State, instead of signing with a more important school or turning pro. Jake is willing to try – it was his relentless coaching that helped mold Jesus into an athletic marvel – but Jesus has never forgiven him for bringing about his mother's tragic death and will barely speak to him, much less follow his wishes. Jake has a week to get a signed letter from Jesus pledging to enroll at Big State; otherwise he goes back in the slammer. Returning to the city under guard, Jake reestablishes contact with his shattered family and discovers that Jesus is being bombarded with offers from a bewildering number of sports promoters with very questionable motives. The young man's fans are largely black; the power brokers courting him are largely white. The climax of the story is a one-on-one basketball game between father and son, proposed by Jake and carrying high stakes: if Jake wins, Jesus will sign the letter of intent; if Jesus wins, Jake will never interfere in his life again. Jesus wins and Jake lands back in prison. Right afterward, Jesus holds a press conference to announce that he'll attend Big State after all; but Warden Wyatt points out to Jake that Jesus didn't sign the letter of intent, and therefore the governor isn't obligated to give him early parole according to their deal.

On one level, *He Got Game* is a realistic drama centering on (once again) a complex father–son relationship. In terms of family relationships more broadly, the spirit of the deceased wife and mother hovers invisibly over the story, via memories and letters that Jesus cherishes, and Jake takes time out from engineering his son's future to have a fling with Dakota Burns (Milla Jovovich), a prostitute who lives in the miserable Coney Island motel where he stays during his leave from prison. On another level, the film has elements of religious allegory. Naming the young athlete Jesus was hardly a random choice on Lee's part: the offers pushed at Jesus by greedy basketball teams – many laced with enticements of sex, money, and fame – are portrayed as devilish temptations in the urban wilderness; and the worship he receives from his admirers, who chant "*Jesus saves*" in his presence, scornfully reflects people's tendency to seek "salvation" by appealing to physical activities, human personalities, and other unspiritual sources. The film even has a Tech U basketball coach named Billy Sunday (John Turturro) as a character – his moniker is taken from a late-nineteenth-century baseball player who became a famous evangelist in the early years of the twentieth century – and video shown at the Tech U gym includes snippets from George Stevens's biopic about Jesus of Nazareth, *The Greatest Story Ever Told* (1965). All of this said, however, *He Got Game* treats its religious elements in Lee's familiar dialectical manner. It turns out that Jesus's parents named him not after the Son of God but after the New York Knicks star Earl Monroe, who was nicknamed Black Jesus, which fans then shortened to Jesus, during the earlier Philadelphia phase of his career. The religion favored by this movie isn't Christianity, it's basketball.

On what may be its broadest and deepest level, *He Got Game* is an energetic attempt to create a new American mythology. The key to this is Lee's remarkable choice of music: a blend of rap songs by Public Enemy and, much more surprising, renditions of well-known pieces by Aaron

Copland, one of America's most emphatically American composers. It first swells up during the opening montage, displaying young folks of different races, ethnicities, and genders playing basketball across America in all manner of settings and environments. You needn't be a sports fan to be stirred by this invigorating sight, and you needn't be a Copland fan to find his musical Americana an inspired score for the occasion. So imaginatively are Copland and Public Enemy woven into the soundtrack that they usually seem more like partners than competitors, which is quite a feat even for a filmmaker with Lee's strong musical sense.[3]

In his insightful review for *The Nation*, critic Stuart Klawans suggests that *He Got Game* is a closet remake of *Hoop Dreams*, the well-respected 1994 documentary by Steve James in which an "unscripted and real . . . basketball-playing father came back from prison and tried to go one-on-one with his disaffected son." In addition to its general plot outline, Klawans observes, Lee's movie gives Washington "the raggedy hair of the original model, as well as the man's new-found fluency in Scripture" (1998, 35). It is likely that *Hoop Dreams* was indeed an influence on *He Got Game*, but Lee didn't need reminders about the centrality of athletics, and of basketball in particular, to the American ethos. "When I listen to [Copland's] music," he wrote in his liner notes for the 1998 soundtrack album, "I hear America, and basketball is America. It's played on the sides of barns in Indiana [and] wheat fields in Kansas. Hoops is played on the asphalt courts of Philly, Chicago and also Brooklyn." Like the filmmaker, the composer came from Brooklyn and created art that reached out to all America and to every place American culture is known. It was Lee's special brilliance to realize how marvelously well Copland's music – much of it taken from ballet scores and designed from the beginning to accompany human bodies in fluid, graceful motion – would suit the movie that best reflects his own hoop dreams, reveries, and nightmares, and those of America as a whole.

SUMMER OF SAM

Spike bid farewell to the twentieth century with one of his most pessimistic forays into urban life, rivaling *Jungle Fever* and *Clockers* for dystopian gloom. Like such other 1999 releases as Stanley Kubrick's *Eyes Wide Shut*, Sam Mendes's *American Beauty*, and Mark Pellington's *Arlington Road*, it journeys into the heart of American darkness to convey a morally conservative message about the ill consequences of lust, paranoia, and hypocrisy. Perhaps to reduce the boomerang effect of the film's pessimistic vision, Lee locates the story in the Bronx rather than Brooklyn and makes his main characters Italian-American louts rather than African-American louts. This notwithstanding, *Summer of Sam* is a very recognizable Spike Lee joint – the caustic flip side of *Do the Right Thing* in some respects, again set in the middle of a heat wave and again culminating in deadly violence. Coincidentally but appropriately, it had its world premiere at the Cannes film festival about a month after the infamous student massacre at Columbine High School in suburban Denver, Colorado, and a school shooting in Conyers, Georgia, happened on the very day of its Cannes debut.

The story takes place in 1977, and, as usual in Lee's pictures, the key characters are guys. Vinny (John Leguizamo) is a hairdresser married to Dionna (Mira Sorvino), a waitress; to avoid downgrading her from Madonna to whore, Vinny turns to other women for the blowjobs and suchlike that he craves. Ritchie (Adrien Brody) is a neighborhood oddball who has taken to fancying himself as a Sex Pistols-style punk, sporting spiky hair and a dog collar around his neck; he spends his off-hours dancing and turning tricks at a Times Square club called Male World, and grim would be his fate if his friends – already wary of his freaky hairdo and guitar-playing ambitions – got wind of this. Others on the screen include Luigi (Ben Gazzara), a mob boss who looks after the locals; two detectives (Roger Guenveur Smith, Anthony LaPaglia) working on the Son of Sam case; John Jeffries (Lee), a TV reporter; and the unfortunately nicknamed Ruby the Skank (Jennifer Esposito), a woman more on Ritchie's wavelength than anyone except Vinny, who likes Ritchie because it's good to have a friend as weird on the outside as he himself feels on the inside. And of course there is the semi-eponymous Son of Sam (Michael Badalucca), based on the real-life serial murderer (born in Brooklyn, as it happens) who thrilled and terrorized New York with a string of shootings that killed six people and wounded seven in Queens and the Bronx between July 1976 and August 1977, when he was arrested.[4] The murderer, whose real name was David Berkowitz, gained his sobriquet from his claim that he received orders to kill from a demon inhabiting a neighbor's dog. His other famous nickname, the .44 Caliber Killer, related to his choice of weapon.

Summer of Sam reached the screen more than twenty years after Son of Sam was in the headlines, and one might reasonably wonder why Lee chose that particular summer and criminal case as the backdrop for his otherwise fictional story. One likely reason is that it was a dramatic summer in more ways than one. Another actual event portrayed by the film is an electrical blackout (caused by lightning) that darkened most of New York City for up to twenty-five hours in July, bringing episodes of looting and arson that had not occurred during the shorter blackout (about fifteen hours) that hit much of northeastern America in 1965. Spike was twenty in 1977, a time when New York was under great stress from crime, poverty, financial deficits, and other burdens. Bushwick and Crown Heights, both in Brooklyn, were among the neighborhoods most affected by destruction and violence during the blackout, and across the city more than 3,700 people were arrested (Hut). The block party put on by Luigi in *Summer of Sam*, meant to keep the neighborhood calm and orderly during the blackout, reflects the better angels of urban life that Lee doesn't entirely lose sight of in even his harshest stories. But the harshness is almost always present in this picture: when Vinny's friend Joey T (Michael Rispoli) puts together a militia to police the borders, for instance, viewers might well think of Michael Griffith, one of the urban martyrs to whom Lee dedicated *Do the Right Thing*, dying in 1986 while he and his friends were being chased out of a white neighborhood by white men with baseball bats.

To underscore the factual background of *Summer of Sam*, Lee enlisted the New York newspaper columnist Jimmy Breslin to provide a bit of brief narration. Breslin was a player in the Son of Sam saga: he was writing about the ongoing string of shootings for New York's widely read *Daily News* when a hand-written letter arrived on his desk, postmarked in Englewood, New Jersey, on May 30 and purporting to be from the killer. It began, "Hello from the gutters of N.Y.C. which are filled with dog manure, vomit, stale wine, urine and blood," and it ended, "Upon my capture I promise to buy all the guys working the case a new pair of shoes if I can get up the money. Son of Sam." Authorities had divided opinions about the letter's authenticity, but it caused a sensation in New York and brought in thousands of false leads and useless tips when Breslin's tabloid published part of it with permission from the police.

Summer of Sam shows Berkowitz howling at the demonic dog and the dog uttering "*Kill!*" to him, but he's a very minor character in the film. The main engines of the story are Vinny's affair with glorious Gloria (Bebe Neuwirth), a beauty-salon colleague; his discovery of two victims of the .44 Caliber Killer, which makes him think death is breathing down *his* neck as punishment for those blowjobs; and the attempt by Joey T to police the neighborhood's borders with a sort of homegrown militia. Atop these and a few other pivotal ingredients, Lee has stacked a daunting array of personalities, incidents, details, and what can only be called free associations – someone thinks the killer is baseball star Reggie Jackson, because the number on his New York Yankees uniform is 44 – that just barely cohere as a single narrative. The story's dominating emotional current is the tide of xenophobic dread that surges through the area as the murders continue. Ritchie becomes the community's suspect of choice for the obvious reason that he is *different*, and everyone knows that *different* people can never be trusted. In the end he is beaten almost to death before the eyes of his friend Vinny, escaping with his life only because word arrives that the killer has been arrested just outside the city. Lee has never given a more scathing depiction of the havoc wrought by hatred, intolerance, and tribalism among members of a community who share the same color, ethnicity, socioeconomic class, and fiercely defended ignorance of whatever fails to gibe with their insular, dogmatic worldview.

The film's other overarching element is the uproariously insane morality that prevailed in New York City – and in much of America, for that matter – in the second half of the 1970s, when the exciting cultural upheavals of the 1960s had spawned an army of grating, grubby offspring. In place of spirited challenges to outworn tradition, Lee now sees aimless confusion and unruliness; in place of a hopelessly naïve peace generation he now sees a hopelessly stupid status-quo generation; in place of ideals of free love he now sees spasms of brainless fucking; and on it goes, one squalid symptom of social pathology after another. The villains in *Summer of Sam* are not only the .44 Caliber Killer and the witch hunters who stomp Ritchie; they are also the sensationalistic mass media that whip up fears to boost their profits, the kings of commerce who peddle cheap sex and porn, the looters who pillage Brooklyn and Harlem during the blackout, and the entire moral climate of the age, which Lee pictures as a virtually anarchic bedlam that encourages everything from the money-fueled licentiousness of a Manhattan sex club to the belligerently sexist behavior of pretty much every male character. No wonder the movie has to scurry so frenetically from Plato's Retreat to CBGB, from Brooklyn beauty parlor to seedy waterfront, from Martin Scorsese-style ethnology to lurid B-movie shockeroo, from quasi-documentary reportage to the eye-jolting punches of Ellen Kuras's hugely inventive cinematography.

By exposing the paranoid aggressiveness bred by the characters' sadly limited lives, and the way their self-serving ideas are reinforced by contemporary culture as a whole, Lee suggests deep links between the public and private aspects of ethical decay. He also paints a scathing portrait of a male-defined double standard that produces weird combinations of promiscuity and puritanism, with women always on the losing side of the equation. *Summer of Sam* pulls no punches in displaying the dysfunction it attacks, and therein lies its enduring power as high-octane pulp fiction, as genre-bending cinema, and as blistering critique of an America staggering through one of the least admirable periods in its recent history.

BAMBOOZLED

You've been hoodwinked. You've been had. You've been took.
You've been led astray, led amok. You've been bamboozled. –
Malcolm X

Audacious Satire

Lee ushered in the new millennium with *Bamboozled*, a desperately comic treatment of a desperately serious topic. Teeming with ideas, abounding with commentary, and swarming with details, it makes *Summer of Sam* look almost well behaved by comparison. But overstuffed, overambitious jumble that it is, it sets forth more pungent themes, and takes more cinematic risks, than almost any other movie of its day.

The protagonist, Pierre Delacroix (Damon Wayans), is an African-American writer bent on turning his Ivy League degree and creative talent into a successful media career. Taking a job at a cable TV network with perilously low ratings, he scrambles to create a bold new programming concept that will reverse the company's slide. Two options present themselves. He can go to his bosses with the wildest idea he can dream up, on the theory that only an aggressive gamble can save the rapidly sinking ship. Or he can make the ship sink even faster, saving his own skin by getting fired before it goes down for good, thus outfoxing his contract, which doesn't allow him to resign, and humiliating his white boss, Thomas Dunwitty (Michael Rapaport), who considers himself a "soul brother" because his wife is black and he collects African art. Putting both plans into operation, Pierre designs a show so outrageously awful that the network will self-destruct, planning to watch the disaster from the safety of his next job.

The concept Pierre pitches is what makes *Bamboozled* such an audacious satire. The entertainment industry, he reasons, has made a fortune by exploiting African-Americans through demeaning images. So he'll thrust his own fists into that long, scurrilous heritage and steal its most shameless tricks. First he hires two black performers, Manray (Savion Glover) and Womack (Tommy Davidson), off the street. Then he changes their names to Mantan and Sleep'n'eat, makes them conspicuously blacker with splotches of burnt-cork makeup, and christens their act "The New Millennium Minstrel Show," surrounding them with every degrading racial cliché he can find. The characters shuffle, strut, smile, and sing in the manner of stereotypes cut from cardboard; the backup dancers are called the Pickaninnies, the band is called the Alabama Porch Monkeys, and everyone lives in a watermelon patch. Surely this offensive travesty will crash in the ratings, plunging the network into oblivion and allowing Pierre to get on with his career in some setting better suited to his talents. But of course the opposite happens: Dunwitty loves it, audiences love it, and racist images and epithets become the hottest thing in entertainment. Turning on a dime, Pierre basks in the applause, acclaim, and awards that quickly come his way.

Complications ensue, however. Pierre's personal assistant, Sloan Hopkins (Jada Pinkett-Smith), is appalled by these developments, and so are the Mau Maus, a radical rap group led by Sloan's militant brother, Julius Hopkins, aka Big Blak Afrika (Mos Def). Sloan tries to stir Pierre's conscience by assembling a jarring video montage of racist imagery, to no avail. Manray finally rebels against the show – seeing that studio audiences have taken to wearing blackface, he starts refusing to do so – but is kidnapped and killed by the Mau Maus, who show his execution in a live internet feed. Pierre, driven mad by the things he has been through, now broods in his office, wearing blackface and surrounded by the collection of racist toys and artifacts that he has amassed. Fatally wounded by a shot that Sloan has inadvertently fired from Julius's gun, he dies while watching her video montage, which constitutes a guided tour through the racist imagery manufactured, circulated, and savored by generations of white American society, ranging from caricatured "coon" artifacts to movie and TV clips that reflect (and have crucially shaped) the country's racial unconscious. The sequence does not just preach but actually *proves* the culpability of mainstream culture in an interminable process of spiritual and psychological genocide, inflicted on minority citizens by hegemonic media shot through with greed, complacency, and irresponsibility.

Lee said that *Bamboozled* was inspired by Elia Kazan's *A Face in the Crowd* (1957) and Sidney Lumet's *Network* (1976), both classics of media-related cinema. He must also have thought of Mel Brooks's boisterous farce *The Producers* (1968), about two Jewish con artists who stage an impossibly absurd show called "Springtime for Hitler," which presents a historically unhinged portrait of the Führer as a benevolent leader with a smile on his face and a song in his heart; the producers plan to abscond with the money they've collected from investors when the show inevitably closes on opening night, but as in *Bamboozled*, the audience finds it hilarious, stopping the swindle in its tracks. I find *The Producers* as insufferable as "Springtime for Hitler" is supposed to be, and Susan Stroman's musical remake (2005) is even worse. Its premise is a good one, though, and Lee works enough changes and variations on it to make it feel fresh. More important, he outdoes all precedents in the lengths to which he pushes his satire, going far beyond ordinary limits of taste. Scene after scene mixes in-your-face comedy with over-the-top plot twists and outspoken, often bitter social commentary, culminating in the barrage of blatantly racist film clips and pop-culture artifacts that are as disturbing to see as they are impossible to dismiss.

Bamboozled was and is a controversial film. Leaving aside its mixed reception on ordinary movie-review grounds – critical opinions were divided about the acting, scripting, and so forth – it has struck many commentators as a stinging revelation of and rebuke to the racial bigotry woven through

American life, and it has struck many others as a self-indulgent replication of cultural sins that are better contemplated in educational and political settings than in the malls and multiplexes where Hollywood movies are consumed. The film clips in the concluding montage are culled from a broad array of movies, newsreels, cartoons, and TV programs, with legendary performers like Judy Garland, Bing Crosby, and Mickey Rooney smearing blackface makeup on their features. Displaced from their usual mainstream venues and slotted into this film's context, black-oriented entertainments as seemingly innocuous as *The Jeffersons* (CBS, 1975–85) and *The Cosby Show* (NBC, 1984–92) take on dubious overtones not normally associated with them. The militant Mau Maus are a grim parody of gangsta rappers, whom Lee attacks in his DVD commentary track for *Bamboozled*, calling their acts "the twenty-first century minstrel show." (He points to Mos Def, who plays Julian in the film, as an example of the constructive rappers who are trying to extricate hip-hop lyrics from their own swamp of stereotyping.) Commercials seen on "The New Millennium Minstrel Show" lampoon the mass marketing of products made by whites to customers who are black: African-Americans chug forty-ounce bottles of The Bomb Malt Liquor, and Timmy Hillnigger promotes clothing that is "so authentic, we include the bullet holes." The film references such other faddish items as the hula hoop, the yo-yo, and the Pokemon franchise, using their popularity to suggest, as critic Marcus Gilmer notes, that it may not actually be impossible for something as idiotic as blackface to become a trend.

Not a Repro

Along with its moving-image clips and parodies, *Bamboozled* incorporates an ongoing critique of racist Americana by way of objects, specifically the objects that "are generally designated Sambo art, negro memorabilia, or black collectibles: the Aunt Jemima cookie jars, the Jocko hitching posts, the canisters and salt and pepper shakers, the hot pad holders, most infamously the Jolly Nigger bank," as Bill Brown, the leading scholar of thing theory, summarizes them. Whereas the minstrel show animates the "plantation darky" stereotype, Brown observes, "these objects might be said to deanimate it, to arrest the stereotype, to render it in three-dimensional stasis, to fix a demeaning and/or romanticizing racism with the fortitude of solid form." Significantly, the sardonic present that Sloan gives to Pierre is a "Jolly Nigger Bank," and not a "repro" but the genuine "circa turn-of-century" item. She loves those black collectibles, she adds, because they recall "a time of our history in this country when we were considered inferior, subhuman, and should never forget." Hoping the gift will open Pierre's eyes to the enormity his show is inflicting on black America, she has selected the most widely manufactured and purchased variety of iron-bust bank. But this only feeds Pierre's enthusiasm for gathering more such things, imitating the likes of Oprah Winfrey, Magic Johnson, and Henry Louis Gates Jr., who famously keep collections of this kind (B. Brown 183–4, 185, 188, 194).

Late in the film, Pierre's madness first registers as a vision of the bank taking on its own life: in voiceover he says, "When I thought or imagined that my favorite Jolly Nigger bank, an inanimate object, a piece of cold cast iron, was moving by itself, I knew I was getting paranoid." Now the kind of manufactured object that freezes and deanimates the racial stereotype is itself becoming animated, and the process goes into overdrive when the march of the toys concludes the film. Lee meant the spectacle to unveil the "hatred of the minds that made this stuff," but, as Brown astutely notes, the sequence manifests much more than this. Animated several times over by their machinery, by the camera, and by the music, he writes, "each figure, whether gorgeous or grotesque, seems caught, frantically dancing or fiddling, bouncing or swinging, swallowing pitched balls, grinning and smiling, unable to stop. No longer part of that mute chorus witnessing the repetition of history, the individuated objects bespeak a life of things that is no social life, only the hyperactive persistence of the past" (195, 207)

This is powerful magic, open to many interpretations, and it is not surprising that critics have hailed it and condemned it in about equal measures.[5] *Bamboozled* is so far over the top, Roger Ebert (2000) wrote, that "people's feelings run too strongly and deeply for any satirical use to be effective. The power of the racist image tramples over the material and asserts only itself. By contrast, Stuart Klawans (2000) found that Lee had "applied his erudition to this American tradition and discovered not just how it wounds but also how it entertains. With the intellectual acuity of the Menippean satirist, he's shown that the entertainment *is* the wound – the louder the laughter, the worse the damage." As so often with a Spike Lee joint, the intricacy of the work flummoxes consensus, and that is all to the good. *Bamboozled* marked the end of another stage in Spike's career, characterized by an intense focus on the complexities of African-American experience – and of white American experience in *Summer of Sam* – viewed through the lenses of various and sundry genres.

A DOCUMENTARY JOINT

In addition to producing such major works as *He Got Game* and *Summer of Sam*, the late 1990s marked Lee's emergence as a nonfiction filmmaker to be reckoned with. Leaving aside his minute-long contribution to the omnibus film *Lumière and Company* made by forty-one directors in 1995, his first foray into documentary was *4 Little Girls*, funded by 40 Acres & A Mule Filmworks and HBO for both theatrical and TV exhibition. Coproduced by Lee and Sam Pollard, then his regular film editor, the 1997 release gives a meticulous account of the racist bombing that destroyed the 16th Street Baptist Church in Birmingham, Alabama, on September 15, 1963, while a Sunday school session was in progress. The blast killed four young girls – three were fourteen, one was eleven – and injured many other churchgoers, stunning African-Americans and decent non-black people across the country. This was far from the first outbreak of virulent racial hatred in the city, where the infamously bigoted Eugene "Bull" Connor was chief of police and the Ku Klux Klan was a flourishing enterprise. No one was arrested or charged with the crime until 1977, and in 1980 the United States Department of Justice issued a report indicating that J. Edgar Hoover, director of the Federal Bureau of Investigation until his death in 1972, had blocked evidence that would have been invaluable to investigators and prosecutors.

This project had roots in Lee's film-student days, when he realized the enormity of the crime and started giving it serious thought, contacting the father of the youngest victim and suggesting a film about the tragedy. The idea came to fruition years later, when Lee went to Birmingham with Pollard and cinematographer Ellen Kuras to do research and begin filming. The film goes considerably beyond the church bombing itself, drawing out longtime Birmingham residents on what it was like to live there under segregation, and what it was like to initiate children into the awful fact that a majority of their fellow citizens regarded them as less than fully human. Seeing morgue photographs of the little girls in an Alabama public library, Lee was jolted despite his familiarity with the case. "You can imagine what twenty sticks of dynamite can do,"

he said later. After debating whether to display the dreadful
photos in his film, he decided to show them in quick, fleeting
shots, to "reinforce the horror" of the crime (Judell 143). *4
Little Girls* is very conventional in style, but the story it tells
remains an urgent one in an America that bears heavy scars
from race-based evils of the past and present.

THEATRICAL JOINTS

The late 1990s and early 2000s brought Lee's first ventures
into filmed theater. He and John Leguizamo had not yet collaborated on *Summer of Sam* when Leguizamo opened his
solo comedy-drama *Freak* at the Cort Theatre on Broadway
in February 1998. The show played for 144 performances
before the curtain went down on the Fourth of July, earning
the Drama Desk Award for Outstanding Solo/One-Person
Show as well as Tony Award nominations for best actor and
best play. Lee liked the show, which presents a frenetic string
of faux-autobiographical scenes involving funky friends and
dysfunctional family members, and felt that documenting it
on film might further his ambition of moving 40 Acres &
A Mule into TV production, a potentially profitable field
of operation.[6] His game plan was modest, seeking only "to
show [Leguizamo's] talent and try to transfer that to the
tape" without hindering the performance in any way. The
show was recorded twice before live audiences, and Lee's
frequent film editor, Barry Alexander Brown, cut the tape
so as to show each of Leguizamo's personas from a different
perspective (Aftab 243). The result has pleased many viewers who find Leguizamo's in-your-face performing style and
rude-and-crude humor more endearing than I do. Looking
at the larger picture, intense involvement with this energetic
Latino celebrity – Leguizamo hails from Bogotá, Columbia,
although his family migrated to the United States when

he was four – surely deepened Lee's exposure to a facet of American ethnicity that overlaps to some extent with his African-American background.

The Original Kings of Comedy, a 2000 release coproduced by 40 Acres & A Mule Filmworks and MTV Films for theatrical distribution by Paramount Pictures, was a more ambitious filmed-theater project. It documents a show featuring four black standup comedians – D.L. Hughley, Cedric the Entertainer, Steve Harvey, and Bernie Mac – that had been playing all around America for three years, becoming what Harvey described as "the highest-grossing comedy tour ever." Paramount was edgy about entering such unfamiliar territory, but the comics were confident that Lee would show them off perfectly without asking them to change their styles or material. Harvey told Lee's biographer that the show was important in cultural as well as commercial terms, calling it "an inside peek, for those who are not in the urban culture, at a lot of the ways we as a community view situations. And never before had there been such a diversified viewpoint of our culture." Lee again shot two performances, using fifteen cameras and dedicating some of them to shots of the audience, with the stipulation that if a cutaway showed someone laughing, the laugh had to be in response to the joke actually happening at that moment. The movie cost about $3 million to make and earned almost $40 million in American theaters (Aftab 257). *That's* entertainment!

These projects notwithstanding, Lee's heart remained primarily in the world of theatrical narrative films. The next chapter looks at his most recent phase, which brought a larger number of stories dealing entirely or mostly with white characters. In an ironic twist, this period gave birth to his most phenomenal hit and his most phenomenal flop, followed by the worst impasse in feature-film financing he had ever faced.

6

CRIME, WAR, MIRACLES

The most important thing to observe about Spike Lee's theatrical filmmaking in the 2000s has been his ability to rebound almost miraculously from misguided and miscalculated projects, following them with vastly better and more confident films . . . until he couldn't, for reasons largely beyond his control. Two years after the box-office failure of *Bamboozled* in 2000 he completed the extraordinary *25th Hour*, which is arguably his most mature, intelligent, and profoundly moving film to date. Two years after the negligible *She Hate Me* he released his first major-studio genre film, *Inside Man*, scoring at the box office as never before. But two years after that came *Miracle at St. Anna*, the World War II movie he had dreamed of making. Audiences fled as if a hostile battalion was firing live ammunition at their eyes and ears, and critics retreated to their foxholes muttering words of displeasure to the few who cared enough to listen. Lee did not rise quickly after this ringing defeat. Plans for a sequel to the hugely popular *Inside Man* disintegrated, as did other possibilities, and he fell back on shorts, documentaries, television, and filmed-theater ventures. His spirits did not sag, however. He stayed as busy as ever, and the two most prominent productions of the period stand with his most fully realized films.

Lee's first project after *Bamboozled* was one of his very best filmed-theater TV works. *A Huey P. Newton Story*, televised in 2001 by Starz! Encore Entertainment, documents a one-person play by Roger Guenveur Smith, a gifted character actor whose roles in Spike's joints range from Smiley in *Do the Right Thing* and Gary in *Get on the Bus* to Big Time Willie in *He Got Game* and Detective Atwater in *Summer of Sam*. The eponymous protagonist of *A Huey P. Newton Story* is the militant African-American leader who founded the Black Panther Party for Self Defense with Bobby Seale in 1966, became a highly visible activist on behalf of black power and what he dubbed "revolutionary humanism," wrote a large number of poems and essays, had serious run-ins with the law related to violence and murder, earned a Ph.D. in social philosophy at the University of California at Santa Cruz in 1980, and was shot to death in 1989 by a young member of the Black Guerilla Family, another radical black-nationalist organization. Smith etches a complex and nuanced portrait of Newton in his play, smoothly shifting among various dramatic modes – skillful impersonation, in-depth psychological acting, presentational address to the audience – in a manner that the theater theoretician Bertholt Brecht would surely have enthusiastically applauded. Smith had performed it some six hundred times before Lee and cinematographer Ellen Kuras shot it in an old synagogue on the Lower East Side of Manhattan, before an audience separated from the stage by security grilling and dressed all in black at Kuras's request. "Spike . . . has always been a big supporter of my work on stage," Smith remarked later, "and that work has been very political. I think that we have seen eye to eye on a lot of things in the political realm and we have been able to weave our passions together successfully in many regards" (Aftab 270–1). *A Huey P. Newton Story* is definitely such an occasion.

By contrast, the 2002 TV documentary *Jim Brown: All American* is a highly conventional and hagiographic affair with few strong Spike Lee touches and little interest for those not already fascinated with the football star's life and career. The feature-length TV drama *Sucker Free City*, made for the Showtime Networks in 2005, is more substantial. Lee left New York for the other side of America, shooting in San Francisco for the first time. Scripted by Alex Tse and set in the African-American neighborhood of Hunter's Point, the story centers on a white family that faces problems from the black V-Dub gang until a local drug dealer and CD pirate (Anthony Mackie) cozies up to the young man of the household (Ben Crowley) because he needs help with the technological end of his media-bootlegging operation. A parallel storyline concerns an enforcer (Ken Leung) for a Chinese mobster (George Cheung) who gets into trouble with his ruthless boss. Tightly directed and capably acted by a multiracial cast, the drama shows Lee's guerilla filmmaking chops to be in very good shape.

Two other TV projects reflect the didactic side of Lee's artistic personality. The amiable *Miracle's Boys*, a six-part miniseries shown in 2005 on the teen-oriented channel called The N, deals with three orphaned African-American brothers facing interrelated challenges: twenty-year-old Ty'ree (Pooch Hall), the oldest, has turned down a top-flight college to stay at home and raise the younger boys;

fourteen-year-old Lafayette (Julito McCullum), the youngest, is afraid that his mother's death has somehow erased
his terrific flair for baseball; and Charlie (Sean Nelson), the
middle brother, just served a stretch in a juvenile detention
center that has left him bitter and confused. Lee directed the
first and last episodes, injecting some of his personal touches,
such as the camera-and-actor dolly shot that makes a character appear to be gliding magically through cinematic space.[1]

   Lee's most celebrated TV documentary, *When the Levees
Broke: A Requiem in Four Acts*, premiered on HBO on two
consecutive nights in August 2006. Produced by 40 Acres &
A Mule and HBO, budgeted at $2 million, and running four
and quarter hours, it sets out an exhaustive account of the
miseries undergone by countless residents of New Orleans,
Louisiana, during and after the onslaught of Hurricane
Katrina in 2005, which caused levees to fail and brought
catastrophic flooding throughout the area. Lee interviewed
almost a hundred people for the film, including historian
Douglas Brinkley, sociologist Michael Eric Dyson, journal-
ist Soledad O'Brien, actors Wendell Pierce and Sean Penn,
musicians Wynton Marsalis and Harry Belafonte, United
States Senator Mary Landrieu, Louisiana governor Kathleen
Blanco, New Orleans mayor Ray Nagin, and the Rev. Al
Sharpton, the noted black activist. The crew included such
frequent Lee collaborators as film editor Barry Alexander
Brown, film editor and coproducer Samuel D. Pollard, and
Terence Blanchard, who composed the score and appears as
an interviewee. The film was nominated for six nonfiction
Emmy Awards and won in the categories of exceptional
merit, outstanding directing, and outstanding picture; it also
won an NAACP Image Award and a Peabody Award, and
the Venice Film Festival bestowed two prizes on it.

   Lee returned to New Orleans in the 2010 sequel, *If God
Is Willing and da Creek Don't Rise*, another 255-minute epic.

In addition to its account of problem-plagued rebuilding and relocation efforts during the five years since Katrina, this film broadens its focus to discuss such pertinent matters as the BP oil spill that fouled the Gulf of Mexico and the Louisiana coast in 2010; federal court proceedings against the Army Corps of Engineers for shoddy work on a vital waterway that exacerbated the hurricane's disastrous effects; and charges that the New Orleans Police Department indulged in lawlessness and brutality after the devastating storm. Reception of the sequel was more muted than that of the first film, but it was still welcomed as an important contribution to investigative reporting on one of the most important cataclysms of the early twenty-first century. Neither film is particularly distinctive or distinguished in artistic terms, but together they comprise a work of humanistic cinema that is as laudable as it is monumental.

25TH HOUR

A line in the apartment overlooking the World Trade Center site is very important when Jacob asks Frank, "Are you going to move?" and Frank says, "Fuck that. Bin Laden can drop another one." That's . . . the line of eight million New Yorkers saying, "We're staying here." – Spike Lee (Aftab 281)

David Benioff published his first novel, *The 25th Hour*, in 2000. He wrote the screenplay for Lee's movie soon afterward, staying true to the outlines of the original story.[2] It centers on Monty Brogan (Edward Norton), a young New Yorker spending his last night with friends and family before starting a seven-year prison stretch for drug dealing; he's due to surrender himself at the medium-security Otisville Prison in upstate New York, about seventy miles from New York City, the next morning. Monty's closest male friends

are Frank Slaughtery (Barry Pepper), a Wall Street stock-
broker, and Jake Elinsky (Philip Seymour Hoffman), a prep-
school English teacher who has developed a crush on Mary
D'Annunzio (Anna Paquin), a flirtatious pupil in his poetry
class. Monty's girlfriend, Naturelle Rivera (Rosario Dawson),
is a Latina with Puerto Rican roots. His mother died when
he was eleven, but his Irish-American father, James Brogan
(Brian Cox), is a former fireman and a reformed alcoholic
who still runs a neighborhood bar in Queens, and his Uncle
Nikolai (Levani) is a Russian gangster whose drugs Monty
peddled until the narcs barged into his apartment and went
straight to the stash of dope and cash hidden in the living-
room sofa. Nikolai's enforcer, a Ukrainian thug named
Kostya Novotny (Tony Siragusa), also figures in the story.
Major scenes include a farewell bash at a nightclub, a tense
meeting upstairs between Monty and his Russian mafia cro-
nies, and a fight in which Frank beats Monty up after Monty
implores him to mess up his face so he'll stand a chance of
not being raped the moment he walks through the prison
door. We learn about Monty's history and relationships
through encounters, conversations, and flashbacks. We also
gain insights into his fierce regrets over his wasted past and
his gnawing anxiety about what may be a horrific future.

Although the novel was in print a year before September
11, 2001, the terrorist attacks on the World Trade Center
and the Pentagon were very much on Lee's mind when he
and Benioff went to work on the shooting script; as Lee said
later, he felt that as "responsible filmmakers" they were obligated to mirror the post-9/11 atmosphere in the film. This
brought about various adjustments to the original material:
Frank's apartment directly overlooks the Ground Zero site;
James became a retired firefighter as well as the owner of
a bar, and the bar houses a shrine of photographs memo-
rializing firefighters killed in the WTC attack; phrases like

"Bin Laden: Wanted Dead or Alive" appear on T-shirts, reflecting Lee's observation that "Americans wanted blood" in the wake of the tragedy. Terrence Blanchard's score was also affected. Recorded by an orchestra with such unusual elements as Northumbrian smallpipes and vocalizing by the French-Algerian singer Cheb Mami, it incorporates melodies and textures borrowed from Middle Eastern and Irish musical traditions; as Blanchard explained, "all too often Islamic music and Irish music have been associated with just certain sections of American life, and I guess [Spike] was trying to say, 'All of this is America'" (Aftab 280, 283).

Blanchard's score makes its first appearance during the opening credits, which are visually accompanied by majestic and melancholy views of the two near-vertical shafts of light that memorialized 9/11 in its immediate aftermath. The gravity of the film's intentions is unmistakable from the outset, and the story begins with a scene (later seen to be a flashback) that introduces serious emotion through everyday activity that's just a little out of the ordinary. Monty and Kostya are driving to some sort of drug appointment when they spot a dog that has been severely wounded, probably in a dogfight. Kostya's gun is handy, and Monty wants to put the dog out of its misery. Badly injured though it is, the dog tries to fight him off, instantly winning the affections of Monty, who has an outlaw streak of his own hidden beneath a seemingly harmless demeanor. Naming him Doyle in honor of his Irish ancestry, Monty adopts him as a pet, and once he's rehabilitated they become close companions. This single brief scene sets out several key elements of the film: the blend of decency and rebelliousness in Monty's personality; the fascination with dark sides of New York, such as the physical place where Monty finds the dog and the mental space he inhabits as a dope dealer; and Monty's need for loyalty, which he immediately shows to Doyle and receives from Doyle in return. Loyalty is a key theme of *25th Hour*, since a major subplot arises from the suspicion of Monty's friends that his lover Naturelle is the person who betrayed him to the police. Although a more likely malefactor ultimately proves to have been the traitor, the misgivings about Naturelle are plausible, since the cops clearly knew just what they were seeking and where it was concealed in the apartment that she and Monty shared. Then too, Monty's main reason for entering the drug trade was to raise the payoff money that keeps James's bar safe from mob extortionists. Talking with his dad later in the film, Monty says that the only people he has confidence in besides his father are Jake and Frank, his longtime friends. Trust and betrayal, friendship and loneliness, longing and dread, the vibrancy of urban America and the horror of September 11 do subtle, insinuating dances with one another throughout the film.

The story of Monty and the theme of 9/11 are most fully integrated during two indelible scenes. In one of them, Monty stands before a restroom mirror and reflects on all the people he might blame for the rotten turn his life has taken. This episode has been controversial because of its similarity to a scene in *Do the Right Thing* – the so-called "race rant," where the story stops in its tracks while characters holler race-baiting slurs, smears, insults, and epithets directly into the camera, foregrounding the banality, inanity, and sheer emptiness of the abusive language that lies coiled within ordinary discourse like a species of reptile always eager to spew its venom. This scene and the analogous one in *25th Hour* do have resemblances: both are Brechtian interludes that interrupt the narrative for didactic as well as aesthetic purposes. But the likeness ends there. The race rant in *Do the Right Thing*, colorfully acted by familiar characters, is a comic scene, geared to amuse the audience with its seemingly random string of rude, crude obscenities rendered silly and harmless by standing outside the story of the film. The restroom scene in *25th Hour* is a sharper, more dangerous affair. Monty is not outside the story; on the contrary, he is undergoing a psychological crisis when he enters the lavatory and thinks the darksome thoughts that we hear on the soundtrack and see illustrated by images materializing in the mirror before his eyes. Monty is not inveighing against abstract caricatures, moreover; his stream-of-consciousness tirade boils with overwhelming rage against very real people, from Osama bin Laden and his terrorist ilk to "nigger" gangs, "towel-head" taxi drivers, and all of the Others who populate a city that was filled not long ago with white immigrants like his father, like his friends, like himself. Seen from behind as his body slumps into a stooped posture reflecting his humiliation, Monty excoriates them all in the strongest imaginable terms before admitting that his guilt stems from his own actions and that his fate rests on his own shoulders. The proper curse, he realizes, is not *fuck you* but *fuck me.* The scene is vastly more powerful than its quasi-counterpart in *Do the Right Thing* owing to the excellence of its execution and to Lee's characteristic boldness in unmasking the prejudices embedded in American culture, in world history, and (one suspects the filmmaker is acknowledging) in himself. A good first step toward eradicating intolerance in America might be for people with established power to think a sincere and hearty *fuck us all.*

Another scene with extraordinary force occurs when Monty's friends Frank and Jake converse in Frank's apartment overlooking the starkly spotlighted Ground Zero site, which is relentlessly visible as the dialogue unfolds in a single bravura shot. Their unsparing discussion of Monty touches on everything from the great potential his life once held to the question of whether he'll kill himself rather than suffer in prison. In sum, they are gazing at a blasted, annihilated

*In 25th Hour, Frank Slaughtery (Barry Pepper) and Jacob Elinsky
(Philip Seymour Hoffman) overlook Ground Zero in lower Manhattan
while talking about the awful destiny of their best friend, who is about
to begin a long prison sentence – a discussion of a blasted life against the
background of a blasted place.*

place and conducting a mournful post mortem on a blasted,
annihilated life.

Eventually the camera moves slowly toward the window,
recalling the stunning single-take scene in *Do the Right Thing*
when Sal talks with his son Pino before a window looking
out on their Bed-Stuy street; in both cases Lee is pointing
to the inescapable links between individuals and the troubled
environments in which their lives unfold. What took place
at Ground Zero is, of course, immeasurably more horrific
than anything that could happen to Monty or to any single
person, if only because the pain and anguish were inflicted
on such a large number of bodies and minds in such a concentrated period of time. The specter of Monty's incarcera-
tion is real and terrible all the same, and it's made even more
frightening by what has hitherto been one of his best assets
in life: the strong, healthy body and handsome, appealing
face that are sure to get him promptly and repeatedly raped.
Film critic David Edelstein states this theme's importance in
overly sweeping terms, writing that the whole story is "fueled

by the threat of anal rape," but that threat is obviously at
the front of Monty's mind, driving his desperate demand
for Frank to make him ugly the night before his sentence
begins.[3] Frank thinks Monty may commit suicide rather than
face seven years of such horror, and when Jake says they'll
all renew their friendship when he returns to society, Frank
rejects the possibility out of hand, doubting that Monty will
survive the Otisville ordeal even if he doesn't choose to take
his own life.

We never learn what does happen, because *25th Hour*
concludes in a manner at once daringly open-ended and
emotionally gratifying. James has insisted on driving Monty
upstate, so Monty climbs into his father's car for the fate-
ful journey. After driving north toward Otisville for a while,
James unexpectedly says that he could just as easily turn west
and keep on going, bringing Monty to some distant destination where he can start a new, anonymous life. Dazed and
exhausted after a sleepless night and the beating he forced
Frank to give him, Monty dozes as his father's monologue
spins on. The screen fills with James's fantasy, envisioning
a utopia untainted by bygone errors and pregnant with the
possibilities that America holds out to free, unfettered spirits brave enough to grasp them. Historical missteps recede,
races commingle in domestic harmony, and new generations
build ways of living untarnished by the wrong decisions of
their forebears. The film's final shot reveals the daydream's
phantasmal nature, showing the car still heading north
toward the prison. Spike Lee knows better than to embrace
a sanguine view of a country that is scarred to this day by
uncountable quantities of social, cultural, political, and all-
too-human mistakes and misdeeds going back to the time
when avaricious, imperialistic, genocidal white men first set
foot on the North American continent. Yet despite all this
– and here is one of the foremost qualities that make Lee

one of the most expansive, generous-minded artists of our time – he remains acutely aware of the spiritual and psychological riches that America incontestably *should* and someday *may* give to its residents as a birthright. *25th Hour* is a quintessential expression of Lee's unique capacity for finding the political in the personal, the timeless in the quotidian, and worlds of potential splendor in the America shared by black folks, white folks, all folks.

SHE HATE ME

Ever unpredictable, Lee followed the inspired *25th Hour* with a trifle called *She Hate Me*. The title refers to a player for the short-lived XFL football league who nicknamed himself They Hate Me, shortened to He Hate Me so he could display it on his jersey. True to its gender-bent title, the movie deals with homosexuality, featuring eighteen lesbians and then some as characters. Roger Ebert, one of the few critics with good things to say about the picture, started his 2004 review by admitting that after his first viewing he felt it "contains enough for five movies, but has no idea which of those movies it wants to be." His breakdown of the five movies adds up to a plot synopsis freewheeling enough to suit the film:

> Movie One: The story of a corporate whistleblower (Anthony Mackie), and an indictment of the corporate culture. Movie Two: The hero inexplicably becomes a stud who is hired to impregnate lesbians at $10,000 a pop. Movie Three: He impregnates a Mafia daughter (Monica Belluci), and John Turturro turns up as her father, to do a Marlon Brando imitation. Movie Four: A free-standing sidebar about Frank Wills (Chiwetel Ejiofor), the Watergate security guard who brought down the Nixon administration and reaped nothing but personal unhappiness. Movie Five:

How a black man steps up to the plate and accepts responsibility for raising his kids, by bonding with his lesbian
ex-girlfriend (Kerry Washington) and her lover, who have
both borne one of his children.

It is interesting that one of Lee's savviest critics has to create
a sort of five-shot montage to get across the picture's content. Ebert is also one of Lee's most understanding critics,
though, and he ultimately praises the film for attacking things
that Lee and most of us dislike – stereotypes, platitudes,
genre formulas – by embodying them instead of launching
just another liberal attack on them, much as *Bamboozled* both
incorporated and excoriated certain kinds of entertainment,
but doing so in less obvious ways, hoping that *She Hate Me*
would avoid the dismal box-office fate of *Bamboozled*. It's a
good argument, and to some extent I buy it. I do think the
movie is disorganized in concept and execution, however.
Lee's box-office strategy was also flawed: *Bamboozled* has
reaped about $2,275,000 to date, the least of any Lee movie
except *She Hate Me*, which has a lifetime gross of $366,037,
a truly pathetic sum.[4]
    Lee evidently felt a need to take on sexuality, alterity, and
the multifaceted plight of those with minority status in a more
aggressive manner than he had essayed before. As things
turned out, his aims exceeded his abilities in this instance. A
filmmaker who had rarely succeeded in creating a fully three-
dimensional female character now sketched a roster of caricatures that barely qualify as one-dimensional, much less as
credible figures engaged in plausible activities, the strenuous
efforts of a gifted cast notwithstanding. Oblique references
to recent history, such as the financial problems of the security guard who came upon the Watergate burglary but later
fell into obscurity, add little. *She Hate Me* is an audacious
venture, to be sure, and I applaud its ambitions. That said,

I see no reason to linger on the film. It was, sad to say, one
of the last theatrical films that Ossie Davis completed before
his death in 2005.

INSIDE MAN

Whether or not *She Hate Me* is five movies, *Inside Man* is
two movies, metaphorically speaking. It is Spike Lee's most
financially successful film, as noted earlier, and the one most
unabashedly plugged into the Hollywood studio system, with
funding from Universal Pictures and Imagine Entertainment
as well as Lee's own 40 Acres & A Mule Filmworks in the
mix. At the same time, though, one can't resist seeing it as
one of Lee's most thinly veiled allegories for his aspirations
as a filmmaker – to be an inside man, able to pivot at will
between specialized, personal projects that speak primarily to
his devotees and smoothly machined mass-audience projects
that speak to everyone everywhere.

The title character of *Inside Man* is Dalton Russell (Clive
Owen), an insider *and* outsider who's also a criminal with
a conscience. He begins the story by addressing the audience from some small, claustrophobic space – he calls it a
"tiny cell" in his monologue – that could be anything from
a jail cell to a hideout (it turns out to be the latter), and he
ends it by striding through the scene of the crime under
the very nose of dedicated detective Keith Frazier (Denzel
Washington), who has been working like mad to lay hands
on him and bring him to justice. The bulk of the movie
details Russell's daylight raid on a huge Manhattan bank,
where he and his gang seize all of the customers present as
hostages, gain access to the vault, and control the situation
by maintaining an atmosphere of terror. In the meanwhile,
Frazier communicates with Russell about demands and hostages, and finds time to brood about corruption charges

that hang over him in connection with a completely different case; they are bogus, but if they hold up they'll stymie a promotion he needs to marry his fiancée, Sylvia (Cassandra Freeman), and settle down with her in a nice home. Slightly scrambling its own timeline, the film punctuates the unfolding story with brief, semi-improvised scenes showing Frazier interviewing people taken from the bank when the robbery ended, hoping to find that some of them are perpetrators posing as former hostages. Much of the movie's suspense comes from uncertainty over how the endgame will play out. Russell has demanded an airplane and buses, but he surely knows that police never give in to demands like that. How does he think he will escape? Why does he seem to be stalling for time, when that's normally what the *cops* do as they search for solutions to a hostage crisis?

The most important subplot centers on Arthur Case (Christopher Plummer), chairman of the bank's board of directors, and Madeleine White (Jodie Foster), a fixer hired by Case when he hears about the robbery under way. His safe-deposit box is in that branch of the institution, he tells her, and it contains priceless heirlooms that must be safeguarded at all costs. White sets up her own line of communication with Russell, who informs her in a roundabout way that her prosperous, powerful, universally esteemed employer started his fabulous career by collaborating with Nazis when he worked at a Swiss bank during the Holocaust, stealing from Jewish victims and covering up his vicious crimes afterward. Eventually we learn that the items in the safe-deposit box are indeed priceless, but only to Case, whose reputation, position, and fortune would vanish in a flash if their incriminating nature became public knowledge. And the ruin of this craven capitalist, we further learn, is the real motivation for the ostensible bank-vault robbery that Dalton Russell has engineered. The narrative's chess game grows ever more

complicated as the film proceeds, involving certain hostages,
various police officers – most notably Frazier's partner, Bill
Mitchell (Chiwetel Ejiofor), and commanding officer John
Darius (Willem Dafoe) – and New York City's mayor (Peter
Kybart), over whom White has a remarkably high degree of
influence.

Auteurs

The major-studio backing and Russell Gewirtz screenplay of *Inside Man* notwithstanding, director Spike Lee is
clearly the movie's auteur. Washington is the star; gifted
African-American players like Ejiofor and Freeman have
well-written roles; characteristic observations about race and
class pepper the dialogue and situations; and the ability of
white-controlled money to bring about evil consequences is
a dominating theme. Just as clearly, character Dalton Russell
is the auteur of the film's fictional matrix, exercising full
creative control over the scenario (the bank raid), the crew
(his accomplices), the cast (their hostages), and the audience
(police officers, media reporters, the public) within the world
of the story. And neither of the enterprises we are watching – Lee's big-studio joint, Russell's audacious robbery – is
just about money. The felon and the filmmaker have grander
goals, and gaining entrance to a rich, rock-solid institution by any means necessary is only a first step for each of
them. If they achieve their ultimate aims, America will be
a better place: Russell will have brought down a fabulously
powerful, unspeakably immoral capitalist, and Lee will have
broken down the barrier between personal film and genre
film, art film and mainstream film, African-American film
and American film. Against the odds, both artists succeed.

It was a short-lived victory, however. Two years later,
he parlayed the success of *Inside Man* into support from

Touchstone for *Miracle at St. Anna*, which returned less than $8 million domestically (and a bit more than $9 million worldwide) on its $45 million investment, joining the same unprofitable league as *Bamboozled* and *She Hate Me*. Bearing out the truism that in Hollywood one's prospects are precisely as good as the grosses of one's last picture, Hollywood slammed on the financial brakes, indefinitely stalling at least three projects – a film about prizefighter Joe Louis, a biopic about football great Jim Brown, and a sequel to *Inside Man* – in various stages of development. As successful as *Inside Man* was, moreover, it may not have been quite successful enough, falling short of the $100 million in domestic earnings that Hollywood holds dear.[5] "I haven't made a feature film in three years," Lee lamented to Charlie Rose in June 2011. "*Inside Man* was my most successful film. . . . But we can't get the sequel made. And one thing Hollywood does well is sequels. The film's not getting made. We tried many times. . . . [M]oney is a big part of film, unlike a lot of other art forms" (Obenson). This is one indicator of the damage that the well-intentioned but misguided *Miracle at St. Anna* inflicted on Lee's career.

MIRACLE AT ST. ANNA

We're on the highway to heaven up here. Sitting ducks. For what? For nothing. Over a scam. That's what this war is. A scam. . . . The Negro don't have doodleysquat to do with . . . this devilment, this war-to-free-the-world shit. . . . They better not talk that boogie-joogie to me. White folks own the world, goddamit. We just rentin'. – Sergeant Bishop Cummings (McBride 167)

Filling in the blanks of African-American history is one of Lee's longstanding interests, as we have seen. His feature films have recounted Malcolm X's career and traveled by bus to the Million Man March, while his documentaries have explored everything from the racist bombing of an Alabama church to the horrors experienced by black residents of New Orleans when Hurricane Katrina revealed emergency officials to be incompetent and apathetic. This was the impulse behind *Miracle at St. Anna*, Lee's effort to celebrate the heroism of African-American soldiers who fought and died in the European theater during World War II – a topic virtually unknown by most Americans and virtually ignored by Hollywood for more than a century.

Adapted by the African-American journalist, author, and musician James McBride from his eponymous 2002 novel, *Miracle at St. Anna* focuses on soldiers serving in the all-black 92nd Infantry Division, a segregated unit known as the Buffalo Soldiers, after the Native American nickname for black men who fought in the United States Cavalry on the American frontier. The actual unit did its first fighting in France as World War I was nearing its conclusion. During World War II it was the only black infantry division to fight in Europe, serving in the Italian campaign from September 1944 until April 1945. Its men engaged with German troops in the Po Valley and the northern Apennines, and in December 1944 they fought a ferocious battle near St. Anna of Stazzema, a small village in the area. McBride's novel and Lee's film depict events related to the plight of four soldiers trapped in the town as winter settles in. One of them, the gentle and slow-witted Private Sam Train (Omar Benson Miller), is determined to help a badly wounded Italian boy (Matteo Sciabordi), complicating a situation that is growing ever more perilous as the enemy closes in; and racism is rampant among the unit's white commanders, who are shockingly careless with the lives of their Negro men. The title refers to the town of St. Anna and to intimations of the

divine that enter the story when Train befriends the traumatized boy and continue during the slaughter of 450 men,
women, and children who refuse to turn over an anti-Nazi
partisan leader.

Spike versus Clint

In further pursuit of his mission to correct the historical
record, Lee used the impending premiere of *Miracle at St.
Anna* as an opportunity to attack a pair of World War II
movies released in 2006 by Clint Eastwood, another major
American auteur. *Flags of Our Fathers* deals with the famous
1945 photograph of six Marines planting the American flag
atop Mt. Suribachi during the Battle of Iwo Jima, spotlight-
ing the deceptive nature of the image – the flag was not put
up in the heat of combat but was raised, taken down, and
raised a second time for the camera – and following three of
the soldiers (the other three were killed) as they reluctantly
toured America to raise money for the war effort, coerced
into papering over the horrific realities of combat and
promoting their own heroism at the expense of fallen com-
rades. That film's companion piece, *Letters from Iwo Jima*,
recounts the American invasion of Iwo Jima from the perspectives of Japanese soldiers, including General Tadamichi
Kuribayashi, who was in charge of Japanese forces on the
island, and some of the rank-and-file combatants under his
command.

Both are strikingly humane and compassionate dramas,
refuting and rejecting most of the clichés and platitudes that
characterize the great majority of Hollywood war movies.
Viewing them through a race-conscious lens, however, Lee
saw much to criticize. Visiting the Cannes International Film
Festival to promote *Miracle at St. Anna* a few months before
its premiere, he engaged Eastwood in a rhetorical battle that

unfolded in separate statements to the media by the two directors. Put into dialogue form it goes like this:

> **Lee:** Clint Eastwood made two films about Iwo Jima that ran for more than four hours total, and there was not one negro actor on the screen. If you reporters had any balls you'd ask him why. There's no way I know why he did that. ... But I know it was pointed out to him and that he could have changed it. It's not like he didn't know. ... Many veterans, African-Americans, who survived that war are upset at Clint Eastwood. In his vision of Iwo Jima, Negro soldiers did not exist. Simple as that. I have a different version. (Lewis)
>
> **Eastwood:** Has he ever studied the history? ... He was complaining when I did *Bird* [the 1988 biopic of Charlie Parker]. Why would a white guy be doing that? I was the only guy who made it, that's why. He could have gone ahead and made it. Instead he was making something else. ... [The small detachment of black troops on Iwo Jima as part of a munitions unit] didn't raise the flag. The story is *Flags of Our Fathers*, the famous flag-raising picture, and they didn't do that. If I go ahead and put an African-American actor in there, people'd go: "This guy's lost his mind." I mean, it's not accurate. ... A guy like him should shut his face. (Dawson)
>
> **Lee:** [T]he man is not my father and we're not on a plantation either. He's a great director. He makes his films, I make my films. The thing about it though, I didn't personally attack him. And a comment like "a guy like that should shut his face" – come on, Clint, come on. He sounds like an angry old man right there. ... If he wishes, I could assemble African-American men who fought at Iwo Jima and I'd like him to tell these guys that what they did was insignificant and they did not exist.

I'm not making this up. I know history. And I know the
history of Hollywood and its omission of the one million African-American men and women who contributed
to World War II. . . . Not everything was John Wayne,
baby. . . . I never said he should show one of the other
guys holding up the flag as black. I said that African-
Americans played a significant part in Iwo Jima. For
him to insinuate that I'm rewriting history and have one
of the four guys with the flag be black . . . no one said
that. It's just that there's not one black in either film.
And because I know my history, that's why I made that
observation. (Marikar)

Lee is right: black soldiers needn't have been completely
scrubbed from the screen. Eastwood is right: the story told
in *Flags of Our Fathers* (like that told in *Letters from Iwo Jima*)
did not call for much of an African-American presence.[6]

Beyond the squabbling, what we find in this disagreement
are complementary critiques of America's hypocrisy with
respect to war. Lee mounts a counteroffensive against the
culture industry's elision of African-American heroism and
patriotism, while Eastwood makes a similar move on behalf
of Japanese sacrifice, suffering, and death in *Letters from Iwo
Jima* and attacks the culture industry's readiness to lie, mis-
lead, and propagandize in *Flags of Our Fathers*. Lee is also
correct about his broader point, however, regarding the all-
white version of World War II that Hollywood has peddled
ever since the time of the war itself. "This is the same shit
they were doing back in the forties, fifties, and sixties," he
said of Eastwood's films. "Really, until Jim Brown was in *The
Dirty Dozen*, in 1967. *Home of the Brave* was a great film with
a great African-American character in it. But if you look at
the history of World War Two films we're invisible. We're
omitted" (Colapinto).[7] Eastwood isn't to blame for this state

of affairs, but as Lee said, he hasn't helped to correct it. Lee did work to set the record straight, and it is a sad irony of his career that the resulting movie proved far too uninvolving and unconvincing to serve his cause well.

Miracle at St. Anna received unfavorable reviews from critics who focused on its cinematic quality, and somewhat better ones from critics who gave more weight to its good intentions, historical significance, and intermittent moments of effective filmmaking. "It remains a wonder," Todd McCarthy (2008) wrote in *Variety*, "that no one, from Lee to the various producers and studio execs, demanded that someone whip this story into more sensible shape before the cameras rolled, so obvious are its excesses and indulgences." *Washington Post* critic Ann Hornaday found the picture overwrought, overproduced, overbusy, and overlong, concluding that it "suffers from the worst filmmaking sin of all: the failure of trust, in the story and the audience." She also wrote that Private Train is "particularly problematic as an example of the 'magical Negro' stereotype that has bedeviled movies from *The Green Mile* to *Million Dollar Baby*." Wesley Morris, the African-American film critic of the *Boston Globe*, said the film 'is not a work of outrage or joy. It's something distressingly new for the filmmaker: a work of obligation. It feels like a movie Lee made in order to say he did it." By contrast, the African-American critic Lisa Kennedy gave the film a favorable review in the *Denver Post*, saying that it takes "a sophisticated gift to depict the myriad wrinkles of race and identity captured in this addition to the 'Greatest Generation' pantheon." Other critics with good things to say about *Miracle at St. Anna* included Carrie Rickey of the *Philadelphia Inquirer* and A.O. Scott of the *New York Times*, but few showed a great deal of enthusiasm for the film. In an especially thoughtful review, *Wall Street Journal* critic Joe Morgenstern contrasted it with Rachid Bouchareb's *Days of Glory* (*Indigènes*, 2006), an Algerian–French–Moroccan–Belgian coproduction about "four Algerian soldiers in the French army fighting bravely against the Nazis for the nation they love while their fellow French soldiers treat them like scum, and their casually despicable racist officers use them as cannon fodder." Bouchareb allows the bitter absurdities of the situation to speak for themselves, however, whereas Lee hammers them home "with agitprop fervor and clumsy actors playing racist officers as crude cartoons." Audiences agreed with the nay-sayers, and Lee's standing as a bankable filmmaker did not begin to recover until 2011, when reports of a new project – a remake of a South Korean thriller, of all things – came as heartening news to his admirers.

EPILOGUE: EXPANDING HORIZONS

People think I'm this angry black man walking around in a constant state of rage. – Spike Lee in 2008 (Colapinto)

Spike Lee's America is a diversified place, populated not only by African-Americans but also by Asian-Americans, Italian-Americans, and other-Americans, by women as well as men, by gays as well as straights. Yet even after the critical success of *Summer of Sam* and the commercial success of *Inside Man*, he has remained more an African-American filmmaker than simply an American filmmaker in the minds of many movie-goers, and this perception has surely been a factor in the lackluster box-office records of many of his joints. After the good (not excellent) showing of *Malcolm X* in 1992, ticket sales for Lee's films followed a general downward trend. "It got to where people would come up to me and say, 'Hey, when's your next movie coming out?' – and I had one open-ing the next day," he told *New Yorker* writer John Colapinto just *before* the premiere of *Miracle at St. Anna* in 2008.

The perception of Lee as an *angry* black man (throwing garbage cans through windows) and as an angry black *man* (poorly representing women and gay people) is fed by shortcomings in his films, which revolve almost entirely around straight males, and by intemperate remarks, as when he dubbed the Warner Bros. studio "The Plantation" at the very time it was preparing to distribute *Malcolm* X in American theaters. *Miracle at St. Anna* was, among other things, a rare Spike Lee stab at broadening his cultural horizons by exploring American characters in a non-American setting, as he had done in *Malcolm X* but hardly at all since. If the war movie had succeeded, it could have expanded Lee's public image beyond its previous boundaries while maintaining his status as the cinema's most reliable chronicler of African-American life.

At this writing, it appears that Lee will be expanding his horizons in a direction few would have predicted, directing an American version of *Oldboy*, a 2003 thriller by Chan-wook Park, one of South Korea's most internationally respected directors. According to industry scuttlebutt, Josh Brolin will play the protagonist, Joe Douchett, a man who is kidnapped and imprisoned in a room without explanation for fifteen years, and then abruptly released, whereupon he sets about finding his captor and exacting revenge. Adrian Pryce is expected to play Sharlto Copley, the villain, and Elizabeth Olsen may join the production in the female lead. The screenplay, based on the Japanese manga comic by Garon Tsuchiya and Nobuaki Minegishi, is by Mark Protosevich, a thoroughly commercial writer whose credits include Wolfgang Petersen's *Poseidon* (2006) and Kenneth Branagh's *Thor* (2011). The major stars, hot Hollywood screenwriter, and Asian provenance of the story are an interesting combination of elements for Lee to manage, and interest in the project is high.

Even in his off periods, Lee has remained a hard worker and a determined artist. Difficulties and disappointments after the failure of *Miracle of St. Anna* blocked off pathways to theatrical films for a few years, but the following year he documented the Broadway production of *Passing Strange* and made the feature-length TV documentary *Kobe Doin' Work*, about Los Angeles Lakers basketball star Kobe Bryant, for the ESPN sports network. In 2010 he made the two-part TV documentary *If God Is Willing and da Creek Don't Rise*, the sequel to *When the Levees Broke*, and directed *Da Brick*, an HBO television drama. A new feature film, *Red Hook Summer*, opened in August 2012. It centers on Flik Royale (Jules Brown), an unhappy Atlanta boy spending the summer in the Red Hook neighborhood of Brooklyn, where his poor but spirited grandfather, Da Good Bishop Enoch Rouse (Clarke Peters), wants to make him a Christian believer. The old man's undertaking is hindered by Flik's first impressions of inner-city hardship and dysfunction, but the boy becomes less cynical through his friendship with Chazz Morningstar (Toni Lysaith), a lovely girl who sees good things beneath the borough's hard-edged surface. The film was promoted as a new instalment in Spike Lee's Chronicles of Brooklyn, and its pedigree is clear in everything from names – Lee plays Mr. Mookie, for instance, and Da Good Bishop recalls The Good Reverend Doctor in *Jungle Fever* – to its fundamentally affectionate portrait of what remains Lee's favorite place on earth.

In another nice irony of his career, Lee is sometimes compared with one of the most relentlessly white-centric writer-directors in American film: Woody Allen, who likewise favors New York City locations and also releases about a movie a year, although he doesn't have anything like Lee's workaholic schedule in other media as well, and he doesn't have a major gig like Lee's position as artistic director of

New York University's graduate film program (yet another ironic development in Spike's career, given his complaints about his experiences as a student there) . "He is able to accomplish so much in part because he often rises at 5 a.m.," Colapinto reports. "You want to get a lot done, you gotta get up in the morning," Lee told the journalist. The rest, he said, is "time management."

It is impossible to predict whether the most important part of Lee's legacy will lie in the seventeen features he created during the twenty-two years between *She's Gotta Have It* and *Miracle at St. Anna*, or whether those productions will be eclipsed by works made in the later phases of his career. If the former is the case, it's safe to speculate that he will be honored as the writer-director of an incontestable masterpiece, *Do the Right Thing*, and an indispensable historical biopic, *Malcolm X*, as well as lesser works that look more impressive and exciting with every passing year, such as the irrepressible college satire *School Daze*, the heartbreaking urban melodrama *Clockers*, and the morally charged thriller *Inside Man*. It is also likely that *25th Hour* will increasingly be seen as a pivotal film of the early twenty-first century and an inspired summation of Lee's deepest, richest intuitions about America in all its breadth, variety, exasperating imperfection, and near-infinite promise for those who, like Spike Lee, put anger and striving aside from time to time and open themselves to currents of imagination, creativity, and the possibility that America will someday embrace the equality for which Lee's great heroes, Malcolm and Martin, gave their lives.

NOTES

Introduction: Challenging Questions, No Easy Answers

1 Bobo's sources include *American Film, Black Enterprise, Boxoffice, Film Comment, The New York Times, Variety,* and *The Wall Street Journal.* The figures represent theatrical income only, excluding ancillary rights (e.g., DVD sales, foreign distribution) and product tie-ins.

2 François Truffaut and Jean-Luc Godard, who, like Lee, did their greatest work in the first ten years of their careers, are among the more notable members of this company; founders of auteurism in theory and practice, they had firm creative control over every aspect of their canonical films.

3 Taubin's ten-best-of-the year lists for the *Village Voice* have included *Crooklyn, Clockers, He Got Game, Bamboozled,* and *Do the Right Thing,* the last of which is the focus of the article I quote from.

4 Spike is the book's credited author, but it presents a third-person account of his career, which suggests that

Aftab actually wrote it. Shades of Gertrude Stein and *The Autobiography of Alice B. Toklas!*

Chapter 1 The Early Joints

1 Unless otherwise indicated, box-office figures are taken from the website Box Office Mojo (http://boxofficemojo. com) and other standard sources.

Chapter 2 The Right Thing and the Love Supreme

1 The Sharks, the Jets, and Officer Krupke are characters in the American stage and movie musical *West Side Story*, choreographed by Jerome Robbins.

2 The first music in *Do the Right Thing* arrives before the opening titles, when a tenor saxophone (a key instrument in both jazz and rock'n'roll) plays a riff on "Lift Every Voice and Sing," an important African-American anthem; it was written in 1900 by poet and activist James Weldon Johnson and composer John Rosamond Johnson, his brother (Wilson). Various points in my discussion of music in *Do the Right Thing* benefit from Johnson's analysis.

3 Sun City, located in the North West Province of South Africa, was a favored target of anti-apartheid protesters, including musician Steven Van Zandt's organization Artists United Against Apartheid, in the 1980s.

4 Mister Señor Love Daddy's complete declaration lists Boogie Down Productions, Rob Base, Dana Dane, Marley Marl, Olatunji, Chuck D, Ray Charles, EPMD, EU, Alberta Hunter, Run-DMC, Stetsasonic, Sugar Bear, John Coltrane, Big Daddy Kane, Salt-n-Pepa, Luther Vandross, McCoy Tyner, Biz Markie, New Edition, Otis Redding, Anita Baker, Thelonious Monk, Marcus Miller, Branford Marsalis, James Brown, Wayne Shorter, Tracy Chapman, Miles Davis, Force MDs, Oliver Nelson,

Fred Wesley, Maceo, Janet Jackson, Louis Armstrong, Duke Ellington, Jimmy Jam, Terry Lewis, George Clinton, Count Basie, Mtume, Stevie Wonder, Bobby McFerrin, Dexter Gordon, Sam Cooke, Parliament-Funkadelic, Al Jarreau, Teddy Pendergrass, Joe Williams, Wynton Marsalis, Phyllis Hyman, Sade, Sarah Vaughn, Roland Kirk, Keith Sweat, Kool Moe Dee, Prince, Ella Fitzgerald, Dianne Reeves, Aretha Franklin, Bob Marley, Bessie Smith, Whitney Houston, Dionne Warwick, Steel Pulse, Little Richard, Mahalia Jackson, Jackie Wilson, Cannonball and Nat Adderley, Quincy Jones, Marvin Gaye, Charles Mingus, and Mary Lou Williams.

5 It's interesting to note that, except for race, as Jerome Christensen points out, the one denominator common to Buggin Out's suggested black candidates for the Wall of Fame – Malcolm X, Nelson Mandela, and Michael Jordan – is celebrity (588).

Chapter 3 Deeper into Politics

1 The person who inspired Flipper's character appears to have been Lee's friend and cinematographer Ernest Dickerson, who majored in architecture at Howard University (P.L. Brown).

2 The drug charge was eventually dismissed. "I'm glad I was arrested," Bill Lee said in 1994. "It woke me up. . . . Dope was not part of my life until I was 40 years old." But he also said, "I don't have anything to do with Spike now." Some relatives sided with him against Spike in the father–son conflict. The same *Los Angeles Times* article quotes Spike's half-brother Arnold Lee, the son of Bill Lee and Kaplan, as saying Spike was "not even [ours] anymore" and Kaplan-Lee as saying, "I've never been a Spike Lee fan," wearing a *Do the Right Thing* jacket while she spoke (Mandell).

3 The circumstances of the murder were evidently more complicated than press reports often made it sound. According to John DeSantis in his 1991 book *For the Color of His Skin: The Murder of Yusuf Hawkins and the Trial of Bensonhurst*, a black Bensonhurst man helped assemble the arsenal of baseball bats, and the gathering of thugs was an outgrowth not only of generalized racism but also of an internal neighborhood feud. The white woman whose actions touched off the violence "was an 'admitted crack addict' who often invited 'a fast crowd of drug users who were mostly black and Latino' to her block" (Shipler).

4 I noted in *The Christian Science Monitor* (1992a) that Lee's pro-male bias shows through in the film's finale, which "seems more male-dominated than necessary, accompanying talk of black 'manhood' with schoolroom shots that privilege boys over girls."

5 Merriam-Webster defines a "buppie' as "a college-educated black adult who is employed in a well-paying profession and who lives or works in or near a large city." This actually does sound like Lee.

6 The nastiness between Baraka and Lee grew partly from what happened when Lee asked Baraka to write about *Mo' Better Blues* for a collection of essays on his films written by African-American critics. "I told him he wouldn't like anything I had to say about his work," Baraka recalled later. "He wrote a piece that was 100 percent negative . . . so . . . I said, I ain't running this," Lee recalled later (Ansen 1991).

7 Perhaps the most tantalizing proposal was floated by Richard Pryor in 1983, offering Marvin Worth a package deal with Warner Bros. whereby Pryor would play Malcolm and Lumet would direct from David Mamet's screenplay. Worth and Warner's backed away from

Mamet's script, though. Lumet described it as very stylized, "full of mad, marvelous speeches" (Thompson, 28).

8 The play was first staged by the Negro Ensemble
Company in New York, with Denzel Washington and
Samuel L. Jackson in the cast. Washington was in the film
version as well.

Chapter 4 Brownstones in the Nabe, Projects in the Hood

1 hooks's argument oscillates between getting the point
and missing the point, often lapsing into formulations
that block and frustrate whatever clear meanings might
emerge from more organized thinking and writing. We
learn in one sentence that Lee creates "representations
that challenge and oppose racist stereotypes," for instance,
and in the next that he frames these with "representations
that forcibly reinscribe stereotypical norms" (36). And so
on, most notably in observations about Troy that waver
between recognition of her complexity and complaints
about her inconsistency.

2 *Amos 'n' Andy* was a hit on radio and then television from
the 1920s through the 1950s, and hooks doesn't specify
which iteration(s) she has in mind.

3 The point of view in Price's novel alternates between Strike
and Rocco; in Price's original screenplay, Rocco's point of
view takes over; but Strike's takes over in the final shooting
script credited to both Lee and Price (Massood 190).

4 Taubin refers to the legal philosopher Jeremy Bentham's
eighteenth-century designs for a "panopticon" penal complex, which is best known today as a metaphor developed
by Foucault to represent the way modern societies install
mechanisms of physical and psychological surveillance
throughout the environment, thereby encouraging people
to police their own behaviors lest outside forces observe,
discipline, and/or punish them (Foucault 195–228). In

NOTES TO PAGES 139–42

the panopticon, cells holding prisoners are positioned in a ring around a central guard tower, and each prisoner knows that someone in the tower might be observing him or her at any hour of the day or night. The housing project inverts this model, placing alleged wrongdoers in the center and their potential observers along the circumference. Foucault performs the same inversion in his figural use of the panopticon designs.

Chapter 5 Women and Men, Blacks and Whites

1 Actual attendance at the march was estimated at 837,000 (with a ± 20 percent margin of error) by the Center for Remote Sensing at Boston University. The Nation of Islam claimed that between 1.5 million and 2 million attended, while an initial estimate by the National Park Service indicated that 400,000 were there (BU Center).

2 According to a transcript of a 1984 sermon by Farrakhan published by *The New York Times*, the minister said, "Now that nation called Israel never has had any peace in 40 years and she will never have any peace because there can be no peace structured on injustice, thievery, lying and deceit and using the name of God to shield your dirty religion under His holy and righteous name" (Shipp 1984). Farrakhan denied having said this, and the controversy devolved into a squabble over whether the adjective had been "gutter" or rather "dirty," which is about as petty as ideological quarreling can get. One of Farrakhan's more widely known denials came in a letter he sent in 1997 to Jude Wanniski, an economist, conservative pundit, former *Wall Street Journal* editor, and Farrakhan supporter. "Over the centuries," the minister wrote,

the evils of Christians, Jews and Muslims have dirtied their respective religions. True Faith in the laws and Teaching

of Abraham, Jesus and Muhammad is not dirty, but, practices in the name of these religions can be unclean and can
cause people to look upon the misrepresented religion as
being unclean. In the same way, I have throughout my
life referred to Hitler as a wicked man, yet, the national
news media insists that I called him a "great man," with the
implied inference that "great" means "good." However, I
did refer to him as "wickedly great." In the same sense that
Ghengis Khan stands out in history. (Wanniski)

Farrakhan had made similar disclaimers in the years before
Get on the Bus was written and produced, so at worst Rick
is believing what he wants to believe, and at best he is
uncritically accepting a dubious claim. It's interesting
that Aftab's as-told-to biography of Lee flatly asserts that
Farrakhan made the inflammatory "gutter religion" and
Hitler remarks.

3 The music by Copland comes from numerous sources,
including the "Interlude" from *Music for the Theatre*
(1925), the 1940 Orchestral Suite from the 1938 ballet
Billy the Kid, the "Grover's Corner" portion of the score
for Sam Wood's movie *Our Town* (1940), *John Henry*
(1940/1952), *Lincoln Portrait* (1942), the "Hoe-Down" that
concludes the ballet *Rodeo* (1942), the ballet *Appalachian
Spring* (1944), *Letter from Home* (1944/1962), *Orchestral
Variations* (1957), the ballet *Dance Panels* (1959/1962), and
Fanfare for the Common Man (1942), an overused warhorse
that Spike should not have trotted out. (Music critic Greg
Sandow speaks highly of the latter piece in his liner notes
for the *He Got Game* soundtrack CD, but, as he points
out, it has been performed "by everyone from the US Air
Force Band to Emerson, Lake and Palmer.")

4 He initially confessed to killing six people and wounding
several others in the course of eight shootings, but later

changed the confession to say that he had committed only two shootings, killing three victims and wounding one. He has been behind bars since his arrest in 1977.

5 Reviews aggregated on the Rotten Tomatoes website show a favorable/unfavorable split of 52/48 percent among "all critics" (96 reviews) and 50/50 percent among "top critics" (32 reviews).

6 Spike made the PBS documentary *Pavarotti & Friends 99 for Guatemala and Kosovo* in 1999 for the same reason, drawing this comment from his brother David, who couldn't get over Spike's hectic schedule: "I was just reading the newspaper one day and I saw Spike was in Italy with Luciano Pavarotti. I didn't even know he'd left the *country*. But there it was, he was in Italy with the Three Tenors. I *still* don't know what that was" (Aftab 243).

Chapter 6 Crime, War, Miracles

1 The other episodes were directed by Bill Duke, Neema Arkadie, LeVar Burton, and former Lee cinematographer Ernest R. Dickerson.

2 This was Benioff's first screenplay. Since then he has written or cowritten original or adapted scripts for Wolfgang Petersen's *Troy* (2004), Marc Forster's *Stay* (2005) and *The Kite Runner* (2007), Gavin Hood's *X-Men Origins: Wolverine* (2009), and Jim Sheridan's *Brother* (2009), and he is cocreator of the HBO television series *Game of Thrones* (2011–).

3 Edelstein's review bears the nudge-nudge-wink-wink title "Back Door Blues" and the pseudo-tell-all subtitle "What Spike Lee's *25th Hour* is really about." Edelstein manages to miss the whole point of the movie's 9/11 theme, saying that Monty's "syncopated harangue against the city's sundry ethnic groups" is a "jarring note" because "it's not clear what any of these tribes have to do with Monty's

predicament – he's an educated white boy who works for Russians." One might as well ask why Lee brings racism into the picture, since neither Monty nor the Russians are black. Perhaps living in urban America has something to do with it?

4 The budget for *Bamboozled* was $10 million, and for *She Hate Me* it was $8 million.

5 *Inside Man* grossed a bit more than $88.5 million domestically on a $45 million budget, although its worldwide earnings came to almost $185 million.

6 Historians estimate that between seven hundred and nine hundred black servicemen participated in the Iwo Jima battle, out of a total of thirty thousand troops (Colapinto).

7 *The Dirty Dozen* was directed by Robert Aldrich. *Home of the Brave*, a 1949 release produced by the liberal message-movie specialist Stanley Kramer, was directed by Mark Robson and written by Carl Foreman, based on Arthur Laurents's play. Lee presumably takes it as an exception to the omission of which he speaks.

FILMOGRAPHY

Student Films

Last Hustle in Brooklyn (1977)
Director: **Spike Lee**

The Answer (1980)
Director: **Spike Lee**
With: Ernest Rayford.
Production: New York University

Sarah (1981)
Director: **Spike Lee**
Production: New York University

Joe's Bed-Stuy Barbershop: We Cut Heads (1983)
Director: **Spike Lee**
Producers: **Spike Lee,** Zimmie Shelton
Screenplay: **Spike Lee**
Cinematography: Ernest R. Dickerson

Film editor: **Spike Lee**
Art director: Felix de Rooy
Music: Bill Lee
With: Monty Ross (Zack Homer), Donna Bailey (Ruth Homer), Stuart Smith (Thaddeus), Tommy Redmond Hicks (Nicholas Lovejoy), Horace Long (Joe Ballard), LaVerne Summer (Esquire), Africanus Rocius (Spinks), Robert Delbert (Fletcher)
Production: 40 Acres & A Mule Filmworks, New York University
Color, 60 min.

Theatrical Features

She's Gotta Have It (1986)
Director: **Spike Lee**
Producer: Shelton J. Lee (**Spike Lee**)
Screenplay: **Spike Lee**
Cinematography: Ernest Dickerson
Film editor: **Spike Lee**
Art director: Ron Paley
Production design: Wynn Thomas
Costume design: John Michael Reefer
Music: Bill Lee
With: Tracy Camilla Johns (Nola Darling), [Tommy] Redmond Hicks (Jamie Overstreet), John Canada Terrell (Greer Childs), Raye Dowell (Opal Gilstrap), Joie Lee (Clorinda Bradford), **Spike Lee** (Mars Blackmon), Bill Lee (Sonny Darling)
Production company: 40 Acres & A Mule Filmworks
B&W/Color, 84 min.

School Daze (1988)
Director: **Spike Lee**
Producer: **Spike Lee**

Screenplay: **Spike Lee**
Cinematography: Ernest Dickerson
Film editor: Barry Alexander Brown
Art director: Allan Trumpler
Production design: Wynn Thomas
Costume design: Ruthe Carter
Music: Bill Lee
With: Larry Fishburne (Dap Dunlap), Giancarlo Esposito (Julian "Big Brother Almighty" Eaves), Tisha Campbell (Jane Toussaint), Kyme (Rachel Meadows), Joe Seneca (President McPherson), Art Evans (Cedar Cloud), Ellen Holly (Odrie McPherson), Ossie Davis (Coach Odom), Bill Nunn (Grady), James Bond III (Monroe), Branford Marsalis (Jordan), Kadeem Hardison (Edge), Eric A. Payne (Booker T.), **Spike Lee** (Half-Pint), Joie Lee (Lizzie Life), Cinqué Lee (Buckwheat), Samuel L. Jackson (Leeds)
Production companies: 40 Acres & A Mule Filmworks, Columbia Pictures Corporation
Color, 121 min.

Do the Right Thing (1989)
Director: **Spike Lee**
Producer: **Spike Lee**
Screenplay: **Spike Lee**
Cinematography: Ernest Dickerson
Film editor: Barry Alexander Brown
Production design: Wynn Thomas
Costume design: Ruth Carter
Music: Bill Lee
With: Danny Aiello (Sal), Ossie Davis (Da Mayor), Ruby Dee (Mother Sister), Richard Edson (Vito), Giancarlo Esposito (Buggin Out), **Spike Lee** (Mookie), Bill Nunn (Radio Raheem), John Turturro (Pino), Paul Benjamin (ML),

Frankie Faison (Coconut Sid), Robin Harris (Sweet Dick Willie), Joie Lee (Jade), Miguel Sandoval (Officer Ponte), Rick Aiello (Officer Long), John Savage (Clifton), Rosie Perez (Tina), Sam Jackson (Mister Señor Love Daddy), Roger Guenveur Smith (Smiley), Martin Lawrence (Cee), Steve Park (Sonny)
Production company: 40 Acres & A Mule Filmworks
Color, 120 min.

Mo' Better Blues (1990)
Director: **Spike Lee**
Producer: **Spike Lee**
Screenplay: **Spike Lee**
Cinematography: Ernest Dickerson
Film editor: Sam Pollard
Production design: Wynn Thomas
Costume design: Ruth E. Carter
Music: Bill Lee
With: Denzel Washington (Bleek Gilliam), **Spike Lee** (Giant), Wesley Snipes (Shadow Henderson), Giancarlo Esposito (Left Hand Lacey), Robin Harris (Butterbean Jones), Joie Lee (Indigo Downes), Bill Nunn (Bottom Hammer), John Turturro (Moe Flatbush), Dick Anthony Williams (Big Stop Gilliam), Cynda Williams (Clarke Betancourt), Nicholas Turturro (Josh Flatbush), Jeff "Tain" Watts (Rhythm Jones), Samuel L. Jackson (Madlock), Leonard Thomas (Rod), Charles Q. Murphy (Eggy), Steve White (Born Knowledge), Rubèn Blades (Petey) Abbey Lincoln (Lillian Gilliam), Raye Dowell (Rita), Zakee L. Howze (Young Bleek/Miles)
Production companies: Universal Pictures, 40 Acres & A Mule Filmworks
Color, 130 min.

Jungle Fever (1991)
Director: **Spike Lee**
Producer: **Spike Lee**
Screenplay: **Spike Lee**
Cinematography: Ernest Dickerson
Film editor: Sam Pollard
Production design: Wynn Thomas
Costume design: Ruth E. Carter
Music: Stevie Wonder, Terence Blanchard
With: Wesley Snipes (Flipper Purify), Annabella Sciorra (Angie Tucci), **Spike Lee** (Cyrus), Ossie Davis (The Good Reverend Doctor Purify), Ruby Dee (Lucinda Purify), Samuel L. Jackson (Gator Purify), Lonette McKee (Drew), John Turturro (Paulie Carbone), Frank Vincent (Mike Tucci), Anthony Quinn (Lou Carbone), Halle Berry (Vivian), Tyra Ferrell (Orin Goode), Veronica Webb (Vera), Michael Imperioli (James Tucci), Nicholas Turturro (Vinny), Debi Mazar (Denise), Tim Robbins (Jerry), Brad Dourif (Leslie), Rick Aiello (Officer Long), Miguel Sandoval (Officer Ponte), Queen Latifa (Lashawn)
Production companies: 40 Acres & A Mule Filmworks, Universal Pictures
Color, 132 min.

Malcolm X (1992)
Director: **Spike Lee**
Producers: Marvin Worth, **Spike Lee**
Screenplay: Arnold Perl, **Spike Lee**; based on *The Autobiography of Malcolm X* as told to Alex Haley
Cinematography: Ernest Dickerson
Film editor: Barry Alexander Brown
Art director: Tom Warren
Production design: Wynn Thomas
Costume design: Ruth Carter

Music: Terence Blanchard
With: Denzel Washington (Malcolm X), Angela Bassett (Betty Shabazz), Albert Hall (Baines), Al Freeman Jr. (Elijah Muhammad), Delroy Lindo (West Indian Archie), **Spike Lee** (Shorty), Theresa Randle (Laura), Kate Vernon (Sophia), Lonette McKee (Louise Little), Tommy Hollis (Earl Little), James McDaniel (Brother Earl), Ernest Thomas (Sidney), Debi Mazar (Peg), Joe Seneca (Toomer), Wendell Pierce (Ben Thomas), Giancarlo Esposito (Thomas Hayer), Roger Guenveur Smith (Rudy), Shirley Stoler (Mrs. Swerlin), Raye Dowell (Sister Evelyn Williams), Zakee Howze (Young Malcolm), Vincent D'Onofrio (Bill Newman), Christopher Plummer (Chaplain Gill), Peter Boyle (Captain Green)
Production company: 40 Acres & A Mule Filmworks
Color, 202 min.

Crooklyn (1994)
Director: **Spike Lee**
Producer: **Spike Lee**
Screenplay: Cinqué Lee, Joie Susannah Lee, **Spike Lee**
Cinematography: Arthur Jafa
Film editor: Barry Alexander Brown
Art director: Chris Shriver
Production design: Wynn Thomas
Costume design: Ruth E. Carter
Music: Terence Blanchard
With: Alfre Woodard (Carolyn Carmichael), Delroy Lindo (Woody Carmichael), David Patrick Kelly (Tony Eyes/ Jim), Zelda Harris (Troy), Carlton Williams (Clinton), Sharif Rashed (Wendell), Tse-Mach Washington (Joseph), Christopher Knowings (Nate), José Zúñiga (Tommy La La), Isaiah Washington (Vic), Ivelka Reyes (Jessica), **Spike Lee** (Snuffy), Frances Foster (Aunt Song), Joie Susannah

Lee (Aunt Maxine), Vondie Curtis-Hall (Uncle Brown), Bokeem Woodbine (Richard), Tracy Vilar (Monica)
Production companies: 40 Acres & A Mule Filmworks, Child Hood Productions, Universal Pictures
Color, 115 min.

Clockers (1995)
Director: **Spike Lee**
Producers: Martin Scorsese, **Spike Lee**, Jon Kilik
Screenplay: Richard Price, **Spike Lee**; based on the novel *Clockers* by Richard Price
Cinematography: Malik Hassan Sayeed
Film editor: Sam Pollard
Art director: Tom Warren, Ina Mayhew
Production design: Andrew McAlpine
Costume design: Ruth Carter
Music: Terence Blanchard
With: Harvey Keitel (Rocco Klein), John Turturro (Larry Mazilli), Delroy Lindo (Rodney), Mekhi Phifer (Strike), Isaiah Washington (Victor), Keith David (Andre the Giant), Pee Wee Love (Tyrone), Regina Taylor (Iris Jeeter), Tom Byrd (Errol Barnes), Sticky Fingaz (Scientific), Fredro (Go), E.O. Nolasco (Horace), Lawrence B. Adisa (Stan), Hassan Johnson (Skills), Frances Foster (Gloria), Michael Imperioli (Jo-Jo), Lisa Arrindell Anderson (Sharon), Paul Calderon (Jesus at Hambones), Brendan Kelly (Big Chief), Mike Starr (Thumper), **Spike Lee** (Chucky)
Production companies: 40 Acres & A Mule Filmworks, Universal Pictures
Color, 128 min.

Girl 6 (1996)
Director: **Spike Lee**
Producer: **Spike Lee**

Screenplay: Suzan-Lori Parks
Cinematography: Malik Hassan Sayeed, John Corso
Film editor: Sam Pollard
Production design: Ina Mayhew
Costume design: Sandra Hernandez
Music: Prince
With: Theresa Randle (Girl 6), Isaiah Washington (Shoplifter), **Spike Lee** (Jimmy), Jenifer Lewis (Lil), Debi Mazar (Girl #39), Peter Berg (Bob), Michael Imperioli (Scary Caller #30), Naomi Campbell (Girl #75), Gretchen Mol (Girl #12), Richard Belzer (Caller #4), Madonna (Boss #3), John Turturro (Murray), Quentin Tarantino (Director #1), Ron Silver (Director #2), Joie Susannah Lee (Switchboard Operator), Halle Berry (herself), Susan Batson (Acting Coach), John Cameron Mitchell (Rob)
Production company: 40 Acres & A Mule Filmworks
Color, 108 min.

Get on the Bus (1996)
Director: **Spike Lee**
Producers: Rueben Cannon, Bill Borden, Barry Rosenbush
Screenplay: Reggie Rock Bythewood
Cinematography: Elliot Davis
Film editor: Leander T. Sales
Production design: Ina Mayhew
Costume design: Sandra Hernandez
Music: Terence Blanchard
With: Richard Belzer (Rick), DeAundre Bonds (Junior), Andre Braugher (Flip), Thomas Jefferson Byrd (Evan Thomas Sr.), Gabriel Casseus (Jamal), Albert Hall (Craig), Harry Lennix (Randall), Hill Harper (Xavier), Bernie Mac (Jay), Wendell Pierce (Wendell), Roger Guenveur Smith (Gary), Isaiah Washington (Kyle), Steve White (Mike),

Ossie Davis (Jeremiah), Charles S. Dutton (George), Joie
Lee (Jindai), Susan Batson (Dr. Cook)
Production companies: 15 Black Men, 40 Acres & A Mule
Filmworks
Color, 120 min.

He Got Game (1998)
Director: **Spike Lee**
Producers: Jon Kilik, **Spike Lee**
Screenplay: **Spike Lee**
Cinematography: Malik Hassan Sayeed
Film editor: Barry Alexander Brown
Art director: David Stein
Production design: Wynn Thomas
Costume design: Sandra Hernandez
Music: Aaron Copland
With: Denzel Washington (Jake Shuttlesworth), Ray Allen
(Jesus Shuttlesworth), Milla Jovovich (Dakota Burns),
Rosario Dawson (Lala Bonilla), Hill Harper (Coleman
"Booger" Sykes), Bill Nunn (Uncle Bubba), Ned Beatty
(Warden Wyatt), Jim Brown (Spivey), Thomas Jefferson
Byrd (Sweetness), Roger Guenveur Smith (Big Time
Willie), Lonette McKee (Martha Shuttlesworth), Zelda
Harris (Mary Shuttlesworth), Joseph Lyle Taylor (Crudup),
Michele Shay (Aunt Sally), John Turturro (Coach Billy
Sunday), Arthur J. Nascarella (Coach Cincotta), Travis
Best (Sip), Walter McCarty (Mance), John Wallace
(Lonnie), Rick Fox (Chick Deagan), Al Palagonia (Dom
Pagnotti), D'Andre Mackie (Leonard Roberts), Saul Stein
(Prison Guard Books), Ron Cephas Jones (Prison Guard
Burwell), Jade Yorker (Jesus Shuttlesworth – Age 12),
Shortee Red (Booger – Age 12), Coach Dean Smith (him-
self), Coach Lute Olson (himself), Coach John Chaney
(himself), Coach John Thompson (himself), Coach Roy

Williams (himself), Coach Nolan Richardson (himself), Coach Denny Crum (himself), Coach Tom Davis (himself), Coach Clem Haskins (himself), Coach George Karl (himself), Coach Jim Boeheim (himself), Coach Rick Pitino (himself), Coach Robert "Bobby" Cremins (himself), Dick Vitale (himself), Bill Walton (himself), Shaquille O'Neal (himself), Reggie Miller (himself), Charles Barkley (himself), Scottie Pippen (himself), Michael Jordan (himself), Robin Roberts (himself)
Production companies: 40 Acres & A Mule Filmworks, Touchstone Pictures
Color, 136 min.

Summer of Sam (1999)
Director: **Spike Lee**
Producers: Jon Kilik, **Spike Lee**
Screenplay: Victor Colicchio, Michael Imperioli, **Spike Lee**
Cinematography: Ellen Kuras
Film editor: Barry Alexander Brown
Art director: Nicholas Lundy
Production design: Thérèse DePrez
Costume design: Ruth E. Carter
Music: Terence Blanchard
With: John Leguizamo (Vinny), Adrien Brody (Ritchie), Mira Sorvino (Dionna), Jennifer Esposito (Ruby), Anthony LaPaglia (Detective Lou Petrocelli), Bebe Neuwirth (Gloria), Patti LuPone (Helen), Ben Gazzara (Luigi), John Savage (Simon), Michael Badalucco (Son of Sam), Michael Rispoli (Joey T), Mike Starr (Eddie), Roger Guenveur Smith (Detective Curt Atwater), Saverio Guerra (Woodstock), Brian Tarantina (Bobby Del Fiore), Jimmy Breslin (himself), Al Palagonia (Anthony), Joe Lisi (Tony Olives), James Reno (Crony), Arthur Nascarella (Mario), Michael Imperioli (Midnite), Ken Garito (Brian),

Spike Lee (John Jeffries), Reggie Jackson (himself), Bill Raymond (Father Cadilli)
Production company: 40 Acres & A Mule Filmworks
Color, 142 min.

Bamboozled (2000)
Director: **Spike Lee**
Producers: Jon Kilik, **Spike Lee**
Screenplay: **Spike Lee**
Cinematography: Ellen Kuras
Film editor: Sam Pollard
Art director: Harry Darrow
Production design: Victor Kempster
Costume design: Ruth Carter
Music: Terence Blanchard
With: Damon Wayans (Pierre Delacroix), Savion Glover (Manray), Jada Pinkett-Smith (Sloan Hopkins), Tommy Davidson (Womack), Michael Rapaport (Thomas Dunwitty), Thomas Jefferson Byrd (Honeycutt), Paul Mooney (Junebug), Sarah Jones (Dot), Gillian Iliana Waters (Verna), Susan Batson (Orchid Dothan), Mos Def (Julius Hopkins), Johnnie L. Cochran Jr. (himself), Rev. Al Sharpton (himself), Matthew Modine (himself), Mira Sorvino (herself),
Production company: 40 Acres & A Mule Filmworks
Color, 135 min.

25th Hour (2002)
Director: **Spike Lee**
Producers: Tobey Maguire, Julia Chasman, **Spike Lee**, Jon Kilik
Screenplay: David Benioff; based on the novel *The 25th Hour* by David Benioff
Cinematography: Rodrigo Prieto

Film editor: Barry Alexander Brown
Art director: Nicholas Lundy
Production design: James Chinlund
Costume design: Sandra Hernandez
Music: Terence Blanchard
With: Edward Norton (Monty Brogan), Philip Seymour
Hoffman (Jacob Elinsky), Barry Pepper (Francis Xavier
Slaughtery), Rosario Dawson (Naturelle Riviera), Anna
Paquin (Mary D'Annunzio), Brian Cox (James Brogan)
Production companies: 25th Hour Productions, 40 Acres & A
Mule Filmworks, Gamut Films, Industry Entertainment,
Touchstone Pictures
Color, 135 min.

She Hate Me (2004)
Director: **Spike Lee**
Producers: Preston Holmes, **Spike Lee,** Fernando Sulichin
Screenplay: Michael Genet, **Spike Lee**; story by Michael
Genet
Cinematography: Matthew Libatique
Film editor: Barry Alexander Brown
Production design: Brigitte Broch
Costume design: Donna Berwick
Music: Terence Blanchard
With: Anthony Mackie (John Henry "Jack" Armstrong),
Kerry Washington (Fatima Goodrich), Ellen Barkin
(Margo Chadwick), Monica Bellucci (Simona Bonasera),
Jim Brown (Geronimo Armstrong), Ossie Davis (Judge
Buchanan), Jamel Debbouze (Doak), Brian Dennehy
(Chairman Billy Church), Woody Harrelson (Leland
Powell), Bai Ling (Oni), Lonette McKee (Lottie
Armstrong), Paula Jai Parker (Evelyn), Q-Tip (Vada
Huff), Dania Ramirea (Alex Guerrero), John Turturro
(Don Angelo Bonasera), Chiwetel Ejiofor (Frank Wills),

Sarita Choudhury (Song), Joie Lee (Gloria Reid), Michael Genet (Jamal Armstrong)
Production companies: 40 Acres & A Mule Filmworks, Rule 8
Color, 138 min.

Inside Man (2006)
Director: **Spike Lee**
Producer: Brian Grazer
Screenplay: Russell Gewirtz
Cinematography: Matthew Libatique
Film editor: Barry Alexander Brown
Art director: Chris Shriver
Production design: Wynn Thomas
Costume design: Donna Berwick
Music: Terence Blanchard
With: Denzel Washington (Detective Keith Frazier), Clive Owen (Dalton Russell), Jodie Foster (Madeleine White), Christopher Plummer (Arthur Case), Willem Dafoe (Captain John Darius), Chiwetel Ejiofor (Detective Bill Mitchell), Carlos Andrés Gómez (Steve), Kim Director (Stevie), James Ransome (Steve-O), Bernard Rachelle (Chaim), Peter Gerety (Captain Coughlin)
Production companies: Universal Pictures, Imagine Entertainment, 40 Acres & A Mule Filmworks, GH Two
Color, 129 min.

Miracle at St. Anna (2008)
Director: **Spike Lee**
Producers: Roberto Cicutto, **Spike Lee**, Luigi Musini
Screenplay: James McBride; based on *Miracle at St. Anna* by James McBride
Cinematography: Matthew Libatique
Film editor: Barry Alexander Brown
Art directors: Carlo Serafini, Donato Tieppo

Production design: Tonino Zera
Costume design: Carlo Poggioli
Music: Terence Blanchard
With: Laz Alonso (Corporal Hector Negron), Derek Luke (Staff Sergeant Aubrey Stamps), Omar Benson Miller (Private First Class Sam Train), Michael Ealy (Sergeant Bishop Cummings), Pierfrancesco Favino (Peppi Grotta), Valentina Cervi (Renata), John Turturro (Detective Tony Ricci), Joseph Gordon-Levitt (Tim Boyle), John Leguizamo (Enrico), Kerry Washington (Zana Wilder), Walton Goggins (Captin Nokes), Christian Berkel (Captain Eichholz), Waldemar Kobus (Colonel Pflueger), Omero Antonutti (Ludovico), Robert John Burke (General Ned Almond), John Hawkes (Herb Redneck), Alexandra Maria Lara (Axis Sally), D.B. Sweeney (Colonel Driscoll)
Production companies: 40 Acres & A Mule Filmworks, On My Own, Rai Cinema, Touchstone Pictures
Color, 160 min.

Red Hook Summer (2012)
Director: **Spike Lee**
Producer: **Spike Lee**
Screenplay: James McBride, **Spike Lee**
Cinematography: Kerwin Devonish
Film editor: Hye Mee Na
Art director: Sila Karakaya
Production design: Sarah Frank
Costume design: Emilio Sosa
Music: Bruce Hornsby; Hammond B-3 organ music by Jonathan Batiste
With: Clarke Peters (Da Good Bishop Enoch Rouse), Jules Brown (Flik Royale), Toni Lysaith (Chazz Morningstar), Nate Parker (Box), James Ransome (Kevin), Thomas

Jefferson Byrd (Deacon Zee), Heather Alicia Simms (Sister Sharon Morningstar), Colman Domingo (Blessing Rowe), Tracy Camilla Johns (Mother Darling), **Spike Lee** (Mr. Mookie), Daniel Breaker (Cliff)
Production company: 40 Acres & A Mule Filmworks
Color, 121 min.

Oldboy (In Production)
Director: **Spike Lee**
Producers: Doug Davison, Roy Lee, **Spike Lee**
Screenplay: Mark Protosevich; based on the manga by Garon Tsuchiya and Nobuaki Minegishi
With: Josh Brolin (Joe Douchett), Sharlto Copley (Adrian Price)
Production companies: 40 Acres & A Mule Filmworks, Good Universe, Mandate Pictures, Vertigo Entertainment

Television, Performance Films, Miscellaneous Projects
Untitled Segment in *Lumière and Company* (1995; Anthology Film Segment)
Director: **Spike Lee**
Producers: Neal Edelstein, Fabienne Servan-Schreiber
Writer: **Spike Lee**
With: Satchel Lee
Production companies: Cinétevé, La Sept-Arts, Igeldo Komunikazioa, Søren Stærmose AB
B&W, 54 sec.

4 Little Girls (1997; Feature Documentary)
Director: **Spike Lee**
Producers: **Spike Lee**, Sam Pollard
Cinematography: Ellen Kuras
Film editor: Sam Pollard
Music: Terence Blanchard

With: Maxine McNair, Chris McNair, Helen Pegues, Queen Nunn, Arthur Hanes Jr., Howell Raines, Harold McNair, Carole C. Smitherman Esq., Fred Lee Shuttlesworth, Rev. Andrew Young, George Wallace, Nicholas Katzenbach, Ossie Davis, Coretta Scott King, Walter Cronkite, Bill Cosby, Rev. Jesse L. Jackson Sr., Rev. Reggie White
Production companies: 40 Acres & A Mule Filmworks, Home Box Office
Color, 102 min.

They Don't Care About Us (1997; Music Video in Compilation *Michael Jackson: HIStory on Film – Volume II*
Director: **Spike Lee**
Producer: Butch Robinson
Music: Michael Jackson
With: Michael Jackson
Production company: MJJ Productions
Color/B&W, 7 min.

Freak (1998; TV Movie)
Director: **Spike Lee**
Producer: Denis Biggs
Writers: John Leguizamo, David Bar Katz; based on the Broadway production *Freak* by John Leguizamo
Cinematography: Malik Hassan Sayeed
Film editor: Barry Alexander Brown
Production design: Wendell K. Harrington
With: John Leguizamo (himself)
Production company: Lower East Side Films
Color, 89 min.

Pavarotti & Friends for the Children of Liberia (1998; Documentary for TV Series *Great Performances*)

Director: **Spike Lee**
Film editor: David Greenwald
With: Luciano Pavarotti, Jon Bon Jovi, Natalie Cole Vanessa
  Williams, Stevie Wonder, Zucchero, **Spike Lee**
Production companies: British Broadcasting Corporation,
  Public Broadcasting Service, Radiotelevisione Italiana
Color, 105 min.

Pavarotti & Friends 99 for Guatemala and Kosovo (1999;
  TV Documentary)
Director: **Spike Lee**
Executive producer: Andrea Mazzoni
Film editor: David Greenwald
Production design: Luigi Dell'Aglio
Music director: Silvia Rossi
With: Luciano Pavarotti, Mariah Carey, Joe Cocker, Celine
  Dion, Gloria Estefan, B.B. King, Robbie Kondor, Ricky
  Martin, Jose Molina, Lionel Richie, the Spice Girls, Stevie
  Wonder, Zucchero
Color, 99 min.

The Original Kings of Comedy (2000; Feature Documentary)
Director: **Spike Lee**
Producers: David Gale, Walter Latham, **Spike Lee**
Writers: Cedric the Entertainer, Steve Harvey, D.L.
  Hughley, Bernie Mac
Cinematography: Malik Sayeed
Film editor: Barry Alexander Brown
Art director: Tom Warren
Production design: Wynn P. Thomas
Costume design: Denise Marsh
Music: Nelly
With: Steve Harvey (himself), D.L. Hughley (himself),
  Cedric the Entertainer (himself), Bernie Mac (himself)

Production companies: 40 Acres & A Mule Filmworks, Latham
  Entertainment, MTV Films
Color, 115 min.

Fight the Power (2000; Video in Video Compilation *And Ya
  Don't Stop: Hip Hop's Greatest Videos, Vol. 1*)
Director: **Spike Lee**
Cinematography: Ernest R. Dickerson
Music: Public Enemy
With: Public Enemy (themselves), Tawana Brawley
  (herself)
Production company: 40 Acres & A Mule Filmworks
Color, 5 min.

The Making of Bamboozled (2001; Video Documentary)
Directors: **Spike Lee**, Samuel D. Pollard
Producer: Samuel D. Pollard
Cinematography: Dylan Verrechia
Film editor: Tish Giffoni
With: Budd Schulberg, Clyde Taylor, Jack Newfield, Stanley
  Crouch, Thomas Jefferson Byrd, Tommy Davidson,
  Savion Glover, Jada Pinkett Smith, Michael Rapaport,
  Damon Wayans, Judy Aley, Victor Kempster, Sam
  Pollard, Ellen Kuras, **Spike Lee**
Production companies: Luna Ray Films, Lyrical Knockout
  Entertainment
Color, 53 min.

A Huey P. Newton Story (2001; TV Documentary)
Director: **Spike Lee**
Producers: Steven Adams, Bob L. Johnson, Marc Henry
  Johnson
Screenplay: Roger Guenveur Smith; based on the play *A Huey
  P. Newton Story* by Roger Guenveur Smith

Cinematography: Ellen Kuras
Film editor: Barry Alexander Brown
Production design: Wynn Thomas
Costume design: Toni-Leslie James
Music: Marc Anthony Thompson
With: Roger Guenveur Smith (Huey P. Newton)
Color, 86 min.

Come Rain or Come Shine (2001; Documentary Short in
    TV Show **The Concert for New York City**)
Director: **Spike Lee**
Producer: Paul Flattery
Art director: Anne Brahic
Production design: Keith Raywood
Production company: VH1 Television

Jim Brown: All American (2002; TV documentary)
Director: **Spike Lee**
Producer: **Spike Lee**
Cinematography: Ellen Kuras
Film editors: Mark Fason
Music: Terence Blanchard
With: Jim Brown, Art Modell, John Wooten, Joe Frazier,
    Hank Aaron, Karen Brown Ward, Kim Brown, Jim N.
    Brown Jr., Amber Ward, Brandon Well, Chief Oren
    Lyons, Ed Walsh, Dr. Walter Beach, Aris Dallas Brown,
    Monique Brown, Kevin Brown, Raquel Welch, Oliver
    Stone, Bernie Casey, Phil Gersh, Fred "The Hammer"
    Williamson, Stella Stevens, Paul Warfield, James Toback,
    Johnnie L. Cochran Jr., Melvin Van Peebles, Donald
    Bogle
Production companies: 40 Acres & A Mule Filmworks, HBO
    Sports
Color, 140 min.

We Wuz Robbed (2002; Short Film in Anthology Film *Ten Minutes Older: The Trumpet*)
Director: **Spike Lee**
Producer: **Spike Lee**
Cinematography: Chris Norr
Film editor: Barry Alexander Brown
With: Michael Feldman, Nick Baldick, Mike Whouley, David Morehouse, Carter Eskew, Dandra Sobieraj, Donna Brazile, Frank Hunger
Production company: Showtime Networks
B&W/Color, 10 min.

Sucker Free City (2004; TV Movie)
Director: **Spike Lee**
Producer: Preston Holmes
Writer: Alex Tse
Cinematography: Cesar R. Charlone
Film editor: Barry Alexander Brown
Art director: Liba Daniels
Production design: Kitty Doris-Bates
Music: Terence Blanchard
With: Ben Crowley (Nick Wade), Ken Leung (Lincoln Ma), Anthony Mackie (K-Luv), Darris Love (Sleepy), Laura Allen (Samantha Wade), T.V. Carpio (Angela Tsing), Malieek Straughter (Leon), John Savage (Anderson Wade), Kathy Baker (Cleo Wade), James Hong (Kwok), George Cheung (Mr. Tsing), Marguerite Moreau (Jessica Epstein), Artimus Lamont Bentley (Ahmir), Ewan Chung (Edwin Leong), Omari Hardwick (Dante Ponce), Judy Pace (Mama June), Eyal Podell (Stephan Cashen), Stanford Chase (Peter Wu), Emilio Rivera (Detective Zepada), Reynaldo Rosales (Devon), Shay Roundtree (Bonnie), Sam Sarpong (Cue), Eddie Shin (Michael), Avery Kidd Waddell (Yardell), Jim Brown (Don Strickland)

Production company: 40 Acres & A Mule Filmworks
Color, 113 min.

New Charlie and **Bond of Brothers** (2005; Episodes 1 and 6
  of Six-Part TV Mini-series **Miracle's Boys**)
Director: **Spike Lee**
Producer: Leslie D. Farrell
Writers: Kevin Arkadie, Stephen Langford, Dawn Urbont;
  based on the novel *Miracle's Boys* by Jacqueline Woodson
Cinematography: Cliff Charles
Film editor: K.A. Chisholm
Art director: JoAnn Vara
Production design: Ronald L. Norsworthy
Costume design: Donna Berwick
Music: Bud'da
With: Pooch Hall (Ty'ree Bailey), Sean Nelson (Charlie
  Bailey), Julito McCullum (Lafayette Bailey), George Alvarez
  (Discipio), Karole Foreman (Viv), Alexis Iacono (Teacher),
  Kevin Jiggetts (Detective Broadus), Yvonna Kopacz
  (Wilma), Ernest Dancy (Arthur), Doctor Dré (Jinxy Jam)
Production companies: Feralfilms LLC, MTV Networks,
  On-Screen Entertainment
Color

Jesus Children of America (2005; Short in Anthology Film
  All the Invisible Children)
Director: **Spike Lee**
Producers: Mike Ellis, **Spike Lee**
Writers: Cinqué Lee, Joie Lee
Cinematography: Cliff Charles
Film editor: Barry Alexander Brown
Art director: Sarah Frank
Production design: Sarah Frank
Costume design: Donna Berwick

Music: Terence Blanchard
With: Hannah Hodson (Blanca), Coati Mundi (Eneba), Rosie Perez (Ruthie), Natalia Roldan (Lourdes), Andre Royo (Sammy), Charles Socarides (Jim), Robin Taylor (Mike)
Production company: 40 Acres & A Mule Filmworks
Color, 20 min.

When the Levees Broke: A Requiem in Four Acts (2006; Two-Part TV Documentary)
Director: **Spike Lee**
Producer: **Spike Lee**, Samuel D. Pollard
Cinematography: Cliff Charles
Film editors: Barry Alexander Brown, Geeta Gandbhir, Nancy Novack, Samuel D. Pollard
Music: Terence Blanchard
With: Harry Belafonte, Terence Blanchard, Douglas Brinkley, Michael Eric Dyson, Phyllis Montana LeBlanc, Wynton Marsalis, Ray Nagin, Soledad O'Brien, Sean Penn, Wendell Pierce, Al Sharpton, Kanye West, Anderson Cooper, **Spike Lee**, Mike Myers
Production companies: 40 Acres & A Mule Filmworks, Home Box Office
Color, 255 min.

Untitled Pilot for **Shark** (2006; TV Series Episode)
Director: **Spike Lee**
Producers: Robert Del Valle, Robin Gurney
Screenplay: Ian Biederman
Cinematography: Ivan Strasburg
Film editor: Barry Alexander Brown, David C. Cook
Art director: Cat Smith
Production design: Suzuki Ingerslev
Costume design: Ruth Carter
Music: Sean Callery

With: James Woods (Sebastian Stark), Danielle Panabaker (Julie Stark), Sophina Brown (Raina Troy), Sarah Carter (Madeleine Poe), Alexis Cruz (Martin Allende), Sam Page (Casey Woodland), Carlos Gomez (Mayor Manuel Delgado), Melissa Leo (Elizabeth Rourke)
Production companies: Imagine Television, Deforestation Services, 20th Century Fox Television
Color, 42 min.

M.O.N.Y. (2007; TV Movie)
Director: **Spike Lee**
Executive producers: Jim Finnerty, Tom Fontana, Barry Levinson
Writers: Barry Levinson, Tom Fontana
Cinematography: Phil Abraham
Film editor: Barry Alexander Brown
Costume design: Tina Nigro
With: Bobby Cannavale (Joe Capanelli), Carmen Ejogo (Francine Tyson), Arian Moayed (Ates Kiliclioglu), Amy Ryan (Marcie Futterman)
Production companies: The Levinson/Fontana Company, NBC Studios, NBC Universal Television
Color

Lovers & Haters (2007; Short)
Director: **Spike Lee**
Executive producers: Mariah Carey, Benny Medina
With: Mariah Carey (herself), Tommy Cella (Club Patron), Ivonnah Erskine (Mariah's Friend), Brooklyn Freed (Blond Hater), Maya Gilbert (Lover), Kali Hawk (The One), Britten Kelley (Hater), Trystan Angel Reese (Gayer Club Goer)
Production company: 40 Acres & A Mule Filmworks
Color, 15 min.

Passing Strange (2009; Episode for TV Series *Great Performances*)
Director: **Spike Lee**
Producers: Steve Klein, **Spike Lee**, Elizabeth Ireland McCann
Writer: Stew; based on the Broadway musical *Passing Strange* by Stew
Cinematography: Matthew Libatique
Film editor: Barry Alexander Brown
Production design: David Korins
Costume design: Elizabeth Hope Clancy
Music: Heidi Rodewald, Stew
With: Stew (Narrator), Daniel Breaker (Youth), Elisa Davis (Mother), Chad Goodridge (Reverend Jones/Terry/Christophe/Hugo), Rebecca Naomi Jones (Sherry/Renata/Desi), Colman Domingo (Mr. Franklin/Joop/Mr. Venus), De'Adre Aziza (Edwina/Marianna/Sudabey)
Production companies: 40 Acres & A Mule Filmworks, Apple Core Holdings, The Shubert Organization
Color, 135 min.

Kobe Doin' Work (2009; TV Documentary)
Director: **Spike Lee**
Producer: **Spike Lee**
Cinematography: Matthew Libatique
Film editor: Barry Alexander Brown
Music: Bruce Hornsby
With: Kobe Bryant, Lamar Odom, Tony Parker, Pau Gasol, Phil Jackson, Michele Tafoya, Tim Duncan, Derek Fisher
Production companies: 40 Acres & A Mule Filmworks, ESPN Films
Color, 84 min.

If God Is Willing and da Creek Don't Rise (2010; TV Documentary)

Director: **Spike Lee**
Producers: Sam Pollard, **Spike Lee**
Cinematography: Cliff Charles
Film editors: Sam Pollard, Geeta Gandbhir
Music: Terence Blanchard
With: Phyllis Montana LeBlanc, Deuce McAllister, Rita Benson LeBlanc, Calvin Mackie PhD, Garland Robinette, Mitch Landrieu, Terence Blanchard, C. Ray Nagin, Dr. Louis Cataldie, Jacques Morial, Douglas Brinkley, John Barry, Ned Sublette, Anderson Cooper, Brad Pitt, Sean Penn, Wendell Pierce, Rene Preval, Soledad O'Brien, Henry Waxman, Haley Barbour, Mary Landrieu, Arne Duncan, Scott Walker, Dr. John, Bobby Jindal, Ken Salazar, James Carville, Mary Matalin, John Kerry, Eric Holder Jr.
Production companies: 40 Acres & A Mule Filmworks, HBO Documentary Films
Color, 259 min.

Da Brick (2011; TV Movie)
Director: **Spike Lee**
Executive producers: Doug Ellin, **Spike Lee**, Jim Lefkowitz, John Ridley, Mike Tyson
Writer: John Ridley
Cinematography: Malik Hassan Sayeed
Art director: Henry Dunn
Production design: Sarah Frank
Costume design: Donna Berwick
With: John Boyega (Donnie), Kim Brockington (Belinda), Niesha Butler (Kateal), Albert M. Chan (Tim), Mario D'Leon, (Jaci) Kam Dabrowski (Petya), Ilfrenesh Hadera (Saalinge), Rosie Perez (Annalisse)
Production company: HBO Entertainment
Color

Untitled Michael Jackson/*Bad* Documentary (In production; Documentary)
Director: **Spike Lee**
Executive producers: John Branca, John McClain
Music: Michael Jackson
With: Martin Scorsese, Mariah Carey, Kanye West, Quincy Jones, Cee-Lo, Sheryl Crow, Ahmir-Khalib Thompson, Vincent Paterson
Production company: 40 Acres & A Mule Filmworks

REFERENCES

Aftab, Kaleem (2005) *Spike Lee: That's My Story and I'm Sticking to It.* New York: W.W. Norton & Company.

Alighieri, Dante (1949) *The Divine Comedy – 1: Hell*, trans. Dorothy L. Sayers. New York: Penguin Books.

Allon, Janet (2004) "Tonya's Time." *Avenue* (November). http://tonyalewislee.org/avenue_article.html (accessed July 12, 2012).

Anderson, Tammy L. (2008) "Cocaine and Crack," in Vincent N. Parrillo, ed., *Encyclopedia of Social Problems.* Thousand Oaks, CA: SAGE Publications, pp. 136–7.

Ansen, David (1990, August 6) "Spike Lee Almost Blows It." *Newsweek*, vol. 116, no. 6, p. 62.

Ansen, David (1991, April 25) "The Battle for Malcolm X." *Newsweek.* http://www.thedailybeast.com/newsweek/1991/08/25/the-battle-for-malcolm-x.html (accessed July 12, 2012).

Ansen, David (1992, November 15) "From Sinner to Martyr: A Man of Many Faces." *Newsweek.* http://www.thedaily

beast.com/newsweek/1992/11/15/from-sinner-to-martyr-a-man-of-many-faces.html (accessed July 12, 2012).

Aubry, Erin J. (1999, June 30) "Summer of Spike." *LA Weekly*. http://www.laweekly.com/1999-07-08/film-tv/su mmer-of-spike/ (accessed July 12, 2012).

Beauford, Fred (1988) "Spike Lee's *School Daze*." *The Crisis*, no. 95, pp. 6–7.

Berger, Carol (1992, February 10) "Spike Lee's Hot Potato: Director Treads Carefully with *Malcolm X*." *The Christian Science Monitor*. http://www.csmonitor.com/1992/0210/10101.html (accessed July 12, 2012).

Blake, John (2010, May 19) "Malcolm and Martin, Closer Than We Ever Thought." *CNN Living*. http://articles.cnn.com/2010-05-19/living/Malcolmx.king_1_martin-malcolm-blue-eyed-devils-dr-king?_s=PM:LIVING (accessed July 12, 2012).

Bobo, Jacqueline (1991) "'The Subject is Money': Reconsidering the Black Film Audience as a Theoretical Paradigm." *Black American Literature Forum*, vol. 25, no. 2, pp. 421–32.

Bradley, David (1995, September 10) "Spike Lee's Inferno, the Drug Underworld." *New York Times*. http://part ners.nytimes.com/library/film/091095lee-clockers-essay.h tml (accessed July 12, 2012).

Brown, Bill (2006) "Reification, Reanimation, and the American Uncanny." *Critical Inquiry*, vol. 32, no. 2, pp. 175–207.

Brown, Georgia, and Taubin, Amy (1995, September 19) "Clocking In: Two Critics Rate Spike Lee's Ultimate Hood Movie," *Village Voice*, pp. 71, 76.

Brown, Patricia Leigh (1990, November 15) "A Film-in-Progress on a Black Architect." *New York Times*. http://www.nytimes.com/1990/11/15/garden/currents-a-film-in-prog ress-on-a-black-architect.html (accessed July 12, 2012).

Bruckner, D.J.R. (1986, August 8) "Film: Spike Lee's *She's Gotta Have It.*" *New York Times.* http://movies.nytimes. com/movie/review?res=9A0DEFDF143CF93BA3575BC0 A96094826 (accessed July 12, 2012).

BU Center for Remote Sensing (1997) "Million Man March." http://www.bu.edu/remotesensing/research/completed/million-man-march/ (accessed July 12, 2012).

Canby, Vincent (1992, November 18) "*Malcolm X*, as Complex as Its Subject." *New York Times.* http://www.nytimes.com/1992/11/18/movies/review-film-malcolm-x-as-complex-as-its-subject.html?pagewanted=all&src=pm (accessed July 12, 2012).

Christensen, Jerome (1991) "Spike Lee, Corporate Populist." *Critical Inquiry*, vol. 17, no. 3, pp. 582–95.

Chronopoulos, Themis (2011) *Spatial Regulation in New York City: From Urban Renewal to Zero Tolerance.* New York: Routledge.

Colapinto, John (2008, September 22) "Outside Man: Spike Lee's Celluloid Struggles." *New Yorker.* http://www.newyorker.com/reporting/2008/09/22/080922fa_fact_colapinto (accessed July 12, 2012).

Corliss, Richard (1989, July 3) "Hot Time in Bed-Stuy Tonight," *Time*, vol. 134, no. 1, pp. 62–3.

Crouch, Stanley (1989, June 20) "Do the Race Thing: Spike Lee's Afro-Fascist Chic." *Village Voice*, pp. 73–4, 76.

Crowdus, Gary, and Georgakas, Dan (1993) "Our Film Is Only a Starting Point: An Interview with Spike Lee," in Cynthia Fuchs, ed., *Spike Lee: Interviews.* Jackson: University Press of Mississippi, 2002, pp. 65–78.

Daileader, Celia R. (2005) *Racism, Misogyny, and the Othello Myth: Inter-racial Couples from Shakespeare to Spike Lee.* Cambridge, UK: Cambridge University Press.

Dawson, Jeff (2008, June 5) "Dirty Harry comes clean."

Guardian. http://www.guardian.co.uk/film/2008/jun/06/1 (accessed July 12, 2012).

Denby, David (1992) "Spike Lee Vows to Do the Right Thing with an epic *Malcolm X.*" *New York,* vol. 25, no. 36, pp. 50–1.

DeSantis, John (1991) *For the Color of His Skin: The Murder of Yusuf Hawkins and the Trial of Bensonhurst.* New York: Pharos Books.

Dixon, Wheeler Winston (1989) "Urban Black American Music in the 1980s: The 'Word' as Cultural Signifier." *Midwest Quarterly,* vol. 30, no. 2, pp. 229–41.

Doherty, Thomas (1989–90) "*Do the Right Thing.*" *Film Quarterly,* vol. 43, no. 2, pp. 35–40.

Dyson, Michael Eric (1993) *Reflecting Black: African-American Cultural Criticism.* Minneapolis: University of Minnesota Press.

Ebert, Roger (1988, February 12) "*School Daze.*" *Chicago Sun-Times.* http://rogerebert.suntimes.com/apps/pbcs.dll/article?AID=/19880212/REVIEWS/802120303 (accessed July 12, 2012).

Ebert, Roger (1991, June 7) "*Jungle Fever.*" *Chicago Sun-Times.* http://rogerebert.suntimes.com/apps/pbcs.dll/article?AID=/19910607/REVIEWS/106070305 (accessed July 12, 2012).

Ebert, Roger (1992, November 18) "*Malcolm X.*" *Chicago Sun-Times.* http://rogerebert.suntimes.com/apps/pbcs.dll/article?AID=/19921118/REVIEWS/211180301/1023 (accessed July 12, 2012).

Ebert, Roger (1994, August 5) "A Family Tree Grows in Spike Lee's *Crooklyn.*" *Chicago Sun-Times.* http://rogerebert.suntimes.com/apps/pbcs.dll/article?AID=/19940805/PEOPLE/55010320/1023 (accessed July 12, 2012).

Ebert, Roger (1996, March 22) "*Girl 6.*" *Chicago Sun-Times.* http://rogerebert.suntimes.com/apps/pbcs.dll/article?AID

=/19960322/REVIEWS/603220303/1023 (accessed July 12, 2012).

Ebert, Roger (2000, October 6) "*Bamboozled.*" *Chicago Sun-Times.* http://rogerebert.suntimes.com/apps/pbcs.dll/arti cle?AID=/20001006/REVIEWS/10060301/1023 (accessed July 12, 2012).

Ebert, Roger (2004, August 6) "*She Hate Me.*" *Chicago Sun-Times.* http://rogerebert.suntimes.com/apps/pbcs. dll/article?AID=/20040806/REVIEWS/408060304/1023 (accessed July 12, 2012).

Edelstein, David (2002, December 19) "Back Door Blues: What Spike Lee's *25th Hour* is Really About." *Slate.* http://www.slate.com/articles/arts/movies/2002/12/back_door_ blues.html (accessed July 12, 2012).

Eliot, Marc (2008) *Song of Brooklyn: An Oral History of America's Favorite Borough.* New York: Broadway Books.

Farrakhan, Louis (1995, October 17) "Minister Farrakhan Challenges Black Men: Transcript from Minister Louis Farrakhan's Remarks at the Million Man March." *CNN.* http://www-cgi.cnn.com/US/9510/megamarch/10-16/tran script/ (accessed July 12, 2012).

Fine, Elizabeth C. (1991) "Stepping, Saluting, Cracking, and Freaking: The Cultural Politics of African-American Step Shows." *Drama Review*, vol. 35, no. 2, pp. 39–59.

Fine, Marshall (1991) *Bloody Sam: The Life and Films of Sam Peckinpah.* New York: Donald I. Fine.

Foucault, Michel (1979) *Discipline and Punish: The Birth of the Prison*, trans. Alan Sheridan. New York: Vintage Books.

Freedman, Samuel G. (1991, June 2) "Love and Hate in Black and White." *New York Times.* http://movies. nytimes.com/movie/review?res=9D0CE7D81438F931A35 755C0A967958260 (accessed July 12, 2012).

Gabbard, Krin (1992) "Signifyin(g) the Phallus: *Mo' Better*

Blues and Representations of the Jazz Trumpet." *Cinema Journal*, vol. 32, no. 1, pp. 43–62.

Gilmer, Marcus (2004) "The Controversy of Race in Spike Lee's *Bamboozled*." *Not Coming to a Theater Near You*. http://notcoming.com/features/bamboozled/ (accessed July 12, 2012).

Gitlin, Todd (1987) *The Sixties: Years of Hope, Days of Rage*. New York: Bantam Books.

Gleiberman, Owen (1990, August 3) "*Mo' Better Blues*." *Entertainment Weekly*, no. 25. http://www.ew.com/ew/article/0,,3 17864,00.html (accessed July 12, 2012).

Gleiberman, Owen (1992, November 20) "*Malcolm X*." *Entertainment Weekly*, no. 145. http://www.ew.com/ew/article/0,,312418,00.html (accessed July 12, 2012).

Goodman, Paul (1962) "Natural Violence," in Paul Goodman, *Drawing the Line*. New York: Random House, pp. 24–8. (Originally in Paul Goodman, *The May Pamphlet*, Spring 1945.)

Gorbman, Claudia (1987) *Unheard Melodies: Narrative Film Music*. Bloomingdale: Indiana University Press.

Guerrero, Ed (1991) "Black Film: Mo' Better in the '90s." *Black Camera*, vol. 6, no. 1, pp. 2–3.

Hall, James C. (2001) *Mercy, Mercy Me: African-American Culture and the American Sixties*. Oxford: Oxford University Press.

Hentoff, Nat (1966) "*Meditations*: John Coltrane." Liner notes for *Meditations* by John Coltrane, Impulse! Records.

Hill, Logan (2008, April 7) "How I Made It: Spike Lee on *Do the Right Thing*." *New York*. http://nymag.com/anniversary/40th/culture/45772/ (accessed July 12, 2012).

hooks, bell (1996) "*Crooklyn*: The Denial of Death," in bell hooks, *Reel to Real: Race, Sex, and Class at the Movies*. New York: Routledge, pp. 34–46.

hooks, bell (2008) "Whose Pussy is this": A Feminist comment," in Paula J. Massood, ed., *The Spike Lee Reader*. Philadelphia: Temple University Press, pp. 1–9. (Originally in bell hooks, *Talking Back: Thinking Feminist, Thinking Black*. Boston: South End Press, 1989, pp. 134–41.)

Hornaday, Ann (2008, September 26) "*Miracle at St. Anna*." *Washington Post*. http://www.washingtonpost.com/go g/movies/miracle-at-st.-anna,1146328/critic-review.html# reviewNum1 (accessed July 12, 2012).

Howe, Desson (1988, February 12) "*School Daze*." *Washington Post*. http://www.washingtonpost.com/wp-srv/style/longterm/movies/videos/schooldazehowe.htm (accessed July 12, 2012).

Howe, Desson (1992, November 20) "*Malcolm X*." *Washington Post*. http://www.washingtonpost.com/wp-srv/style/longterm/movies/videos/malcolmxpg13howe_a0af39.htm (accessed July 12, 2012).

Hunter, Margaret L. (2002) "'If You're Light You're Alright': Light Skin Color as Social Capital for Women of Color." *Gender & Society*, vol. 16, no. 2, pp. 175–93.

Hut, Katie (2011, July 7) "The 1977 Blackout." *The Brooklyn Historical Society Blog*. http://brooklynhistory.org/blog/2011/07/07/the-1977-blackout/ (accessed July 12, 2012).

Iverem, Esther (1987, December 14) "Bias Cases Fuel Anger of Blacks." *New York Times*. http://www.nytimes.com/1987/12/14/nyregion/bias-cases-fuel-anger-of-blacks.htm l?ref=tawanabrawley (accessed July 12, 2012).

Jackson, Nancy Beth (2002, September 1) "If You're Thinking of Living In Fort Greene; Diversity Culture and Brownstones, Too." *New York Times*. http://www.nytimes.com/2002/09/01/realestate/if-you-re-thinking-living-fort-greene-diversity-culture-brownstones-too.html?src=pm (accessed July 12, 2012).

James, Caryn (1990a) "Spike Lee's Jews and the Passage from Benign Cliché into Bigotry." *New York Times.* http://www.nytimes.com/1990/08/16/movies/critic-s-note book-spike-lee-s-jews-passage-benign-cliche-into-bigotry. html?src=pm (accessed July 12, 2012).

James, Caryn (1990b) "Spike Lee's Middle-Class Jazz Musician." *New York Times.* http://www.nytimes.com/1990/08/03/movies/review-film-spike-lee-s-middle-class-jazz-musician.html?pagewanted=all&src=pm (accessed July 12, 2012).

Johnson, Victoria E. (1991) "Polyphony and Cultural Expression: Interpreting Musical Traditions in *Do the Right Thing.*" *Film Quarterly,* vol. 47, no. 2, pp. 18–29.

Judell, Brandon (1997) "An Interview with Spike Lee, Director of *4 Little Girls,*" *Indiewire* (September 12, 1977), in Cynthia Fuchs, ed., *Spike Lee: Interviews.* Jackson: University Press of Mississippi, 2002, pp. 139–43.

Kael, Pauline (1982) *5001 Nights at the Movies: A Guide from A to Z.* New York: Holt, Rinehart and Winston.

Kempley, Rita (1988, February 12) "*School Daze;*" *Washington Post.* http://www.washingtonpost.com/wp-srv/style/long term/movies/videos/schooldaze.htm (accessed July 12, 2012).

Kempley, Rita (1992, November 18) "Malcolm X." *Washington Post.* http://www.washingtonpost.com/wp-srv/style/longterm/movies/videos/malcolmxpg13kempley_a0a 2f5.htm (accessed July 12, 2012).

Kennedy, Lisa (2008, September 26) "Patriotism But Also Racism." *Denver Post.* http://www.denverpost.com/movies/ci_10549854 (accessed July 12, 2012).

Keough, Peter (n.d.) "*She's Gotta Have It.*" *Chicago Reader.* http://www.chicagoreader.com/chicago/shes-gotta-have-it/Film?oid=1051748 (accessed July 12, 2012).

King, Martin Luther, Jr. (1964, December 11) "The Quest

for Peace and Justice." Nobel Lecture. http://www.nobel prize.org/nobel_prizes/peace/laureates/1964/king-lecture. html (accessed July 12, 2012).

Klawans, Stuart (1998, June 1) "Fanfares." *The Nation*, vol. 266, pp. 35–6.

Klawans, Stuart (2000, November 6) "Amos, Andy 'n' You." *The Nation*, vol. 271, p. 34.

Lee, Spike (1987) *Spike Lee's Gotta Have It: Inside Guerrilla Filmmaking*. New York: Simon & Schuster.

Lee, Spike (1990, August 22) "I Am Not an Anti-Semite." *New York Times*. http://partners.nytimes.com/library/film/082290lee-editorial.html (accessed July 12, 2012).

Lee, Spike (1998) "Why Aaron Copland?" *Spike Lee Presents the Music of Aaron Copland*. Sony CD, SK 60593.

Lee, Spike, and Gates, Henry Louis, Jr. (1991) "Final Cut." *Transition*, no. 52, pp. 176–204.

Lee, Spike, and Gates, Henry Louis, Jr. (1992, May 31) "Just Whose 'Malcolm' Is It, Anyway?" *New York Times*. http://partners.nytimes.com/library/film/053192lee-malco lm-controversy.html (accessed July 12, 2012).

Lee, Spike, with Jones, Lisa (1989) *Do the Right Thing: A Spike Lee Joint*. New York: Fireside.

Lee, Spike, with Jones, Lisa (1990) *Mo' Better Blues: A Spike Lee Joint*. New York: Fireside.

Lewis, Paul (2008, June 5) "Spike Lee Gets in Clint Eastwood's Line of Fire." *Guardian*. http://www.guard ian.co.uk/film/2008/jun/06/usa.race (accessed July 12, 2012).

Lindo, Delroy (1999) "Delroy Lindo on Spike Lee," in Cynthia Fuchs, ed., *Spike Lee: Interviews*. Jackson: University Press of Mississippi, 2002, pp. 161–77.

McBride, James (2002) *Miracle at St. Anna*. New York: Riverhead Books.

McCarthy, Todd (1992, November 9) "*Malcolm X.*" *Variety*.

http://www.variety.com/review/VE1117900017?refcatid=
31 (accessed July 12, 2012).

McCarthy, Todd (2008, September 15) "*Miracle at St. Anna.*"
Variety, http://www.variety.com/review/VE1117938228?
refcatid=31 (accessed July 12, 2012).

McFadden, Robert D. (1988, October 7) "Brawley Made Up
Story of Assault, Grand Jury Finds." *New York Times.*
http://www.nytimes.com/1988/10/07/nyregion/brawley-
made-up-story-of-assault-grand-jury-finds.html?ref=tawan
abrawley (accessed July 12, 2012).

McMillan, Terry (1991) "Thoughts on *She's Gotta Have It*,"
in Terry McMillan, Toni Cade Bambara, Nelson George,
Charles Johnson, and Henry Louis Gates Jr., *The Films of
Spike Lee: Five for Five.* New York: Stewart, Tabori &
Chang, pp. 19–29.

Mandell, Jonathan (1994, April 24) "A Kinder, Gentler
Spike?" *Los Angeles Times.* http://articles.latimes.com/
1994-04-24/entertainment/ca-49825_1_cinque-lee-shelton-
jackson-father-bill-lee (accessed July 12, 2012).

Marikar, Sheila (2008, June 6) "Spike Strikes Back: Clint's
'an Angry Old Man.'" *ABC News.* http://abcnews.go.com/
Entertainment/story?id=5015524&page=1 (accessed July
12, 2012).

Maslin, Janet (1988, February 12) "*School Daze.*" *New York
Times.* http://movies.nytimes.com/movie/review?res=940
DE5DD1639F931A25751C0A96E948260 (accessed July
12, 2012).

Maslin, Janet (1994, May 13) "A Tender Domestic Drama
From, No Joke, Spike Lee." *New York Times.* http://
movies.nytimes.com/movie/review?res=9b05e1dc1e39f930
a25756c0a962958260 (accessed July 12, 2012).

Massood, Paula J. (2003) *Black City Cinema: African American
Urban Experiences in Film.* Philadelphia: Temple University
Press.

Mitchell, Elvis (1991) "Spike Lee: The *Playboy* Interview,"
Playboy (July), in Cynthia Fuchs, ed., *Spike Lee: Interviews*.
Jackson: University Press of Mississippi, 2002, pp. 35–64.

Mitchell, W.J.T. (1990) "The Violence of Public Art: *Do the
Right Thing*." *Critical Inquiry*, vol. 16, no. 4, pp. 880–99.

Morgenstern, Joe (2008, September 26) "In *St. Anna*, Lee
Fumbles Epic of War, Racism." *Wall Street Journal*.
http://online.wsj.com/article/SB122238344981876805.ht
ml (accessed July 12, 2012).

Morris, Wesley (2008, September 26) "*Miracle at St. Anna*."
Boston Globe.

Obenson, Tambay A. (2011, July 1) "Spike Lee: *Inside Man*
Sequel Isn't Happening." *IndieWire*. http://blogs.indiewi
re.com/shadowandact/spike_lee_inside_man_sequel_isnt_
happening_more (accessed July 12, 2012).

Olopade, Dayo (2009, June 23) "The First Couple's First
Flick." *The Root*. http://www.theroot.com/views/first-
couple-s-first-flick (accessed July 12, 2012).

Page, Clarence (1990, August 29) "From Spike Lee, Some
Unfortunate Stereotyping." *Chicago Tribune*. http://arti
cles.chicagotribune.com/1990-08-29/news/9003120922_1
_stereotypes-with-sharks-smiles-white-filmmakers-mo-be
tter-blues (accessed July 12, 2012).

Page, Clarence (1991, June 9) "Mo' Better Hype From Spike
Lee." *Chicago Tribune*. http://articles.chicagotribune.com/
1991-06-09/news/9102210242_1_racism-black-people-wh
ites-only (accessed July 12, 2012).

Pizzello, Stephen (1995) "Between 'Rock' and a Hard Place,"
in Cynthia Fuchs, ed., *Spike Lee: Interviews*. Jackson:
University Press of Mississippi, 2002, pp. 99–111.

Public Enemy (1998) "He Got Game." *PublicEnemy.com*.
http://www.publicenemy.com/index.php?page=page5&ite
m=2&num=102 (accessed July 12, 2012).

Richolson, Janice Mosier (1991) "He's Gotta Have It: An

Interview with Spike Lee," in Cynthia Fuchs, ed., *Spike Lee: Interviews*. Jackson: University Press of Mississippi, 2002, pp. 25–34.

Rickey, Carrie (2008, September 26) "Black GIs in WWII *Miracle.*" *Philadelphia Inquirer.* http://articles.philly.com/2008-09-26/entertainment/24991623_1_buffalo-soldiers-james-mcbride-germans (accessed July 12, 2012).

Rosenbaum, Jonathan (n.d.) "*Malcolm X.*" *Chicago Reader.* http://www.chicagoreader.com/chicago/malcolm-x/Film?oid=1064219 (accessed July 12, 2012).

Ross, Andrew, Diawara, Manthia, Doty, Alexander, Lubiano, Wahneema, Rose, Tricia, Shohat, Ella, Spigel, Lynn, Stam, Robert, and Wallace, Michele (1993) "A Symposium on Popular Culture and Political Correctness." *Social Text*, no. 36, pp. 1–39.

Rule, Sheila (1992, November 15) "Malcolm X: The Facts, the Fictions, the Film." *New York Times.* http://partners.nytimes.com/library/film/111592lee-malcolm-content.html (accessed July 12, 2012).

Rush, George, and Molloy, Joanna, with Anderson, Kasia (2001, November 30) "Spike: My Take on Tawana Was 'Right'." *New York Daily News.*

Saltman, Benjamin (1991–2) "*Jungle Fever.*" *Film Quarterly*, vol. 45, no. 2, pp. 37–41.

Sandow, Greg (1998) "Why Aaron Copland?" *Spike Lee Presents the Music of Aaron Copland*, Sony CD, SK 60593.

Scott, A.O. (2008, September 25) "Hollywood War, Revised Edition." *New York Times.* http://movies.nytimes.com/2008/09/26/movies/26mira.html (accessed July 12, 2012).

Sharpley-Whiting, T. Denean (1997) *Frantz Fanon: Conflicts and Feminisms.* Lanham, MD: Rowman & Littlefield Publishers.

Shipler, David K. (1991, November 10) "A Gentle Young Man Who Would Be 16 Forever." *New York Times*. http://www.nytimes.com/1991/11/10/books/a-gentle-you ng-man-who-would-be-16-forever.html?pagewanted=all &src=pm (accessed July 12, 2012).

Shipp, E.R. (1984, June 29) "Tape Contradicts Disavowal of 'Gutter Religion' Attack." *New York Times*. http:// www.nytimes.com/1984/06/29/us/tape-contradicts-disavo walof-gutter-religion-attack.html (accessed July 12, 2012).

Shipp, E.R. (1988, December 4) "Their Muse Is Malcolm X." *New York Times*. http://www.nytimes.com/1988/1 2/04/arts/their-muse-is-malcolm-x.html?src=pm (accessed July 12, 2012).

Sterritt, David (1989, June 27) "Spike Lee's Hotly Debated New Film." *Christian Science Monitor*. http://www. csmonitor.com/1989/0627/lspike.html (accessed July 12, 2012).

Sterritt, David (1990, August 1) "Spike Lee's Second-Best Movie." *Christian Science Monitor*. http://www.csmoni tor.com/1990/0801/lmo.html (accessed July 12, 2012).

Sterritt, David (1992a, November 18) "Lee's No-Nonsense *Malcolm X*." *Christian Science Monitor*. http://www. csmonitor.com/1992/1118/18141.html (accessed July 12, 2012).

Sterritt, David (1992b, November 24) "Behind the *Malcolm X* Film: A Need to Set Things Straight." *Christian Science Monitor*. http://www.csmonitor.com/1992/1124/ 24011.html (accessed July 12, 2012).

Sterritt, David (1994, May 16) "Spike Lee Unveils His Most Lovable Film to Date." *Christian Science Monitor*. http://www.csmonitor.com/1994/0516/16121. html (accessed July 12, 2012).

Sterritt, David (1995, September 13) "Spike Lee's Urban Playground Feels a Lot Grittier in *Clockers*." *Christian*

Science Monitor. http://www.csmonitor.com/1995/0913/ 13131.html (accessed July 12, 2012).

Sterritt, David (2007) "He Cuts Heads: Spike Lee and the New York Experience," in Murray Pomerance, ed., *City That Never Sleeps: New York and the Filmic Imagination.* New Brunswick, NJ: Rutgers University Press, pp. 136–49.

Stone, Alan A. (1994–5) "Spike Lee: Looking Back." *Boston Review,* December–January. http://bostonreview.net/ BR19.6/spike.html (accessed July 12, 2012).

Strausbaugh, John (2006) *Black Like You: Blackface, Whiteface, Insult and Imitation in American Popular Culture.* New York: Tarcher.

Sundstrom, Ronald R. (2011) "Fevered Desires and Interracial Intimacies in *Jungle Fever,*" in Mark T. Conard, ed., *The Philosophy of Spike Lee.* Lexington: University Press of Kentucky, pp. 144–63.

Taubin, Amy (2002, August) "Fear of a Black Cinema." *Sight and Sound,* vol. 12, no. 8, pp. 26–8.

Thomas, Margaret (1994) "Linguistic Variation in Spike Lee's *School Daze.*" *College English,* vol. 56, no. 8, pp. 911–27.

Thompson, Anne (1991) "Malcolm, Let's Do Lunch." *Mother Jones,* vol. 16, no. 4, pp. 24–9, 57.

Turner, Richard Brent (2003) *Islam in the African-American Experience,* second edition. Bloomington: Indiana University Press.

Uhlig, Mark A. (1987, December 19) "Dinkins Seeks Special Prosecutor to Study Bronx Woman's Death." *New York Times.* http://www.nytimes.com/1987/12/19/nyregion/din kins-seeks-special-prosecutor-to-study-bronx-woman-s-de ath.html (accessed July 12, 2012).

Variety (1985, December 31) *"She's Gotta Have It." Variety.* http://www.variety.com/review/VE11177948

30?refcatid=31&printerfriendly=true (accessed July 12, 2012).

Variety (1987, December 31) "*School Daze.*" *Variety*. http://www.variety.com/review/VE1117794678?refcatid=31 (accessed July 12, 2012).

Vowell, Sarah (1999, June 30) "Vive la diffirence" (sic). *Salon. com.* http://www.salon.com/1999/06/30/sam/ (accessed July 12, 2012).

Wallace, Michele (2008) "Spike Lee and Black Women," in Paula J. Massood, ed., *The Spike Lee Reader.* Philadelphia: Temple University Press, pp. 23–9. (Originally in Michele Wallace, *Invisibility Blues: From Pop to Theory.* New York: Verso, 1990, pp. 100–6.)

Wanniski, Jude (1984) "Letter from Louis Farrakhan." *Polyconomics: The Works and Life of Jude Wanniski.* http://www.polyconomics.com/index.php?option=com_content&view=article&id=2228:letter-from-louis-farrakhan&catid=36:1997&Itemid=30 (accessed July 12, 2012).

Werner, Laurie (1995, September 15–17) "Defusing the Urban 'Powder Keg.'" *USA Weekend*, pp. 10–11.

White, Armond (2006, January 25) "Spike's Joint." *New York Press.* http://www.nypress.com/article-12742-spikes-joint.html (accessed July 12, 2012).

Williams, Patricia J. (1991) *The Alchemy of Race and Rights: Diary of a Law Professor.* Cambridge, MA: Harvard University Press.

Wilmer, Valerie (1962, January) "Conversation with Coltrane." *Jazz Journal*, p. 2.

Wilson, Dr. Sonya Kathryn (2009) "Lift Every Voice and Sing." *Grace and James Weldon Johnson.* http://www.graceandjamesweldonjohnson.org/lift-every-voice/ (accessed July 12, 2012).

X, Malcolm (1964, December 12) "Communication and Reality," in John Henrik Clarke, ed., *Malcolm X: The Man and His Times.* Trenton, NJ: Africa World Press, 1969, pp. 307–20.

X, Malcolm, and Haley, Alex (1999) *The Autobiography of Malcolm X: As Told to Alex Haley.* New York: Ballantine Publishing Group.

Zacharek, Stephanie (2006, March 24) "*Inside Man.*" *Salon.com.* http://www.salon.com/2006/03/24/inside_man/ (accessed July 12, 2012).

INDEX